# Extreme Guns and Babes for an Adult World

By

Jack Corbett

Nirvana Printing Co.

Published by Nirvana Publishing Company

4th Edition

by Jack Corbett

For information address
Jack Corbett
505/21 Moo 5
Naklua Soi 16
Banglamung, Chonburi 20150
Thailand

http://www.alphapro.com
jack.corbett@gmail.com



Fourth edition republish date: October 17, 2020

ISBN-978-0-9848934-5-4

## Other books by Jack Corbett

*Welcome to the Fun House,* Death on the Wild Side,
*Dick Fitswell the Man in Quest of the Perfect Fit, and Pattaya Pattaya Pattaya*
*Confessions of Sin City*

# Dedication

To those who made Extreme Guns and Babes for an Adult World possible, from the entertainers who did such an outstanding job in the photo shoots, to the club owners and managers who proved instrumental at getting them done and the solid backing of the talent agencies representing the models. A very special thanks goes out to Jeremy Mcteague, who had been my editor over at *Xtreme Magazine* and to Andy, the magazine's owner who went along with Jeremy and me. Lastly, many thanks to Vic Meyer and the gun dealers and owners who provided the weapons themselves and who assisted in the photo shoots.

# Table of Contents

# Where the Models came from

Instead of starting everyone off with the usual boring introductions, including all those details about my background, I want to take you inside a Pure Talent Feature Showcase that took place at Big Al's, an adult night club in Peoria, Illinois to give you a better understanding of where my models came from, and why this book is so vastly different from all the rest. As for myself, suffice it to say that I used to write and do photography for adult magazines and topless clubs, and that it was Jeremy McTeague, the editor of *Xtreme Magazine*, a small adult magazine out of Connecticut who put me up to writing all those gun articles that featured beautiful scantily clad women. So what's the big deal about a Pure Talent Feature Showcase that took place in Peoria ten years ago. My hope is that it will justify my own personal feelings about this book to the potential reader, that there is nothing like it in the world and that the main reason for this is that the models were in a class of their own.

At the top of the food chain in the adult entertainment world, there's the feature entertainers. From among their ranks are the superstars of adult entertainment, the special guest performers who are advertised on the radio and the neon signs on adult night clubs across the United States. There's over 3000 such clubs across the U.S. with perhaps one third of these booking feature entertainers for special guest appearances that typically last between three and five nights. The visiting stars typically receive $100 to $500 a show with three shows per evening being a good average. The club that hosts the visiting feature is expected to pay for the feature entertainer's hotel room and travel expenses as well as a fee to the feature entertainment agency that represents her. A feature entertainer's earnings do not end with what she receives per show, however. At the club between her shows she will typically sell her merchandise to customers such as photos, calendars, various mementos with her name and image on them, and photos of herself with her adoring fans she poses with on the spot. Many features also have web sites where they sell their merchandise and digital images.

A feature entertainer's ability to receive a steady stream of lucrative bookings is based on a number of factors such as her audience appeal while doing her shows, her ability to get along well with the hosting club's management and house dancers[1]. Of critical important to a feature's career are the credits she accumulates from appearing on the pages of adult magazines such as *Hustler, Cheri,* or *Xtreme* and from winning trophies and other prizes in night club competitions and other pageants. A long list of credits for a feature entertainer is roughly comparable to a corporate executive's track record.

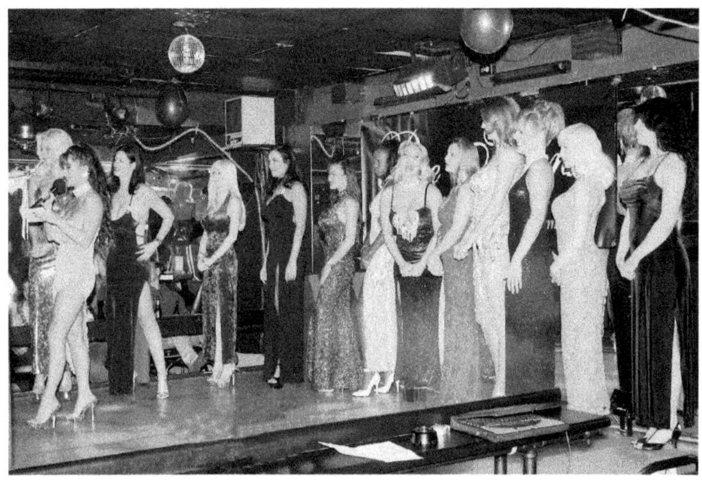

The picture above shows Nina Ferrari being recognized by Anne Marie and Jim Hayek, the owners of the Pure Talent Agency at Big Als October 2002 feature showcase. For several nights in succession 19 feature entertainers performed their shows before visiting club owners who had been invited to the showcase by the agency or Big Al. Each entertainer performed two choreographed shows during the showcase with each show's focus on the entertainer's creativity, organizational skills, beauty and talent.

---

[1]House dancers are the girls who work for any given club on a regular basis. They are typically local girls whereas the feature entertainers are the stars from afar who routinely travel from other states and even foreign countries.

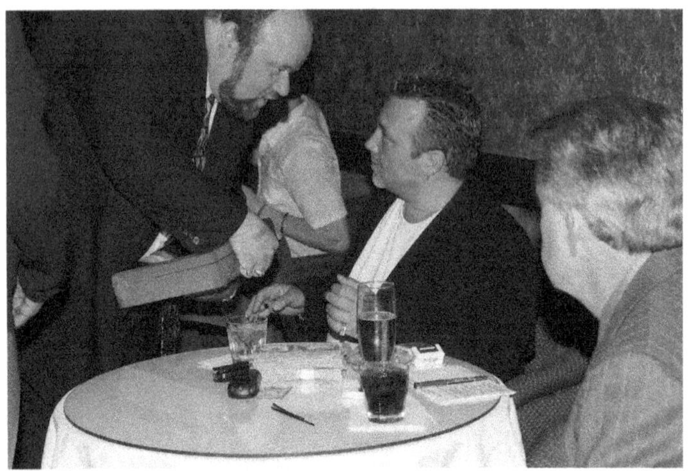

Big Daddy (standing) and Big Al at the feature showcase.

In October 2002, Big Daddy owned a club near Fort Leonard Wood, Missouri, "Big Daddy's Cabaret" which meant he had to drive over 300 miles to get to the feature showcase at Big Al's. Big Daddy would wind up booking at least three of the feature entertainers from this showcase (Casey Cannons, Arianna a del, Carrie Bare) within one year to perform their shows at his night club. Big Daddy would become well acquainted with several more of the Pure Talent entertainers at the May 2003 feature showcase and would book them soon afterwards.

So who gets what in a feature showcase? Obviously an agency such as Pure Talent gets the opportunity to showcase the feature entertainers it represents to visiting club owners such as Big Daddy. The feature entertainers have the chance to show what they can do in front of visiting club owners as well as the opportunity to endear themselves to Anne Marie and Jim Hayek for being reliable team players. Pure Talent collects a fee from the hosting club, in this case Big Al's, as well as 15 % of all future bookings it makes for the entertainers it represents. And as far as Big Al is concerned, well, he gets to pay all those hotel bills (including mine) in addition to Pure Talent's fee for bringing all those entertainers to Peoria.

Within a two year period Big Al would host three feature showcases for Pure Talent. More than anything, Big Al ends up buying a lot of credibility in the adult entertainment world for being a very big player who's willing to go that extra mile and then some. Let me put it this way. On most scorecards Peoria might seem to be pretty small potatoes compared to Chicago, but in the adult entertainment world I can't think of a single

Chicago club that's even on the same map as Big Als.

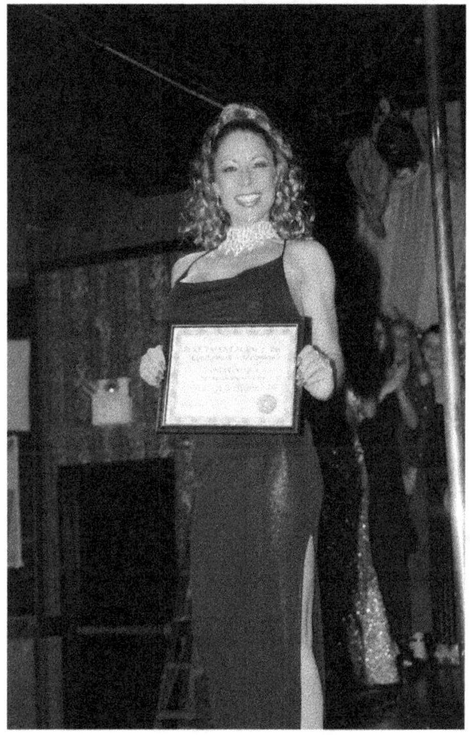

To the left is Montana Steele with her certificate for "Miss Body awarded to her by Pure Talent for her contributions to the Showcase. You will see a lot more of Montana later when she appears in the Winchester lever action rifle article. One month later I would shoot Montana's pictures as she wins first place as M.S. Texas during Club Maximus's M.S. Texas competition. Montana's from Louisville, Kentucky so she's traveled over four hundred miles to participate in this showcase and over a thousand miles to compete for M.S. Texas.

Aspen Reign appears in the next picture after receiving her certificate for having the showcase's best show. Originally Aspen got her start at Big Als where she once worked as a house dancer. Since then she's accumulated too many titles to list here including her being a four time winner of the prestigious Miss Nude World Pageant, Exotic Dancer's 2003 overall entertainer of the year, and Penthouse's Gold G-String Overall Champion (twice).

One might dismiss that long list of Aspen's titles and awards, but I'll say from personal experience that whenever it came time for Aspen to do a show, all the other feature entertainers in the house would immediately drop whatever they were doing to watch her perform. She was the best and everyone knew it.

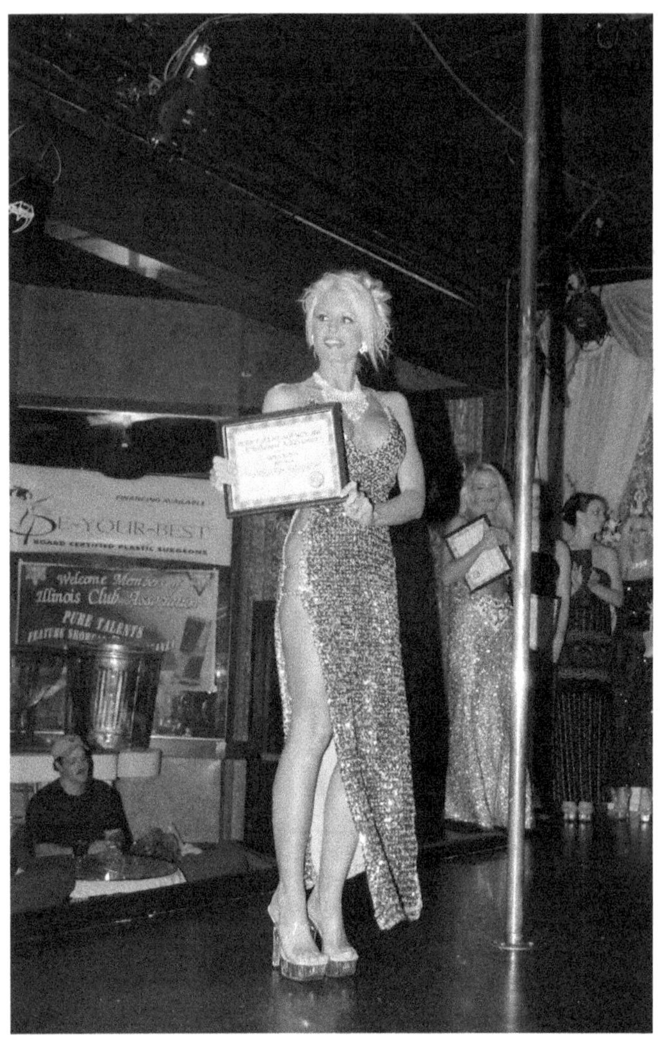


At this point I should mention that none of the 19 entertainers performing at this showcase were paid, and even though Big Al paid for their hotel rooms (with 2 women usually sharing a room), most of the women had to drive themselves to Peoria, no matter how far they had to travel, and that traveling by car simply doesn't cut it for a feature. Most have pickup trucks. Leah Layne, who will appear later on in this book with the Tec 9, used to pull a trailer behind her pickup truck. Montana Steele would drive her pickup filled with saddles and other Western gear and other outfits and props all the way to Wichita Falls, Texas to compete for the M.S. Texas pageant. In Aspen Reign's case, her props and outfits were so extensive that she even had her own Aspen Reign tour bus.

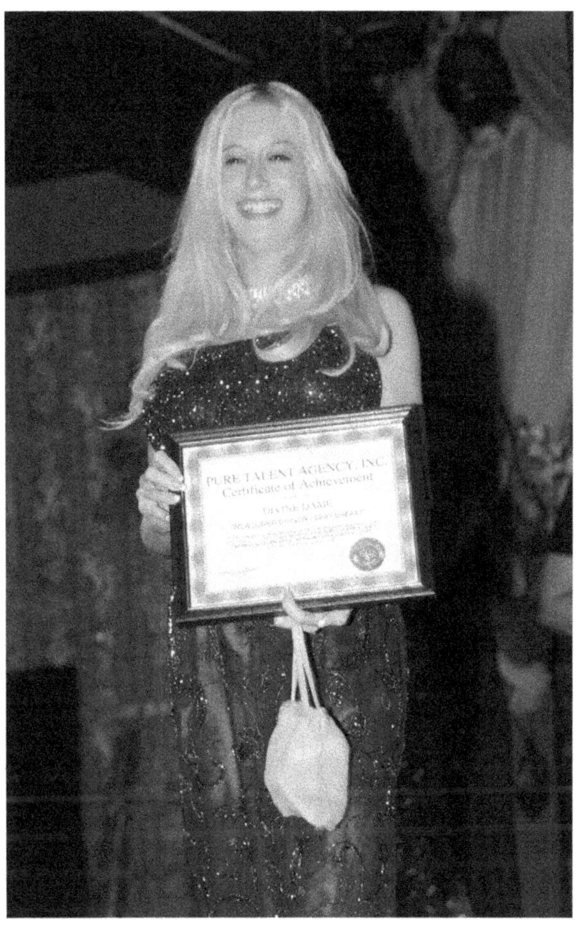


This was Arianna a Del's first outing as a feature entertainer. Notice that her stage name on the certificate is Divine Dame, not Arianna a del. Arianna was simply amazing when it came to taking excellent pictures. I must have taken over 2,000 pictures at this Showcase alone, and of those I took, several hundred were of Arianna doing her shows on the stage. Arianna would drive down from Louisville, Kentucky to do the photo shoots with the M-16 rifle at Vic Meyer's farm and appear in two of my *Xtreme Magazine* articles. Her certificate of achievement is for "Best Breasts".

That's the way it is with these things. Everyone winds up walking away with something. One entertainer gets a certificate for having the best legs, another for best breasts, and still another gets rookie of the year. There's best show, most original show, and so on. An entertainer gets great publicity by getting a lot of credits and by traveling all over the U.S. doing all those feature showcases with Pure Talent which put me in the unique position of having a huge array of fine talent to choose from for the models I'd be using for my gun articles with *Xtreme Magazine* since I'd often be shooting the showcases for Pure Talent.

At the end of the Feature Showcase it seems everyone got a credit, even Big Al, who got the club owner of the year award if I recall. I dimly remember one of his DJ's getting the golden microphone award, or something on that order. Then it was my turn. And I'm sure it must have been L.A. LaMann who put all the Pure Talent girls up to it. She's the blonde in the center of the first row, and she had been one of the Master of Ceremonies for at least one of the nights during the showcase. Someone announced that the entertainers wanted to thank Jack Corbett for all his photography work, and then it happened.

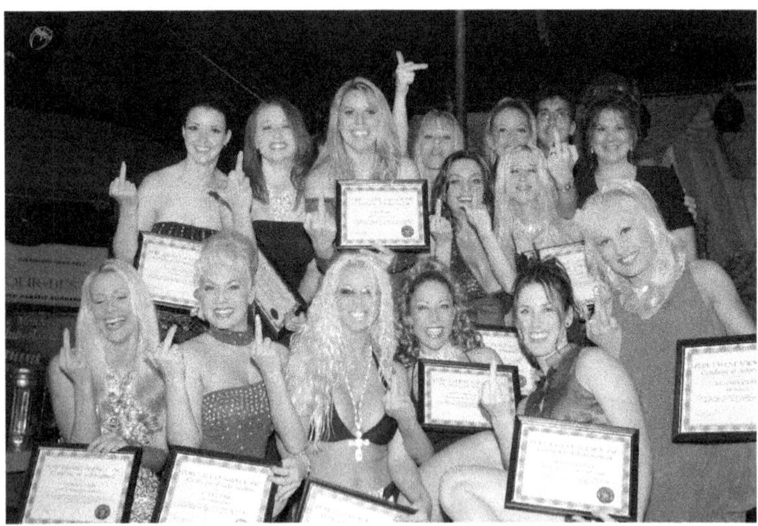

"Thanks Jack, for being our photographer," I heard someone announce. I felt honored. I still do.

Four of the entertainers in the picture will appear in the following gun articles. I'd meet the rest at future feature showcases, while covering other adult industry events such as Nudes-A-Poppin, Exotic Dancer's Annual Las Vegas conventions, the Maximus M.S. Texas Pageants as well as some of my favorite gentlemen's clubs such as PT's Sports in Sauget, PT's Roxys and Platinum Clubs in Brooklyn, IL,, Big Daddy's Cabaret at Fort Leonard Wood, Missouri, and the Lumberyard in Des Moines, IA.

Jack Corbett

# The Tommy Gun

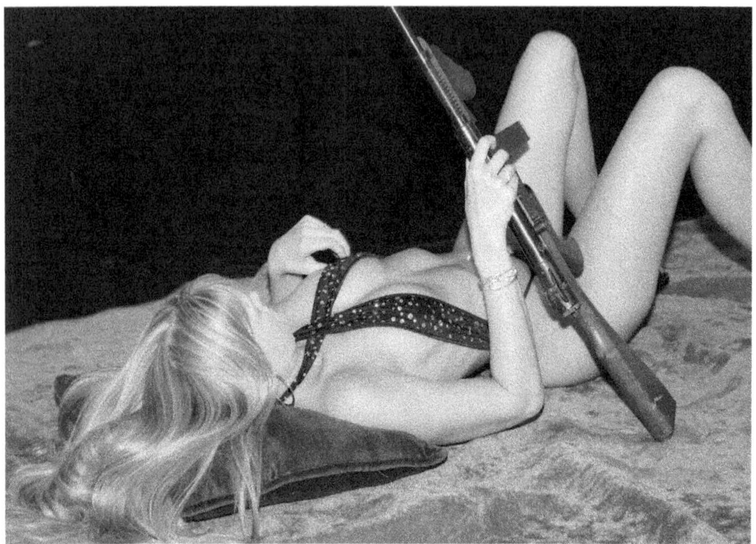

Chandra from Pt's Sports Cabaret where she was a waitress with Thompson look a like at the Belleville Shooting Range. The range had three fully automatic weapons its customers could rent for $15.00 so long as they shot them at the range.

For Americans who grew up watching the "Untouchables" on T.V. and Prohibition era gangster movies, the Thompson, oftentimes called the Tommy Gun or the Chicago Piano, with its ability to deliver a thunderstorm of hard hitting .45 caliber bullets, is the king of submachine guns. During the roaring twenties when rival gangsters were having regular shootouts in the streets it developed a reputation as a horrific manslayer. The favorite of men like John Dillinger, Baby Face Nelson, Pretty Boy Floyd and Machine Gun Jack McGurn, it was the gun that Al Capone's killers used to cut seven members of the Bugs Moran gang to pieces in a few infamous seconds that became known as the St. Valentines Day Massacre. In spite of its fame as the bootlegger's weapon of choice, the general public is completely unaware of the Thompson's initial slow acceptance by the U.S. military or the fact that close to a million Thompsons were ultimately produced by the end of World War II. My mission for *Xtreme* was to get my hands upon a real Thompson, test it on full automatic fire, and to evaluate it as an everyday combat weapon.

In 1917 John T. Thompson became Director of Arsenals after playing a pivotal role in the development and the adoption of the 1911 .45 automatic pistol by the U.S. Armed forces.

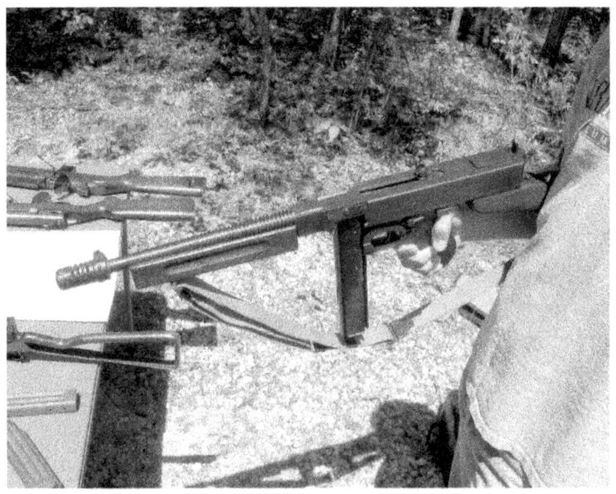

This one's the real thing and the actual submachine gun we tested. The fit and the finish of a genuine Thompson is far superior to what we experienced with the look-a-like.

The close quarter trench warfare of the First World War had convinced Thompson of the need for a trench broom that could deliver massive short range stopping power. In 1919 Thompson formed the Auto Ordinance Company which had a working prototype ready for testing by both the U.S. Army and the Marine Corps in 1920. In the army tests there was only one misfire out of 2,000 rounds with similar results in the Marine Corps tryouts. Most onlookers were impressed but those were the days of American unpreparedness for war when the U.S. Army counted only 30,000 ill-equipped men. Neither the Marine Corps nor the Army was interested in acquiring new weaponry, the new company floundered, and only sales to criminals, the F.B.I. and other law enforcement agencies kept it afloat.

By 1940 Great Britain stood alone against Hitler's Germany. The American lend lease program funneled much needed supplies into a beleaguered Great Britain and other allies. When war with Germany and Japan seemed unavoidable Auto Ordinance dramatically increased its production of Thompson's submachine gun, predicting correctly that the U.S. would soon become the arsenal of democracy. By late 1941 at the time of the Japanese bombing of Pearl Harbor, the U.S. government had ordered 319,000 Thompsons although a sizeable portion had been earmarked for the lend lease program. By the end of the war something like a million Thompsons had been produced.

We tested the Thompson fifty miles southwest of St. Louis Missouri at Vic Meyer's country home along with a fully automatic AK-47, a World War II British Sten gun, a Reising used in the early part of World War II by the Marine Corps, and a World War II M-1 carbine. With the exception of the M-1 carbine, a semi auto which fired just one round each time the trigger was pulled, all the weapons were fully automatic.

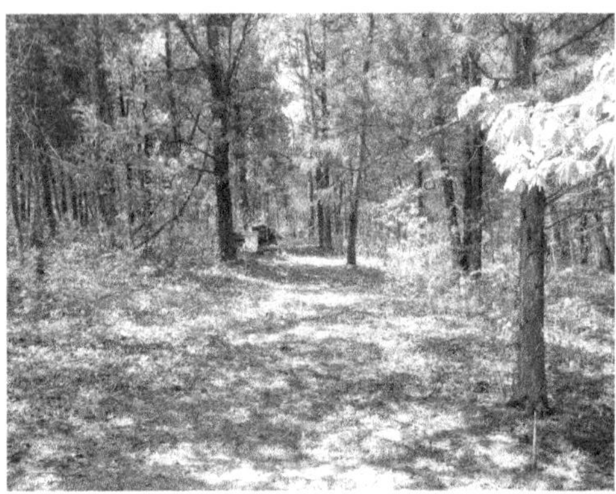

Whether it's in the woods or jungle 100 yards seems a long distance off. Combat is usually at short range in such places

Vic had cleared off a 100-yard firing lane in his timber and had constructed several backstops at varying distances up to the 100-yard limit. In the woods 100 yards seems a good distance out, but in the open fields this doesn't seem like much. Those were Missouri trees and underbrush surrounding it, not jungle. Yet I imagined myself out in the jungles and rain forests of places like Guadalcanal, New Guinea, and the Philippines facing Japanese soldiers hiding in the bushes or up in the trees firing down on me. "How would I have felt armed with the Thompson submachine gun?" I asked myself.

The Thompson is short, compact and heavy weighing more than 10 pounds unloaded. Even more with a 30 round clip of .45 caliber hard ball. It has excellent sights that are state of the art even today. Firing short three and four round bursts at a target 100 yards downrange I was able to keep more than half of my shots in the chest of the man-sized silhouette target. One doesn't ever want to go more than three or four round bursts because the muzzle rises too much on full auto. There's a selector switch one uses to choose between firing full auto and semi automatic. It takes awhile to get onto submachine guns and by now I had fired a few and was able to keep my bursts short and most of my shots on target. Thirty rounds doesn't sound like much when firing on full auto but you can get six to ten bursts out of a Thompson without having to load a fresh clip into the gun. Had I been fighting in the Pacific Theater during World War II, the Thompson would have been my first choice since ranges were typically short and there were a lot of little limbs, leaves, blades of grass, bamboo stalks and whatever for a bullet to travel through. The heavy 45 caliber bullets from the Thompson would have barreled right through a lot of foliage without being deflected by the brush. And those .45 slugs could usually be relied upon to top a man with one hit.

But in the war in the Pacific not all the fighting was done at close range in the jungle. Past a hundred yards the heavy .45 caliber slug drops like a dying swallow. As for fighting the Germans on the Western front, I might have been firing at soldiers a long way off. Out in the open spaces, the M-1 rifle with its long range and accuracy would have been a far better weapon than the Thompson. But for paratroopers dropped behind enemy lines at night, men riding in close confinement in armored vehicles, or any soldier engaging in firefights at close range in the hedgerows of France, in the Ardennes Forest or in house to house fighting for the cities of Italy, France and Germany, the Thompson would have been superior to practically anything else.

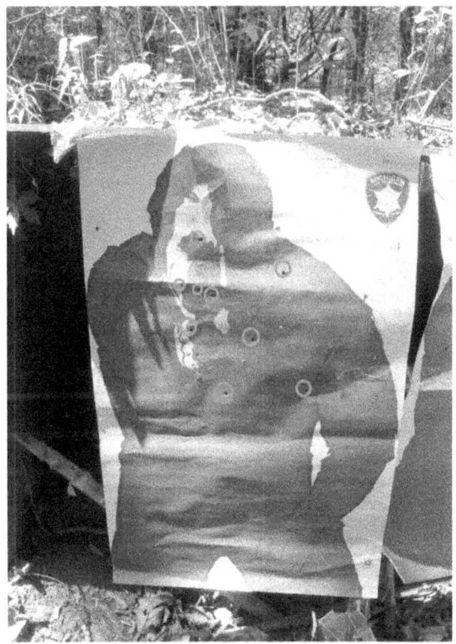
Only 11 out of 20 45 caliber bullets accounted for, but we must keep in mind that the Thompson's been on full auto and the range is 100 yards. After that the .45 slug drops like a rock.

Not once did the Thompson jam whereas the Reising misfired at least once on each clip. One has to pity the Marines who had to use them until enough Thompsons, M-1s and M-1 carbines could be issued to replace them. Even though more than 60,000 Reisings were produced, one Marine commander at Guadalcanal had his units Reisings dumped into the Lunga River rather than have his men have to rely upon them in combat. Like the Thompson, the British Sten Gun and the AK-47 went full auto, clip after clip, without a hiccup.

But if I had to go into combat with the Thompson or the British Sten gun, which is THE SUBMACHINE GUN that supplied the British armed forces during the Second World War, I wouldn't choose the Sten gun even though it proved to be very reliable and efficient. Think I'd risk my life for king or country when my country could only give me a cheap looking gun made from stamped parts crudely welded together? No way. That Thompson's a finely made piece of machinery with close tolerances. It inspires confidence by giving notice that it's a precision tool that can be counted on to deliver a large volume of hard-hitting .45 firepower. If it can't reach out there and touch someone like the M-1 can, at least a soldier could accept its limitations while reveling in its strengths. However, its intricate engineering and superb quality proved its own undoing. It was too expensive to produce and the American war machine proved to be insatiable. Several versions of the Thompson were produced during the War, each one giving up dispensable features that were standard in its predecessor. The Cutts recoil compensator was dispensed with and expensively machined sights gave way to new versions that could be produced more cheaply and quickly. Still unsatisfied with how quickly and cheaply the Thompson could be produced, the U.S. Armed forces thoroughly studied the British Sten gun and came up with its own answer to the Sten, the M-3 submachine gun, that was quickly nicknamed the grease gun because of its uncanny resemblance to the homely tool. As reliable as the Thompson was, the grease gun was even more dependable, especially in harsh environmental conditions. Moreover, because of the grease gun's slower rate of fire it could be more easily controlled on full auto.

During the last year of the Second World War, the official replacement of the Thompson by the grease gun marked the beginning of still a new era in small arms development. The Sten gun and crudely finished submachine guns used by the Soviets started it, but it was the gradual phasing out of the Thompson that really put the handwriting on the wall. The grease gun ushered in a new era of cheaply produced quick firing weapons in which the utmost priority was to be given to raw functionality at the expense of finely crafted weapons such as the Thompson and the M-1 rifle. Nevertheless, the Thompson continued to be revered by those soldiers considering themselves lucky to carry one. We put five World War II through Vietnam era rapid firing military weapons to the test that morning.

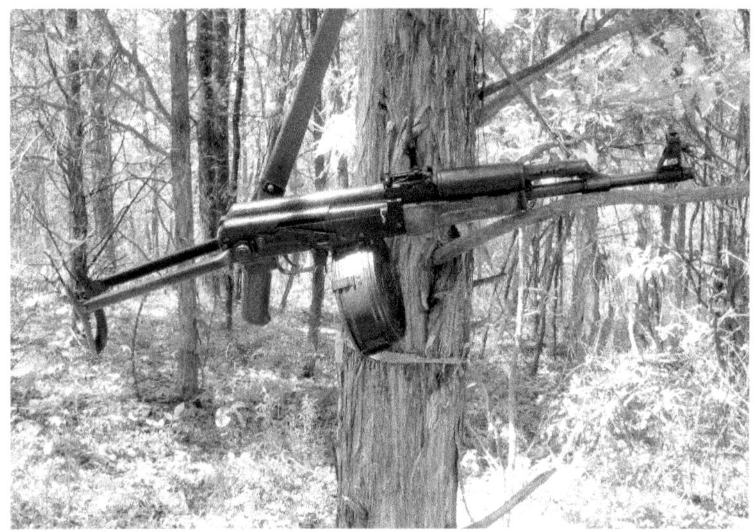
The AK-47 is a lot of fun to shoot on full auto

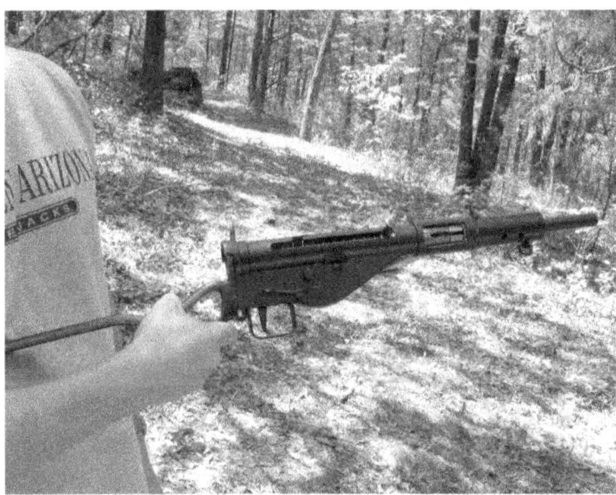
Chambered for 9 mm, the British Sten Gun was crude and could be manufactured from improvised machine shops by Partisans during World War II fighting against the Nazi occupation troops while being equally favored by British commandos, paratroopers. In our estimation it did not measure up to the Thompson or the AK-47.

Far in front of the others in quality, the Thompson had been so popular with the soldiers who used it during World War II, that hardly a sane man among them would have traded his Thompson in for anything else. Stay tuned to a future gun of the month article when I pick one of the four as my weapon of choice, above even the Thompson, in spite of its appearance as a crudely made piece of junk by comparison.

# The Israeli Soldier and his Uzi

> I much prefer that my enemies, if they have any firearms at all, have machine pistols. With a rusty Mauser, a man knows he has to hold and squeeze. With a nice new Uzi, all he feels he has to do is to spray.
>
> Jeff Cooper
>
> (*To Ride, Shoot Straight and Speak the Truth*,)

The MP-38 Schmeisser 9 mm submachine gun was no longer good enough for Hitler's Nazi warriors who by 1944 found themselves hopelessly outgunned, out tanked and outnumbered by the Russian juggernaut. Reeling from vastly superior numbers of often better armed Russian infantrymen, the standard Mauser 98 K bolt action rifle lacked the fire power while the Schmeisser 9 mm machine pistol lacked both the range and the stopping power to deal with the Russian onslaught. To give the German infantryman a better chance German munitions makers began issuing troops with the new MP-44 assault rifle, which combined much of the range and stopping power of the full powered rifle with the rapidity of fire of the machine pistol in a medium sized cartridge. But it was too little, too late.

Shortly after the war, the Russians delivered an improvement on the MP-44 in the form of the Kalashnivov AK-47 assault rifle, which would become the most successful infantry weapon of the second half of the 20$^{th}$ century arming more than half the world and become the yardstick by which all other infantry small arms would be measured by. In 1967 more than twenty years after the introduction of the MP-44, Israel's armed forces overcame the much better supplied and more numerous armies of Egypt, Jordan, and Syria, in six days. I still remember seeing pictures in *Time* and *Newsweek* showing jubilant Israeli troops armed with short, compact submachine guns, which would soon gain worldwide fame and acceptance as the Uzi.

Yet, according to the vast experiences of the German Wehrmacht, and the dictums of Jeff Cooper (editor at large for *Guns and Ammo Magazine*, author of two well-written books laced with Cooper philosophy and World War II colonel in the Marines, and who is widely regarded by firearms devotees as the guru) the submachine gun's usefulness as a mainline infantryman's weapon was long ago buried on the Steppes of Russia. If the Uzi had been obsoleted by the assault rifle, why did Israel accept it as the standard weapon for the IDF (Israel Defense Forces) and how could its forces win such resounding victories with such an antiquated weapon that would later be used by more than 90 countries around the globe?

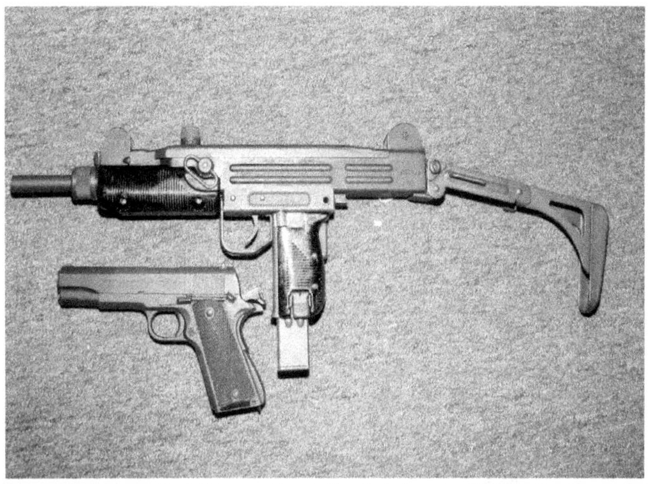

On the left the .45 Colt issued to author's father in WWII. On the right the Uzi the author tested at the Belleville gun range.

Obsolete or not, I had always wanted one, and had been to Israel twice where I had seen them worn on slings by soldiers and civilians alike. And now I had the opportunity to study its effectiveness first hand by firing several hundred rounds through a full auto version.

Make no mistake, the IDF is man for man the finest military organization in the world. It has to be. Hitler did not invent genocide as the "final solution" for what he regarded as the "Jewish problem." He merely perfected it with typical German thoroughness that ended with the murder of six million Jews. For centuries pogroms had been carried out throughout Eastern Europe butchering entire villages of Jews. During World War II while Hitler's death camps went about their deadly business, refugee boats were turned back from the U.S. and other countries to a German occupied Europe where its Jewish passengers would be sent to the death camps. Some refugees made it to a British governed Palestine that was largely occupied by Arabs devoted to a Palestine only for Arabs. The specter of an entire world turning its back upon the slaughter of millions of Jews clearly demonstrated the absolute necessity for a Jewish homeland where all Jews could find sanctuary.

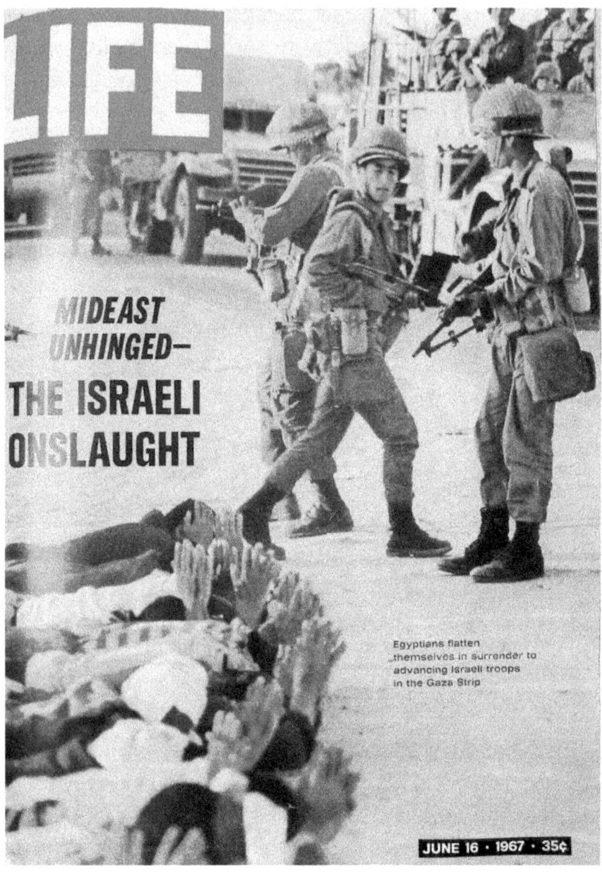


In Palestine where the Arabs outnumbered the Jewish settlers two to one, conflict between Arabs and Jewish settlers had been going on for some time. Both before and after WWII, Palestine's Jewish inhabitants fought for a partitioned Palestine while Britain, the United States, and the Arab nations all opposed it. Big oil was talking and both the U.S. and Britain wanted to appease the surrounding Arab states. In 1948 the British blockaded Palestinian ports against all Jewish bound arms shipments and further immigration of Jews. Repeated Arab massacres of Jewish settlers brought on the War for Independence from Britain in which the superior determination of Jewish settlers won over Arab superiority of numbers and munitions. Britain was forced to relent and Palestine became a partitioned state between Arab occupied Palestine and the new Jewish State of Israel.

In the 1950's Egyptian forces seized the Suez Canal. Until then both the U.S. and Britain had been favoring Israel's enemies, Jordan and Syria both of which received far more Anglo-American munitions than the Israelis. The Egyptians had received an overwhelming supply of modern tanks, artillery and aircraft from the Russians. The U.S. and Britain had committed to mounting a joint air attack on the Egyptians but postponed it when Israel went it alone–and won. It was only after Egypt refused to abandon the Suez Canal and after Israeli troops withdrew that U.S. and Britain launched the promised air attacks, which finished the Egyptians off.

## The Uzi

On the eve of the 1967 six-day war Israel was once again vastly outnumbered by Egypt, Syria and Jordan. Worse, its enemies had at their disposal three times as many tanks and twice as many aircraft. To counter modern Russian tanks the Israelis had to retrofit World War II Shermans they had acquired on the cheap. The Sherman had been outclassed by the German Panzers during World War II but the substantially modified super Sherman was a different animal once larger engines and thicker armor was installed and the 76 mm guns were replaced by 105 mm cannons that could penetrate the Russian armor.

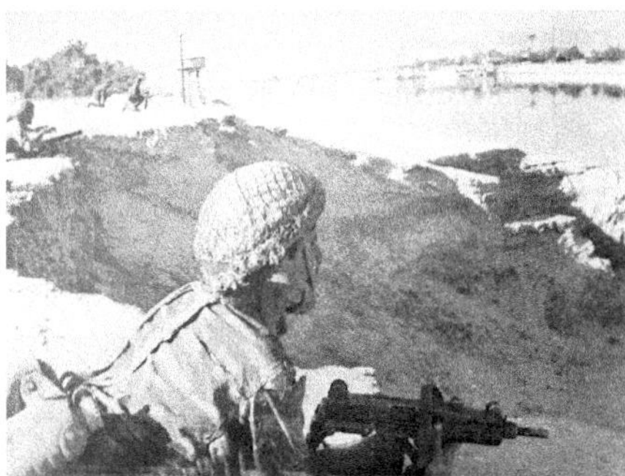

In the background other Israeli soldiers are using weapons such as the FAL the IDF scrounged up from other sources. The Uzi would not be nearly as effective at longer ranges. The first time the author went to Israel in the mid 1980's many troops were still using Uzi's. The second time, he visited the American M-16 armed virtually every solider he encountered.

Artillery was given little attention since it was viewed as too destructive of civilian life where Arabs and Jews lived in close proximity to one another. A great emphasis on intelligence work was placed on the enemy's intentions and troop dispositions. Attack was emphasized at all costs since Israelis had long ago learned they would be abandoned by the Great Powers and that once they had gained the upper hand they would be called off like a dog hovering over a cat it had just wounded.

Night fighting and commando style training was emphasized. To win, Israel tactical doctrine stressed that the IDF must strike first as soon as intelligence sources learned that the Arabs were planning to attack. First priority was given to the Israeli Air Force's destroying enemy air forces on the ground. Tanks supported by Israel's elite infantry would then mop up as Israeli fighter bombers destroyed the enemy's tank formations and fortifications from the air.

Since Israel is at its widest point just seventy-five miles wide, every Israeli soldier knew that Arab armored formations could overrun the entire country in just a single day. Every soldier and civilian was constantly aware that war would be a matter of life and death for everyone. The Arabs had long ago pledged themselves to a Jihad or Holy War against the Jewish state. The IDF had their back against the wall with their wives and children's lives hanging in the balance.

Unlike many past wars in which the infantryman's rifle often won the day, this was to be a war of mobility that would be won primarily in the air. Ground troops would constantly be on the move riding in armored vehicles. Often they would be attacking at night.

At just 25 inches long, the Uzi was perfect for men riding into combat in mechanized vehicles. It was also ideal for night fighting where firing at long range is not paramount. After mounting an overwhelmingly successful attack from the air against the Egyptian air force, Israel's ground forces went into action. Without air cover the Egyptian tanks became sitting ducks for Israeli aircraft and tanks, and breakthroughs by Israeli shock troops were accomplished within hours. Then Israel turned on Jordan and Syria defeating both in piecemeal fashion.

## Firing the Uzi

Boning up on Cooper's writing I had already begun to take a dim view of the submachine gun. Bob, the manager of the gun range I frequented, explained how the Uzi worked. I had never fired a fully automatic weapon before. But what impressed me the most was the gun's sturdiness. It is the sort of thing you can run over with your car, pick it up, and start shooting.

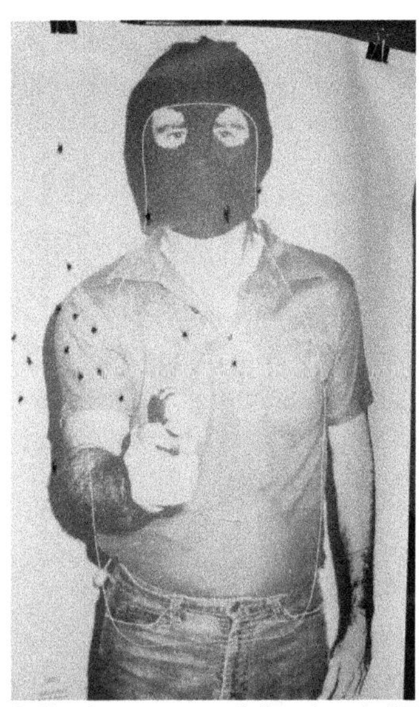
Author's group on full auto at 25 yards. He'd do much better firing the Thompson at 100 yards later on. This might have been his first time firing a weapon on full auto. Nevertheless, he's been shooting since all his life. Someone who's had minimal training would have real problems being effective.

"Look at this," Bob said. "It even has a bayonet lug which should give you an idea of the mind set of these people." Notice that if fires from a closed bolt," Bob continued. "You cock the bolt back a little and you notice that it's ready to fire but you can see that the chamber is open, which is the opposite of the semi automatic pistols we shoot. When the receiver is closed, you are out of ammo. This interferes with the accuracy when you fire a single shot at a time."

I dry fired the Uzi and felt the big spring snap the bolt closed, which jams a round into the chamber and fires it at the same time. Bob went on. "But that's an advantage when you are firing full-auto because when the bolt slams forward the weight distribution goes forward which tends to moderate the gun's recoil."

I took two other guns with me into the firing range. One had been my Dad's World War II 45 auto service auto. The other was my small Kahr 9 mm pistol. Jeff Cooper had long been an admirer of the 45 auto and had claimed that a good shot with a good pistol was more effective than an average shot with a submachine gun.

The 45 auto is no doubt the best service sidearm to ever see combat. I've owned a half dozen of them. Every one of them has had high visibility white outline sights that are easy to see with the exception of the one I have with me. Whereas, the others were produced for the civilian and police markets this one was carried by my Dad in World War II and represents standard Armed Forces issue in both World Wars, Korea and Vietnam. Its sights are small and dark grey making them nearly impossible for me to see the dark silhouette target at twenty-five yards.

Seven shots through the 45 register seven hits to the torso of the man sized silhouette which means I would have hit an adversary seven times. But my group is terrible largely because of the pistol's abysmal sights. The Uzi's next. I have around three hundred hand loads that I'm sure will not function in my Kahr 9 mm which hates hand loads. The Uzi digests them like a goat chewing tin cans.

I've heard that firing long bursts in a submachine gun is a waste of ammo since a submachine gun's barrel will climb and spray bullets all over the place. They're right. Instinctively I hold my bursts to two to four rounds each. The gun shoots higher with each shot. I get 16 hits out of 25 rounds. And I can do it much faster and easier than I can with the 45 auto.

Then Bob takes a turn with the Uzi. Bob's a cop who moonlights by working at the gun range. He gets much tighter groups than I managed with the Uzi. Of course he has much more experience than me with automatic weapons, so I'd get better with practice. I'm impressed with how tight his patterns are. Twenty-five shots in an area the size of a man's head on full auto is not bad at all for twenty-five yards.

My performance with my very light weight Kahr 9 mm is substantially better than it is with the World War II 45 auto, but this is due to its high visibility white sights But I'm a much better pistol shot than average and neither pistol is as easy to hit with as the Uzi which gets its bullets out much faster. Which brings us back to Jeff Cooper's dislike for the submachine gun for most combat situations. Was the Uzi an effective weapon for the Israeli soldiers facing combat during the 1967 six days war? Definitely.

In an era when Israel could not trust the West to be a reliable supplier, having its own arms development and production in house made sense whenever possible. The Uzi is very dependable. It goes bang every time it's supposed to and it is known to keep functioning in the harshest conditions. Exuding quality and indestructible reliability it's a weapon that inspires confidence. Only twenty-five inches long, it is handy and very portable, and therefore ideally suited for soldiers carrying it in vehicles, or paratroopers. And for a war of rapid movement of troops trained to be constantly on the offensive, particularly in night fighting, where combat is at close quarters is the rule rather than the exception, its lack of long-range capability is not the drawback it poses for other armies.

Although the Uzi has largely been supplanted by other weapons in the IDF, primarily by the American M-16, and its shorter variants such as the M-4, it is still widely used as a police weapon throughout the world. The Israeli soldier had every reason to depend upon it. And if the U.S. should suddenly legalize private ownership of automatic weapons, I will be ordering mine today.

# The 454 Casull, One Handed Buffalo Stomper

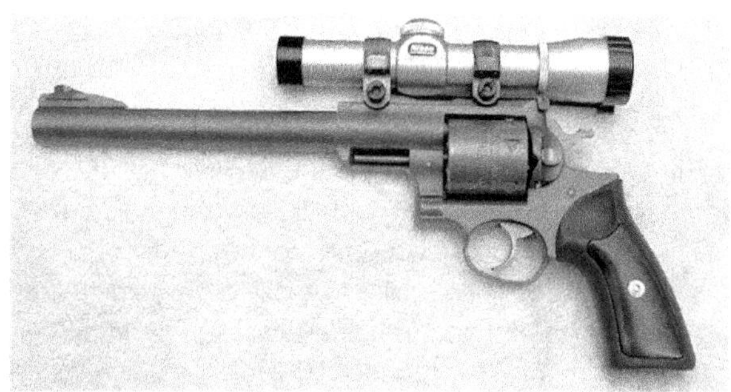

The 454 Casull is a serious handgun prescribed as either primary or backup for the world's most dangerous game such as Alaskan brown bear, elephant or Cape Buffalo that can make confetti out of a man in seconds. Its 250 to 350 grain bullets measure nearly half an inch in diameter and travel 1600 to 1800 feet per second. With ballistics nearly identical to those of the 45-70 Springfields used at Custer's Last Stand and the favorite caliber of buffalo hunters who slaughtered practically every bison on the North American continent, its large bullet moves relentlessly, crushing bones as it destroys a large animal's heart, lungs, and any other vital organs in its path.

The 454 Casull is the most powerful mass-produced revolver in the world, producing nearly twice the muzzle energy of a 44 magnum. Hollow points expand to produce a one inch hole through animals the size of an Elk. To those suggesting that it lacks the power and penetration to handle an Elephant, consider that a custom made 475 Linebaugh revolver reportedly put a cast .475 slug 44 inches through an elephant's head before lodging in the animal's third vertebra. (Penetration Test at the Linebaugh Seminar by Kent M. Bachelor). Penetration for the two calibers show virtually no discernible difference.

The granddaddy of the modern 454 Casull was the Colt Single Action Army Revolver, known as the Peacemaker, which was the

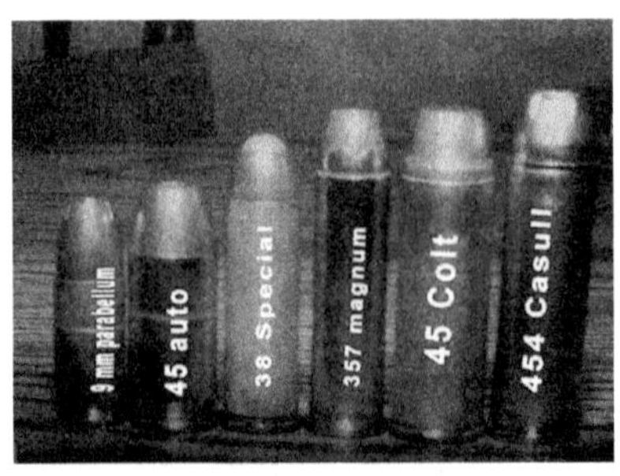


most powerful revolver of its day as chambered for the 45 Long Colt in 1873. More than a hundred years old, this cartridge has had a huge explosion in sales due to the recent popularity of Cowboy Action competitions in which only guns similar to those used in the middle to late 1800's can be used. The 45 Long Colts' cartridge case is huge being much larger than a 44-magnum which is understandable since it was designed to hold 40 grains of black powder, which is far bulkier than the smokeless powders used by today's modern cartridges.

Although the old Peacemaker has been constantly improved, its basic design is virtually unchanged since 1873, when the U.S. military adopted it. Since Samuel Colt never envisioned its handling the pressures of modern smokeless powders, the Single Action Army never could take advantage of the potential of the cartridges cavernous case. In the late 1950's all this started to change when Bill Ruger developed his Single Action Blackhawk: a Peacemaker look-a-like. Ahead of his time, Ruger foresaw the demand for revolvers that not only recaptured the nostalgia of the Old West, but which also could stand the pressures of modern magnum loads. When Ruger chambered his Blackhawk single action in 45 Long Colt, hand loaders wanting the most powerful revolvers for hunting big game, rejoiced. Truth is, when crammed nearly full with smokeless powder, the ancient 45 Colt is an even better big game hunting cartridge than the 44 magnum because of its larger case and bullet.

Dick Casull was one of those pioneers in reaching the true potential of the great 45 Colt cartridge. Not content with getting 44 magnum level performance ot of the cartridge, Dick's efforts led to the founding of the Freedom Arms Company, the development of a lengthened 45 Colt Cartridge that became the 454 Casull and the birth of the finest single action revolver made. This was the Freedom Arms revolver, a weapon specially built to withstand the huge pressures generated by the Casull round. One can compare the 45 Colt cartridges and the 454's to a .357 magnum. The .357 magnum is simply an elongated 38 special driven at higher pressures with a corresponding increase in velocity. At $3000 per gun the Freedom Arms .454 will group inside an inch at 25 yards. Recently, both Taurus and Ruger have marketed much more affordable .454 Casull revolvers in their Raging Bull and Super Redhawk models.

When it dawned on me that I could shoot 45 Long Colts out of a .454 Casull, I decided I had to have one. I already have a pristine Third Generation Colt Single Action Army. With it I can drive a 250 grain slug down the end of a cigarette from 10 feet. When I found a new Ruger Super Redhawk at 50 % off retail I snapped it up and bought 20 rounds of .454 Casull. It was easy to consistently hit a dime sized circle at 25feet with the .45 cowboy loads. The recoil from the Super Redhawk was a piece of cake. But recoil and muzzle blast from shooting the hyper potent .454 loads can only be described as earthshaking. Two men shooting a .44 magnum in the bay next to me at the shooting range said they could feel the concussion from my .454 in their chests. And in spite of the Super Redhawk's comfortable rubberized grips I really believed my skin was about to start peeling off from its recoil. For many who have softer hands than mine, I'd strongly suggest wearing gloves to avoid having them filleted.

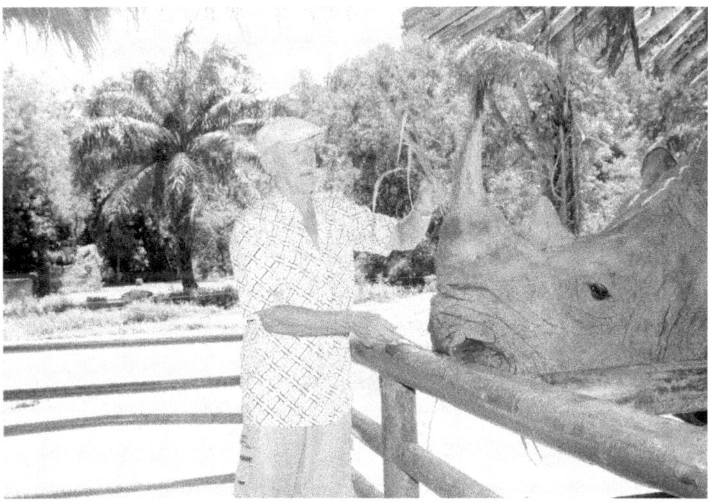

Big game suitable for hunting with the big .454. The author hand feeding a Rhinoceros near his home in Thailand

So what am I going to use this thing for? I'm not going on an

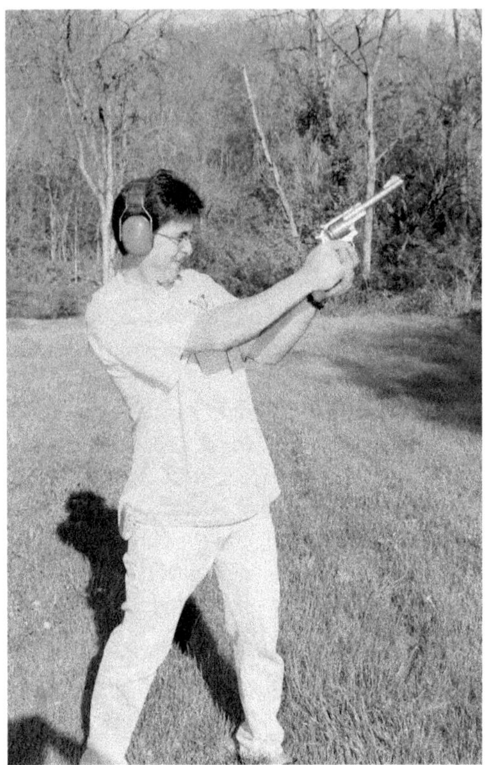

Pure Talent owner Jim Hayek firing 454 Casull while the author was doing a photo shoot of feature entertainers, Carrie Bare, Kelly Taylor and Serenna Starr for the 2004 Xtreme Weapons calendar. Unknown to Jim the author had gone out to get the most potent loads he could find, 260 grain hollow points at 1800 feet per second. As the picture shows the recoil is severe.

African safari, I don't plan on going Elk hunting, and deer are too pretty to kill. But these things are fun to shoot and it's the whole idea of mastery, of a man's putting the heavy slugs exactly where he wants them and overcoming its ferocious recoil with the heaviest loads that does it for me. You can shoot through all kinds of stuff with it and blow things to smithereens. It's too much gun to even be a first rate self defense piece since it takes too long to get back on target from its recoil. But suppose, just suppose that this huge space invader assaulted my apartment and the damn thing was twenty-five feet tall and had thick impenetrable skin? I'd have the most powerful mass-produced revolver on earth and the thing will shoot through and stop practically anything.

# The Roxy's Bomb Girl and 007's Walther PPK

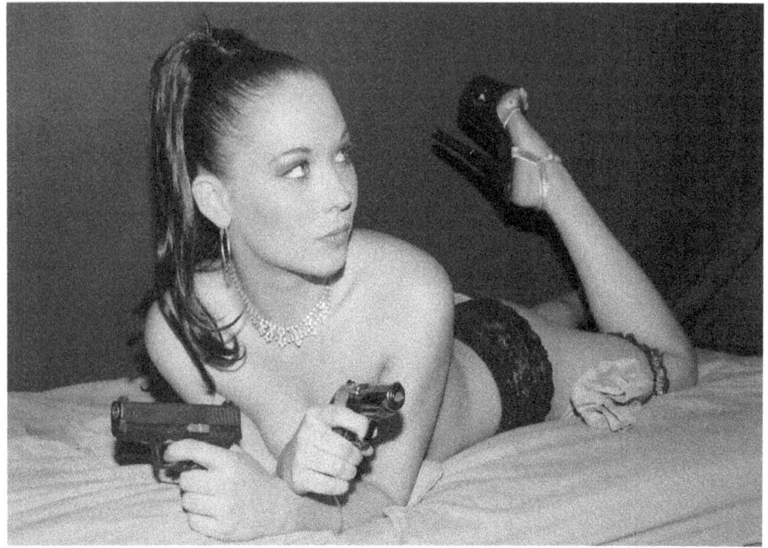

Taylor from PT's Roxy's, one of the author's favorite St. Louis area Clubs, as the Roxy's Bomb Girl.

With James Bond now well past his prime it might be wise for him to turn to younger women such as Taylor dancing at PT's Roxys in Brooklyn, Illinois, who not only has got what it takes to waken James up from the many deep fogs ever since he turned sixty, but is also gravely concerned that his choice of weaponry is too antiquated for him to measure up to his better armed 21st century opponents. The guns of our Roxys Topless Club Bond girl, the subject of this review, are the Walther PPK, the Kahr P 9 and the Seecamp 32 A.C.P.

In Ian Flemming's early Bond novels, 007 is woefully under equipped with a 25-caliber Beretta automatic, a small semi auto which is useful if it is at all, at only point blank range, and even at that offers very poor stopping power against anything larger than a baby rabbit. Q, Flemming's chief armorer for the British Secret Service, insists that Bond replace his pathetic .25 Beretta with the much more powerful PPK in 7.65 mm. For the rest of his career in Flemming's novels, Bond goes about his daily business of shooting the bad guys with his PPK. The reader and later the audience in the 007 movies is assured that Bond is adequately armed for whatever awaits him.

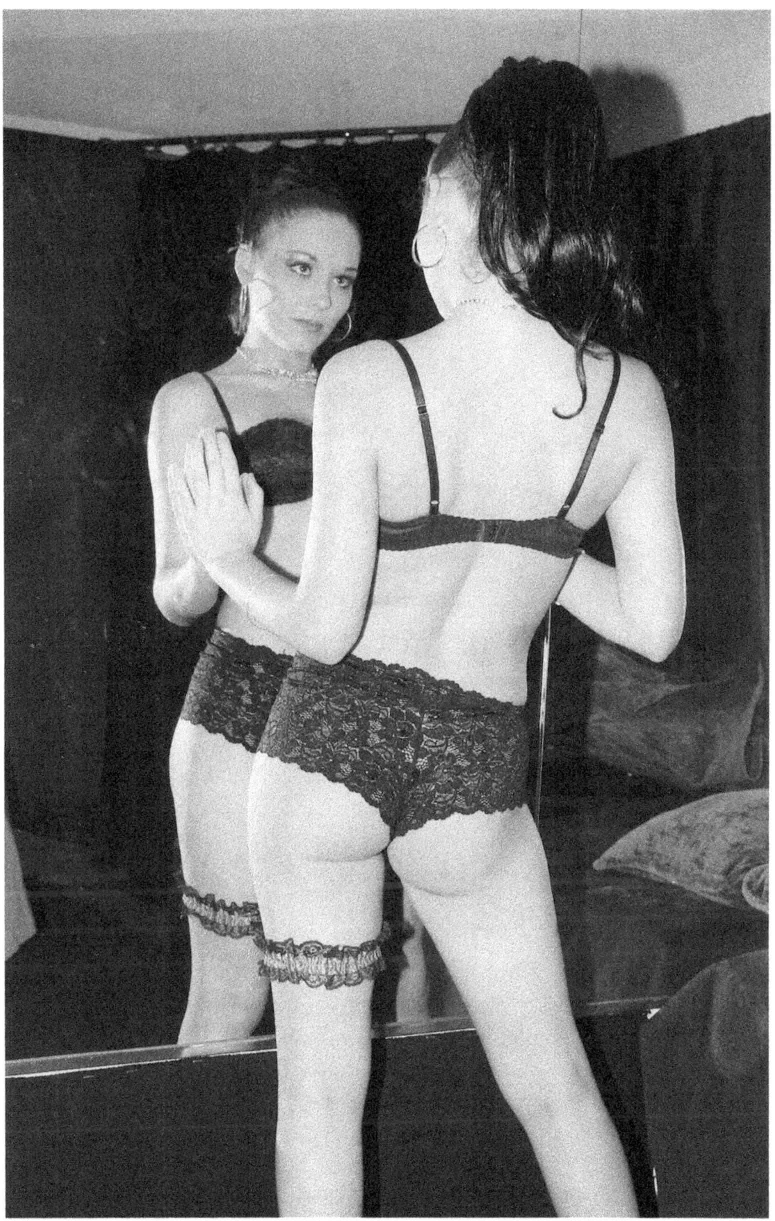

The PPK is a svelte lightweight pocket pistol engineered by the German Walther Arms Company in the 1930's, which started as the model PP, but was shortened to a handier sized version, the PPK. It broke new ground in modern pistol design because it was double action-that is, a bullet could be chambered into the breech, after which one could push a lever that set the trigger in a position so that the gun could not be fired without undertaking a long hard trigger squeeze. Double action refers to a single squeeze of the trigger that both cocks and fires the pistol although later pistol designs such as the Kahr would replace the external hammer with internal striker mechanisms. With the PPK one could also elect to pull the hammer back and fire the piece with an easy pull in single action mode which one accomplishes by pulling the trigger, thus tripping the hammer, which has already been cocked by the shooter, upon the cartridge's primer. The gun's inherent design is very safe since it cannot possibly go off unless the shooter pulls the trigger.

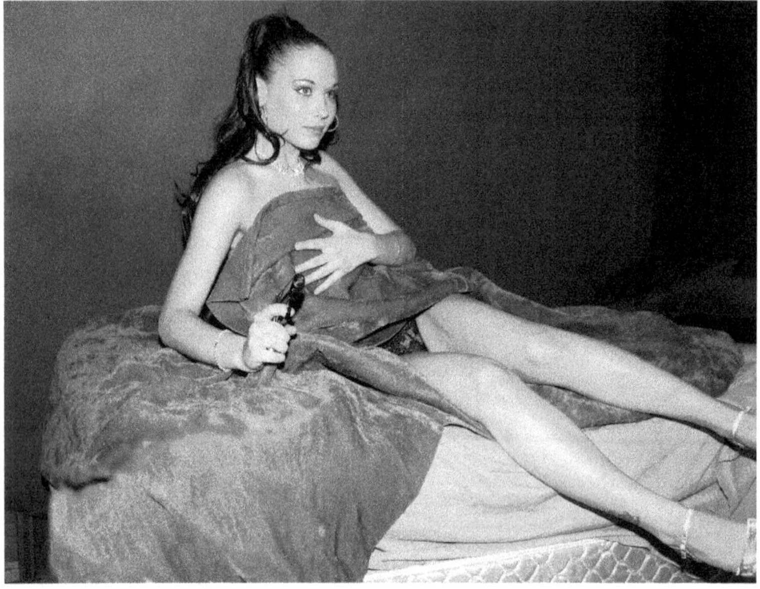

During and after World War II, the German military chose the much more powerful 9mm Parabellum for its service pistols for the most part. The much smaller and lighter PP and PPK models were sometimes used by officers but were more commonly used by the German police, particularly by the Gestapo and other undercover policemen.

A few years ago there were two designs of the PPK on the commercial market. There was the original PPK from Germany in calibers .22, 7.65 mm, and .380 auto and the slightly larger American PPK/S. PPK's are no longer manufactured in Germany. Recently Smith and Wesson became the sole manufacturer and distributor of the PPK/S in the U.S. through a licensing agreement with Walther. Smith and Wesson does not produce the more compact PPK and its PPK/S is currently available in 380 auto only. Prior to

Smith and Wesson's involvement, a company called Interarms imported German made Walthers and subcontracted their manufacture here in the U.S. through a company in Alabama. But quality was not up to German standards and Interarms wound up going belly up. Luckily mine is a pristine German-made PPK in .380 auto, which has a lustrous aftermarket black chrome finish, considered to be more durable than the pistol's original bluing.

The opinion of "gun experts" on the 380 auto's man-stopping ability is divided into two camps. Some consider the .380 auto to be the absolute minimum as a reliable stopper for self-defense whereas many consider it to be inadequate. But nearly everyone who has even a modicum of knowledge about guns deems Bond's first pistol, his beloved .25 Beretta, to be worse than a .22 as a stopper. Keep in mind though that Bond's PPK was chambered in 7.65 mm or what is also known as .32 A.C.P., not 380 auto, a bullet that develops roughly 30 percent more muzzle energy than the .32.

In spite of its deficiencies as a reliable man stopper, the PPK made quite a name for itself for many years. Its lines are trim and seductive, which is probably why Flemming chose the PPK for his suave James Bond character. Its sleek lines combined with relatively low weight made it ideal for concealed carry. Quality of manufacture ensured a reliable weapon that its owner could be proud to carry. And if mine is any indication of most PPK's, its trigger in single action mode is smooth and light compared to most double action semi autos regardless of caliber.

It's a beautiful gun, but the question is, can James Bond do better as he tackles the 21st century? Two likely contenders for Bond's weapon of choice are the Seecamp .32 and the Kahr P-9.

The Kahr P-9 is virtually the same size as the PPK, yet its Polymer frame allows it to weigh in at just 17.7 ounces to the PPK's 21. Of supreme importance is the P-9's chambering in 9 mm which depending on ammo develops anywhere from 350 to 450 foot-pounds of muzzle energy to the .380 Walther's 200. But Bond didn't use a PPK in .380, using instead the even less powerful .32 A.C.P., which develops around 150 foot-pounds at the muzzle.

Which brings up the Seecamp in .32 A.C.P. Seecamp is a small family run operation that has decided not to crank up its production to meet public demand for its excellent little weapon. One can easily wait up to one and a half years for a Seecamp in .32 caliber. I've seen them only once at gun shows and I immediately snapped one up. I've encountered them much more often in .25 auto, which would leave one as poorly armed as James

Bond at the start of his career, who should have been called James Bum for carrying the .25 Beretta in the first place. Only 4 and 1/8th inches long and weighing just 10.5 ounces, the Seecamp is virtually the same size and weight as Bond's hapless Beretta.

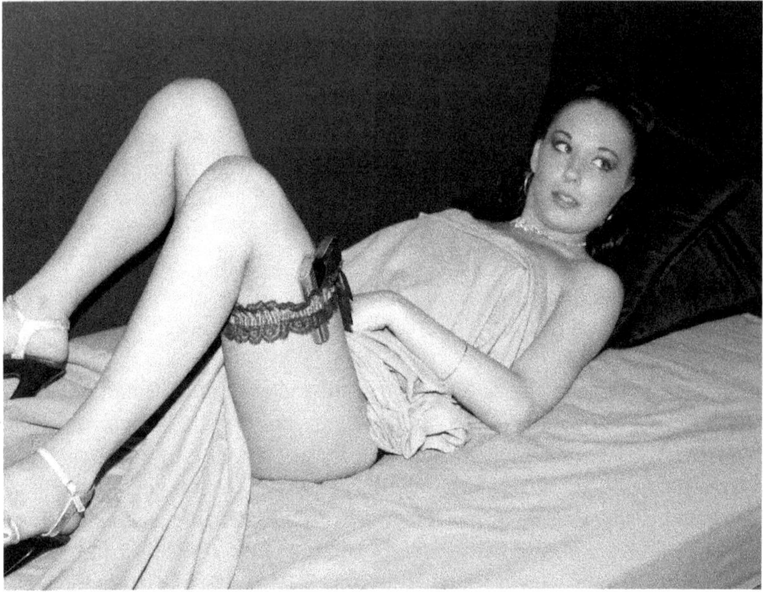

The 32 Seecamp was so highly regarded there was a 2 year wait for delivery

Hailed as the absolute finest small last-ditch close defense pistol ever produced, the principle behind the Seecamp design is that even the most powerful handgun is useless unless its owner has it available when the moment of truth arrives. The Seecamp is so small and unobtrusive, one could carry it to the beach in his swim trunks, hardly noticing it or being noticed carrying it. It doesn't have sights, which can snag in a pocket. It fires in double action mode only, which means a hard long trigger pull, which makes it very safe to carry. There are no external safeties to complicate things or snag in a jacket or pants pocket. And although the .32 A.C.P. is not a .45 or a .357 magnum it's still the same cartridge that Flemming arms Bond with his PPK. The Seecamp is designed around a single hollow point bullet, the 60 grain Winchester Silvertip, which the company guarantees as the only cartridge the Seecamp can fire reliably and this bullet hits more than twice as hard as any .22 or .25 automatic.

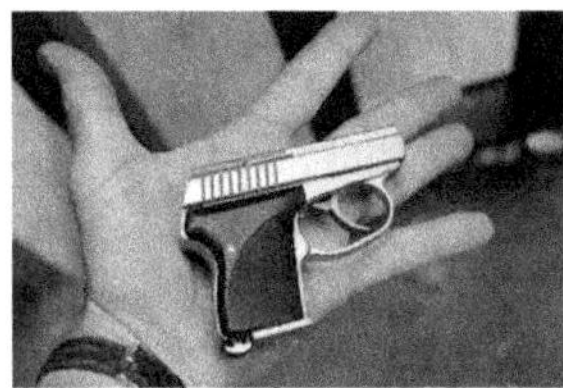

The 32 Seecamp was so highly regarded that there was a 2 year wait for delivery.

Due to its short sighting radius and absence of sights the Seecamp cannot begin to shoot with either the PPK or the Kahr P-9. Its strong suit is it's the utmost in conceivability, a fact dramatized when two police officers once searched my pickup truck for weapons. I had my Seecamp rolled up in my pajamas lying on the floor of the truck. The police officers never found the Seecamp.

The Seecamp is therefore a specialized weapon one has no excuse for not carrying along when one is uncomfortable with carrying larger handguns. So how does the 9-mm Kahr stack up against the PPK?

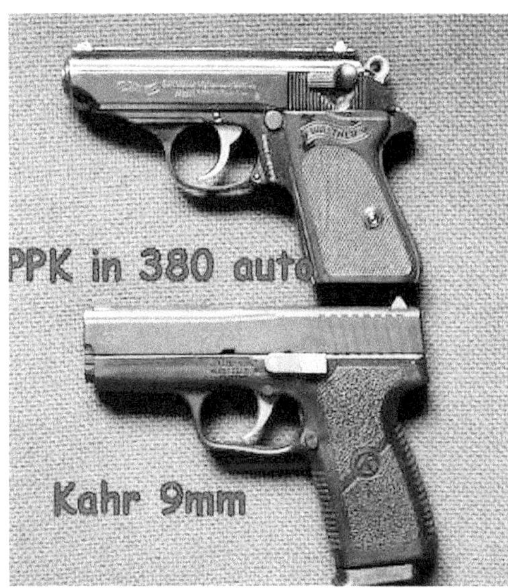


The PPK at first appears to be a much more finely machined pistol than the much more powerful Kahr P-9. Moreover, its sexy lines are prettier than the blocky Kahr. My Kahr has a parkerized slide riding on a polymer (plastic) frame whereas the Walther's black chrome finish is impeccable. Worse, the Kahr fires in double action only which would seem to favor the Walther with its smooth light single action option at the range. But the Kahr shoots the piss out of the PPK. One would think the PPK shoots well for a pocket pistol until one shoots the Kahr. Although the Kahr is double action only, Kahr's double action pistols are the smoothest around. The Kahr also benefits from excellent white high contrast sights that line up quickly and efficiently. In fact, the Kahr is so good, it's competitive with many big name full sized pistols, guns considered far easier to shoot accurately because of their heft and longer sight radius. It's the kind of pistol a shooter can shoot well at twenty-five yards, a distance considered to be outside the range of nearly all pocket pistols.

Although it's only been in existence for a few years, Kahr Arms sales have made it one of the forerunners in modern pistol design. Its P-9 9 mm pistol is roughly the same size as a PPK, yet weighs significantly less. Kahr technology has ensured that it's stone reliable and if the P-9 isn't small enough for an over the hill Bond, who might be tempted to go back to his pitiful 25 caliber Beretta, Kahr has recently introduced an even smaller and lighter version of its P-9. But face it, Bond's getting old,

and rumor has it that he's going for even younger and more beautiful women. With girls as attractive as our Roxys Bomb girl around, it is likely that we will find Bond going around more scantily clad than ever. If James Bond ever clamors for that .25 Beretta again, there's the Seecamp, at the same size and weight, which is much safer to carry, and just as powerful as his old PPK.

# The Dragunov Sniper's Rifle

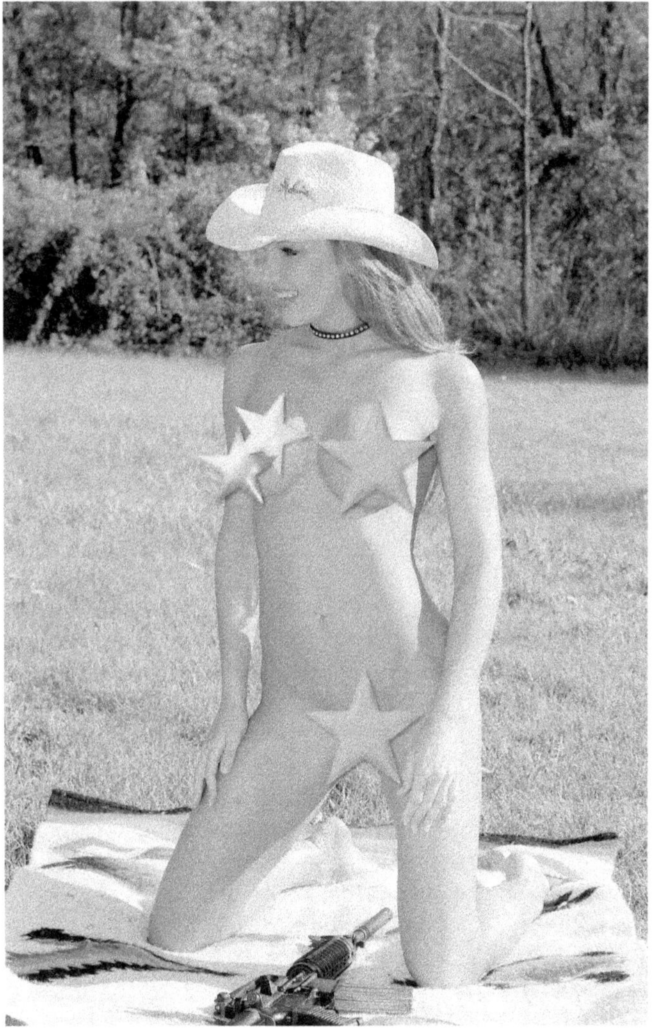

Kelly Taylor poses for the Xtreme Weapons calendar while Pure Talent was holding one of its feature showcases at Big Als gentlemen's club.

His weapon is a highly specialized instrument of death, often a 50 caliber, capable of striking accurately and powerfully at more than 2,000 yards. One of the most feared weapons in warfare is the sniper. Whereas artillery, bombs, and automatic weapons

kill indiscriminately, the sniper has your name on his bullet. Perfectly camouflaged to blend into the foliage, snow drifts, or desert sands of his environment, his mission is to kill the most important soldiers of your unit, i.e. your officers, radiomen directing artillery fire, or the most conspicuously courageous man in your squad. Day or night, the terrifying feeling lurks in the pit of your stomach that a sniper or his spotter is observing you and your comrades through a spotting scope or the cross hairs of a telescopic sight. The modern sniper can be flown by helicopter or parachuted behind your lines where he is able to lurk up to a week, motionless and unseen. If you are unlucky enough to be fighting the American Marines, the sniper you are facing has been specially selected–one out of hundreds makes it through the selection process and some of the most arduous training inflicted by any armed service worldwide. His weapon is a highly specialized instrument of death, often a 50 caliber, capable of striking accurately and powerfully at more than 2,000 yards. As highly evolved as the American art of sniping has become, in many respects long range sniping has been given even greater priority in the Russian Army. The weapon chosen for the long range Russian marksman is the Dragunov, hailed by Western small arms experts as the finest rifle of its kind.

Differing schools of thought on the role of the sniper evolved in the American and Russian armies during World War II, a conflict costing the lives of more than 11 million Soviet combatants and 16 million civilians. Obsolete 1891 bolt action Moisin Nagants were readily available to both the Red Army, and partisans, -irregulars drawn from civilians, who shared in much of the fighting. Nevertheless, by the time of the battle of Stalingrad most Red Army men fought with submachine guns, which gave the Russian infantryman more firepower at close range than any other combatant. Meanwhile, most World War II American infantrymen shouldered the M-1 Garand rifle, the best all around battle rifle since it provided excellent firepower with outstanding long range accuracy. Since the submachine gun's effective range was limited to around 100 yards, the Russians began employing relatively large numbers of skilled riflemen equipped with scope sighted Moisin Nagants to provide the long range capability the Red Army needed.

The sniper is the human equivalent of the submarine–stealthy, hidden from the enemy, and deadly. He strikes suddenly and seldom misses. Just as the invisibility of the submarine enables it to destroy far larger vessels, the sniper, because he is a master at concealment, inspires a terror that is disproportionate to his numbers. Camouflaged in his ghillie suit, he typically operates alone or with a spotter who also operates as a backup armed with a semi automatic or fully automatic rifle. Since officers are favorite big game of the sniper, many officers rip off their badges of rank and refrain from carrying sidearms that give them away as officers. Along with fear, the sniper inspires loathing from his enemies.

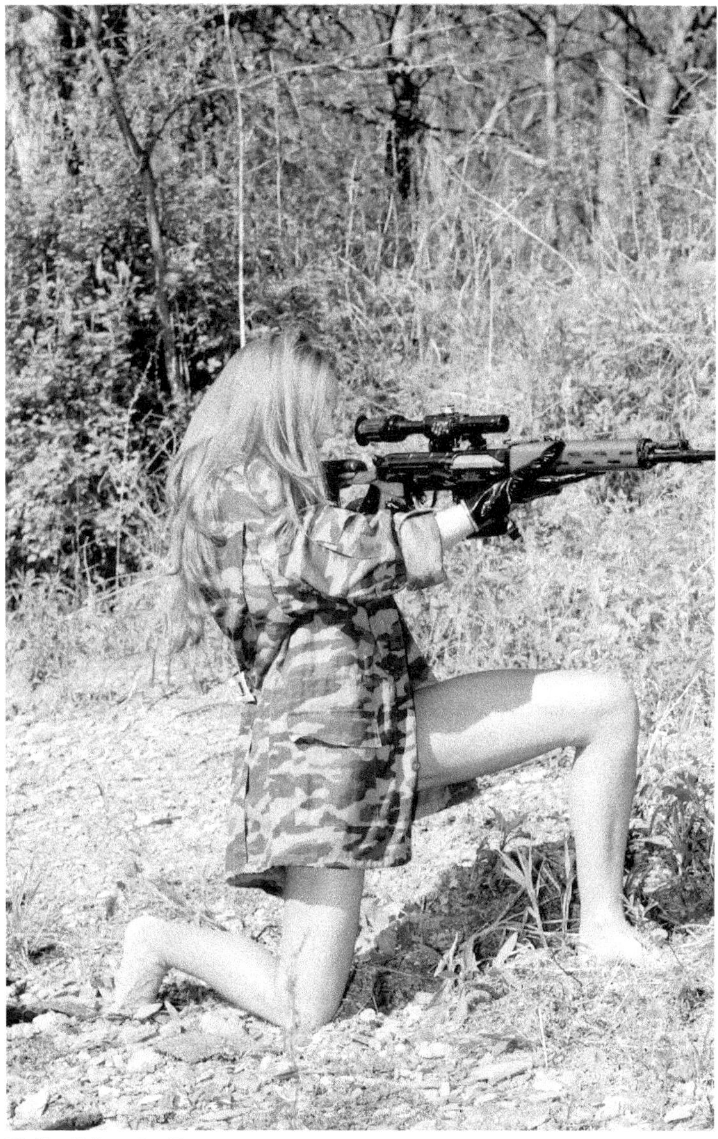

Kelly firing the Dragunov

The proliferation of ghillie suits originally developed by Scottish games keepers, which is composed of burlap strips on which the sniper can easily add grass, or branches and other camouflage added a three-dimensional effect to the sniper's clothing that enable him to appear as a bush or haystack. If you've ever seen one of these things on television or in photos I can guarantee that you will find the thought of men wearing them to stalk his fellow man will inspire strong feelings of terror and revulsion. The sniper is the snake, swift striking and lethal. For the sniper making a single mistake means a swift death, inflicted on him with relish by his intended prey. Very often, that mistake is firing two or more rounds from the same position, which gives his position away, making him the victim of machine gun fire, another sniper, artillery, rocketry or a high velocity round from a tank.

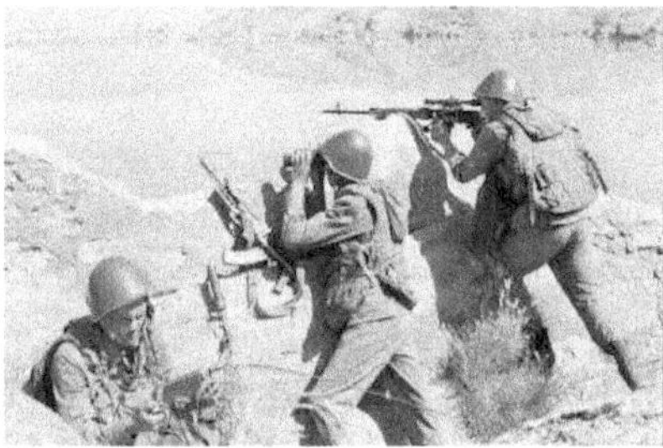

Note how the Dragunov equipped Russian infantryman is providing long range support for his comrades who are using much more compact assault rifles which lack the long range capability of the Dragunov. The AK-47 did not have nearly the long range capability of American standard battle rifles such as the M-1, M-14 and the M-16. Russian tactical doctrine therefore called for more integration into regular units for its snipers whereas the American approach called for its snipers going it alone much more often. A team of two was the general rule with extreme accuracy at very long range being stressed along with rifles that would deliver it.

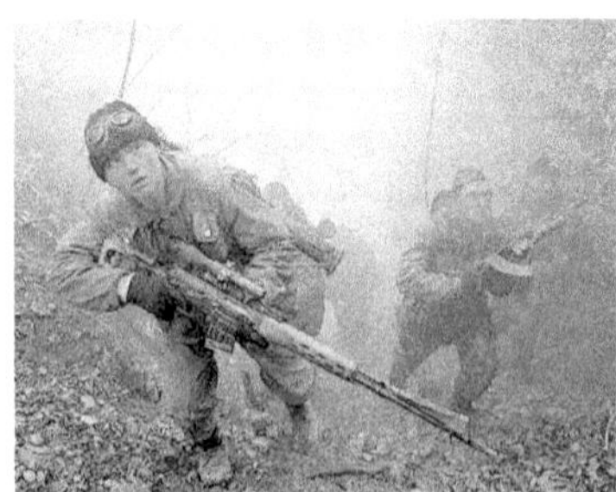

The American school of thought on snipers is that since firing too many rounds from the same position is the kiss of death, the sniper should use the most accurate weapon capable of dealing death at the longest range, and that this end is best served by a tricked out bolt action mounting a high-powered scope. Since the sniper is only going to fire one or two shots before changing his position so that he can remain invisible, the sniper is not thought to be handicapped by the relative slowness of the bolt action compared to the semi auto.

enter the Dragunov, which embodies the Russian school of thought on the matter which is predicated on, "It isn't necessarily so." I remember viewing actual film footage of the bitter street fighting at Stalingrad of a Russian infantryman killing a German soldier with his scope sighted Moisin Nagant bolt action. Several Germans were making a break for it. The Russian sniper got one although he might have killed the other two men had he been armed with a semi-auto. Although the Moisin Nagant was the primary sniper's rifle for the Red Army, many snipers preferred the Tolkarev semi automatic rifle, which although grossly inferior to the American M-1, still permitted fast follow up shots when multiple targets were engaged. In 1947 the Russian Army adopted the AK-47, a magnificently reliable automatic rifle, that is compact enough to be easily carried in armored vehicles, and capable of a high rate of fire, as its main battle rifle. By the late 1960's, the U.S. armed forces had fully embraced the M-16 rifle, capable of the same firepower of the AK-47, although not as reliable. What the M-16 possessed over the AK-47 in spades was greater range, because of the flat trajectory of its high speed .223 bullet and much greater accuracy that enabled it to become one of the most accurate rifles ever devised. So, as with the World War II American soldier with his M-1 Garand, today's typical American infantryman finds himself to be far better equipped than his Russian counterpart for handling his enemy at long range. Not to worry, however, since the Russians had already anticipated this. By 1965 the Dragunov was already fulfilling the Russian scheme of doing things.

# The M-1 Garand, the greatest battle rifle ever

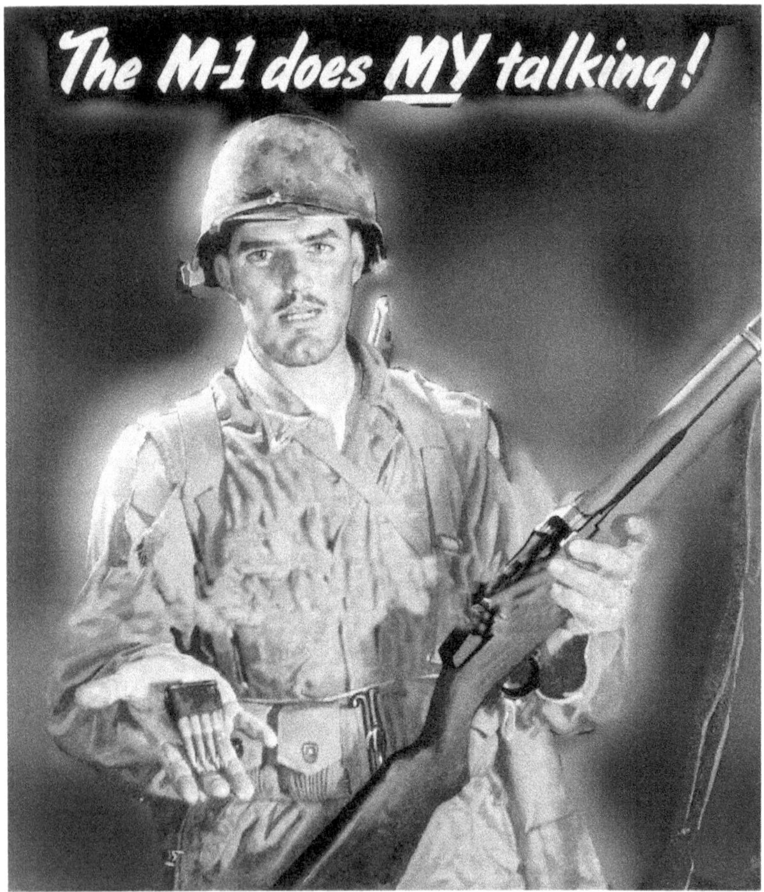


World War II U.S. Armed Forces recruiting poster

General Patton, perhaps the most controversial and brilliant armored warfare tactician during the Second World War, called the M-1 Garand "the greatest battle implement ever devised." And Patton could very well have been right because the M-1 was so good at doing so many things extremely well that it gave the American infantryman a huge advantage over his opponents that his British and Russian allies never had.

The M-1 Garand became the standard American battle rifle of World War II giving the American infantryman much greater firepower over his enemies with reliability and accuracy, and it continued to serve throughout the Korean War, and into the Vietnam War as the M-14, which was essentially an upgraded M-1. And in the war in Iraq the M-14 is still being used in situations where its 22 caliber successors are deficient. But sixty years ago, the main battle rifle of every major combatant during World War II was the bolt action with even the bolt action K-98 Mauser remaining the main battle rifle for the Germany in spite of the German Army's deploying large numbers of submachine guns in order to increase the short range firepower of its fighting men. Meanwhile the Russian Army had almost completely replaced its aging bolt action rifles by the second half of the war with submachine guns that provided the Russian foot soldier with unprecedented short range firepower. Even though we equipped our soldiers with a variety of small arms, it was the M-1 which bore the brunt of most of the fighting. Weighing 9 pounds unloaded the M-1 fired eight shots of powerful 30-06 ammo as fast as a man could pull the trigger. It could be

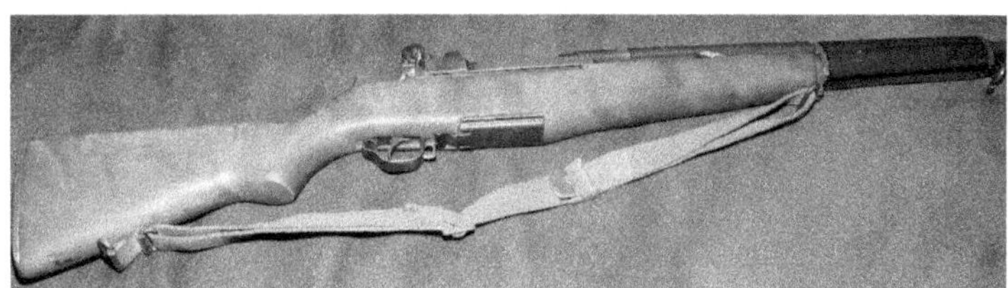

reloaded quickly from eight round clips, shoot through five or six men if they stood in a row and nearly always put a man down with just one shot. The M-1 was so accurate that it replaced the bolt action as a sniper's rifle and today it is still being used in 1,000 yard matches. Ask any World War II or Korean War Veteran who had actually seen combat what weapon he'd choose and you will see his eyes glaze over as he replies, "The M-1 Garand."

Firing one for the first time would be firing a legend while reliving a piece of U.S. History. But I'd be doing more than just firing one for the first time. I had to get my own M-1 to do this article, so I wound up buying one from Vic Meyer who I had just met at a gun show. But I only had it for a couple of days and had not test fired it. Luckily I had new recruit, Skie along, one of the prettiest girls to ever dance on a St Louis Metro East stage. Her assignment would be to handle the submachine gun.

New recruit Skie had just turned twenty just two days before we hit the Belleville, Illinois shooting range. A quick witted willowy five foot six blonde,

I had seen her dance often enough to find her to be a splendid physical specimen. Her first weapon would be the new H & K MP-5 which represents the current state of the art in submachine guns, that is rapidly replacing the Uzi in police and special forces worldwide.

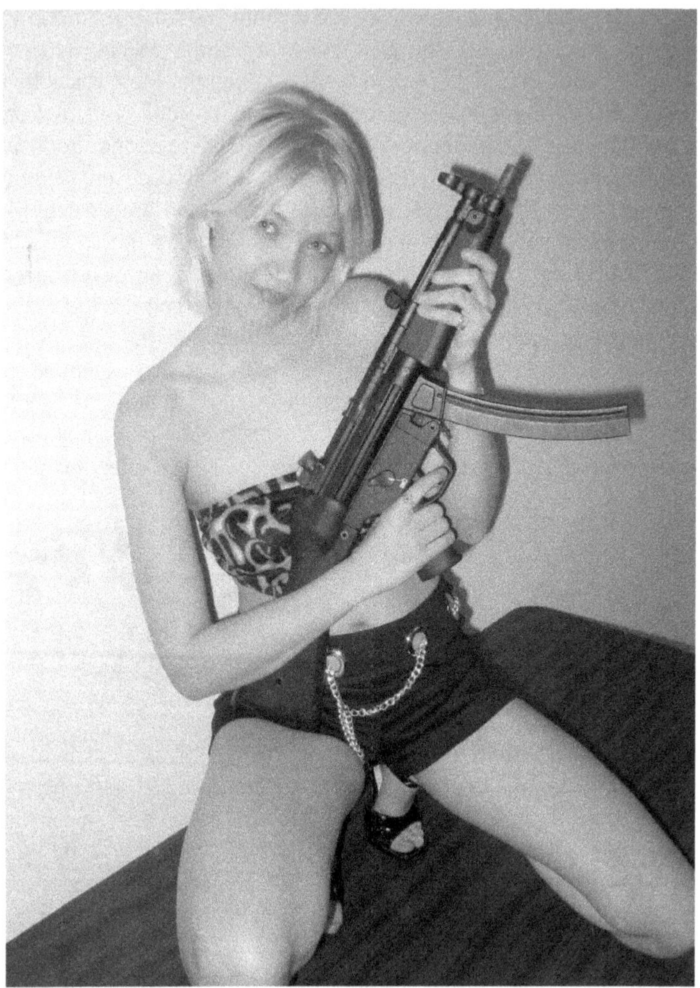

The author met Skie when she was 20 dancing at the Platinum Club. Skie was with him when he first tested his new M-1 Garand at the Belleville gun range and later accompanied him as his photography assistant while he was covering Pure Talent's Feature showcase at Club Fantasies in Providence, Rhode Island

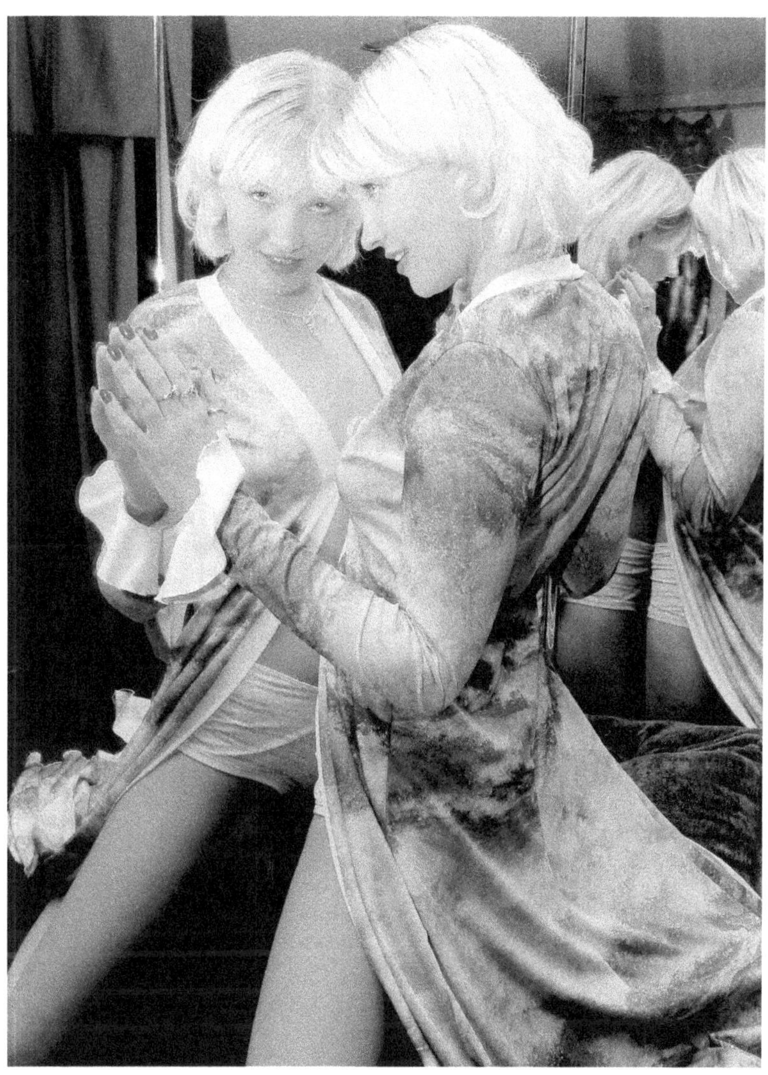

In my hands the MP-5 was short and light, feeling like a finely crafted German toy with the precision of a BMW. In the front room of the gun range, Jim, a police officer, who moonlights by working at the gun range with another police officer, briefed us on how to operate both the MP-5 and my much larger and heavier M-1. Taking one look at the 30-06 ammo I brought with me, Jim shook his head and told me I couldn't use it since it was armor piercing and would go through the range's steel backstop. I ended up getting a good deal on some 30-06 ammo that wouldn't.

New recruit Skie took immediately to the MP-5 as she would to every weapon that she would wind up firing. Although inexperienced with guns

Skie would later keep all her shots inside an area of a man's fist with my Python revolver at thirty-five feet. She moved the MP-5's three position selector lever from "safe" to semi auto. After putting all her shots in the man-sized silhouette target's mid section I advised her to move the selector to full auto. "Aim at where the target's balls would be," I told her. Then just let the gun's recoil move your point of impact up into its chest area. It should do it without your having to do a thing since it's on full auto."

Her first two or three shots on full auto would have castrated a real man. Her first bursts put five our six 9 mm slugs into the target before she could release the trigger. The last shots hit the silhouettes right side which meant that she was allowing the recoil of the MP-5 to twist the gun to her right. I took the clip out and added a few rounds, then handed the gun back to her, telling her to let the MP-5 recoil upwards instead of up and to the right.

Now this raw recruit Skie's quite a gem and I'm not telling anybody where she lives. Catching on immediately she managed to keep all her shots centered on what she was aiming at. She got onto the gun's trigger, limiting her bursts to just three or four rounds, which is considered ideal in combat. But she kept hitting the silhouette where a man's balls would have been. The submachine gun's muzzle just wasn't climbing as much I had expected it to. "Forget shooting it in the testicles," I told her. "Center on its belly or chest."

Her next bursts ripped into the silhouette's mid section. When the clip was empty, I hit the electronic target return button, which started to move the T-bar holding the target back toward us on a steel cable. In addition to the bullet holes in the silhouettes mid section there were two in the middle of its head. "Why did you hit him in the head?" I asked her.

She gave me an impish smile and said: "Because I wanted to see if I could." (I'm still not telling any of you people how to find her because if she can handle a camera's shutter anything like she can handle a gun's trigger, I'm thinking of hiring her as my photographer's assistant).

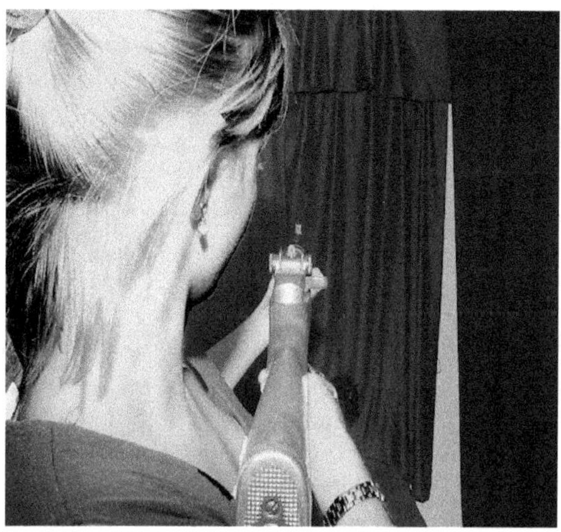

It might not kick all that much but when Skie shouldered the M-1 with the butt away from her shoulder, we decided the much lighter submachine gun would be much better for her

That MP-5 was so cute that I had to take my turn with it. Firing it was like handling a vibrator. But I was saving the best for last--The M-1. Jeff Cooper, the gun writer and ex World War II Marine colonel, who is widely regarded as the founder of modern day defensive pistol technique and considered by many as "The gunner's guru" wrote that any self-respecting real American should have at least one M-1 in his closet. Now Cooper's not just any gun writer. The man's got a Master's in History from Stanford and is just as opinionated as he is brilliant. He has a low opinion of the submachine gun feeling that it is a spray and pray stop gap for troops that just don't know how to shoot.

I laid the rifle across the shelf in front of me on which we were putting our clips and spare ammo. I had sent the silhouette target all the way down to the end of the firing lane twenty-five years away. I then centered the M-1's iron sights just above and between the eyes. The rifle's sights were great allowing for rapid target acquisition and pinpoint aiming when required. "Bam." The 30-06's thunderous report reverberated throughout the indoor range. I could feel the healthy nudge against my shoulder and momentarily lost my sight picture as the muzzle climbed from the gun's recoil. But the rifle's great sights enabled me to quickly line up on my mark as I squeezed the trigger a second time. Had I been shooting a bolt action I would have had to work the gun's bolt to chamber another round which would have jerked the rifle to the left or right off my point of aim.

I kept shooting until the eight round clip ran empty. Because of the gun's semi -automatic action I only had to worry about lowering the rifle slightly to quickly get back on target each time it recoiled. Unlike most semi autos, the M-1 ejects its clip with a loud ping. In other guns you have to manually hit the ejector button to remove the clip. I then inserted another fully loaded clip into the rifle and handed my watch to special recruit Skie. "I took my time just to see how accurate this thing is," I told her. "I am now going to run off a clip into the target's chest area and I'm going to do it quickly. Time me."

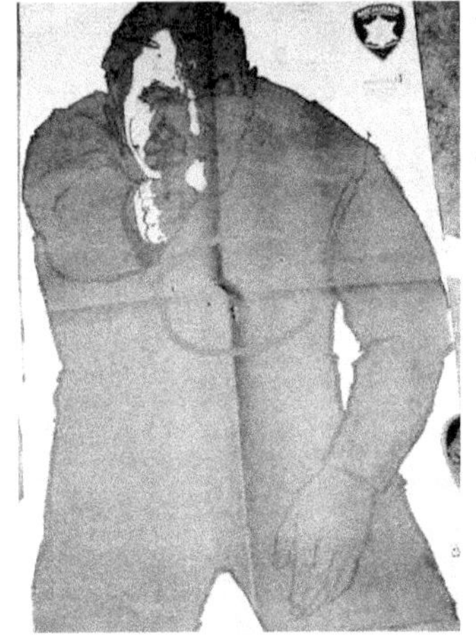

This time I centered on the chest for the first round. As soon as my sight picture moved upwards upon recoil, I lowered the rifle and vaguely sighted in once again on the silhouette's chest as I fired again. The pinging of the ejected clip signaled me when the rifle was empty.

I then pushed the electronic return button which started the target moving back toward us. "How fast was I?" I asked Skie as she studied my watch.

"Ten seconds. Maybe twelve," she replied.

There were eight 30 caliber holes exactly centered above the intersection of the eyes. Seven out of the eight measured just 1.25 inches apart. My rapid fire sequence against the silhouette's chest put eight out of eight rounds in the killing zone. I wanted to shoot the M-1 again and again but Skie and I had pistols to shoot next. "Now that's a rifle," I thought. If an elephant were charging me, I would have eight chances to get one bullet right into its brain or just perforate its chest with rapid fire. This thing will do anything.

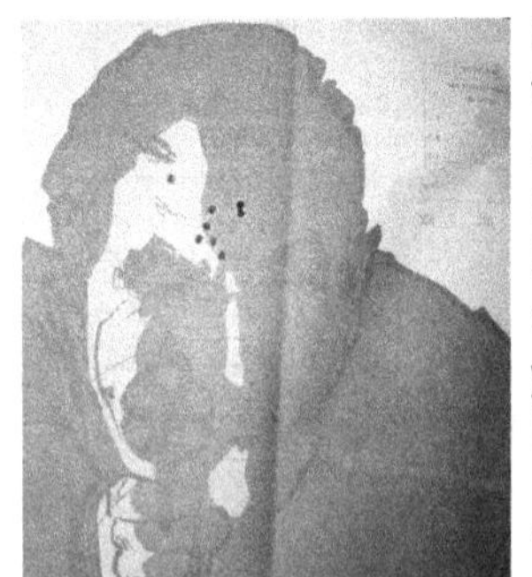

I had never seen a woman take to shooting as fast as Special Recruit Skie. But Jim had felt that she was too inexperienced to handle the M-1's recoil. She helped me pick up the empty brass littering the floor of our shooting bay and put my stuff away. When we returned to the front room, I yelled at Jim: "That MP-5 is a fine weapon but I like the M-1 much better."

"You gotta be crazy," said Jim. "Look, I'm a police officer and we have to be trained to empty out a room with a weapon if necessary. Would you really prefer sweeping a room with that M-1 when you can hose it down with the MP-5?" "Perhaps not," I thought. "But that M-1 will do it all. It fires rapidly and it hits with devastating power and it will reach a long way out there which is something that little 9 mm MP-5 can't do." I paid my bill and Special Recruit Skie said to me as we got into my pickup. "I had fun. I want to go back."

# Queen of Rifles, the Springfield M1 A

"What's a rifle like this doing in a rural cabin? It has the power you need for deer, moose, elk, or bear, so long as there is short enough a magazine in it to conform to the game laws. It also has the power that neutralizes vehicles with judicious shot placement."

Massod Ayoob
Backwoods Home Magazine, May, 1997

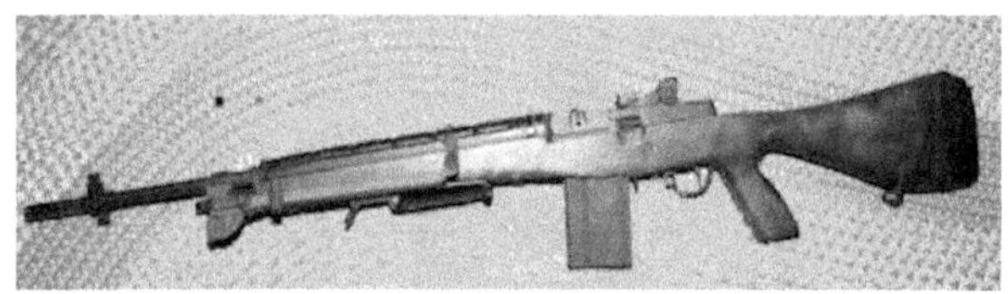

The Springfield M1A is Massod Ayoob's number one choice for a do everything rifle when he's out in the wilds removed from civilization where his very survival might call upon him to hunt big game for food, stop an enraged Grizzly bear or shoot it out with a gang of thugs. Massad mentions using short clips to "conform to the game laws." Twenty shot magazines are readily available, which is just the thing to shoot it out with drug dealers converging on your homestead in thick bodied semi trucks, or hiding behind trees most of which the M 1 A's .308 steel jacketed bullet will drill clean through. Which is not surprising since the M 1A is Springfield Armory's civilian version of the M-14 rifle which had been the U.S. main battle rifle from the late 1950's through the opening years of the Vietnam War. Although obsoleted by the much lighter M-16 rifle, the M-14 was so good that it is still being called upon by elite troops when combat at long range is imminent. An ex cop, Massad Ayoob is one of the most foremost gun writers in the country. Like Massad I had to get my own Springfield M 1 A, which had been my dream rifle since I was eleven. With its muzzle flash suppressor, dark walnut stock, and lengthy twenty-shot magazine, the M-14 looked like something from another planet, a technological marvel to my eleven-year-old mind when I first saw it at the Illinois State fair while checking out the optical sights for the army's latest mortars and recoilless rifles, which I imagined myself firing into the hatch of a Russian tank. "Dad, this M-14 fires a 7.62 mm shell. What's that?" I asked my father.

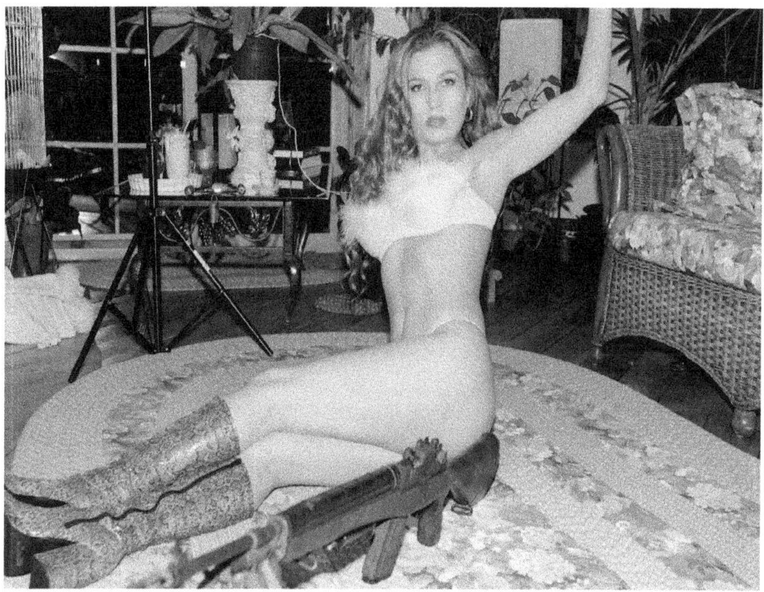

**Feature entertainer Darien Ross with fully automatic M-15 at the Meyer Farm in Missouri. The M-15 is essentially an M-14 with a bipod.**

"It's a new cartridge used by Europeans, including the French," my dad told me.

The prospect of an European cartridge combined with that awesome looking flash suppressor appealed to my 11-year-old mind that was already contemplating the purchase of a Springfield army surplus 30-06 I would get after my 12th birthday with the money I'd make working all Summer on the farm. A doctor living close to us had a Springfield hidden beneath his bed, and after fondling it a few times I had to have one just like it. Its lines were trim and it had sights adjustable to 2700 yards. And that lengthy 30-06 round was just the thing to shoot through anything short of a tank-- perfect for an eleven-year-old living out in the country. This was a much better rifle than that blocky heavy looking M-1 Garand rifle that had replaced it, which I had so far only seen in pictures. As for the M-14-it was the latest thing in the military arsenal, representing what an 11-year-old could never lay his hands on.

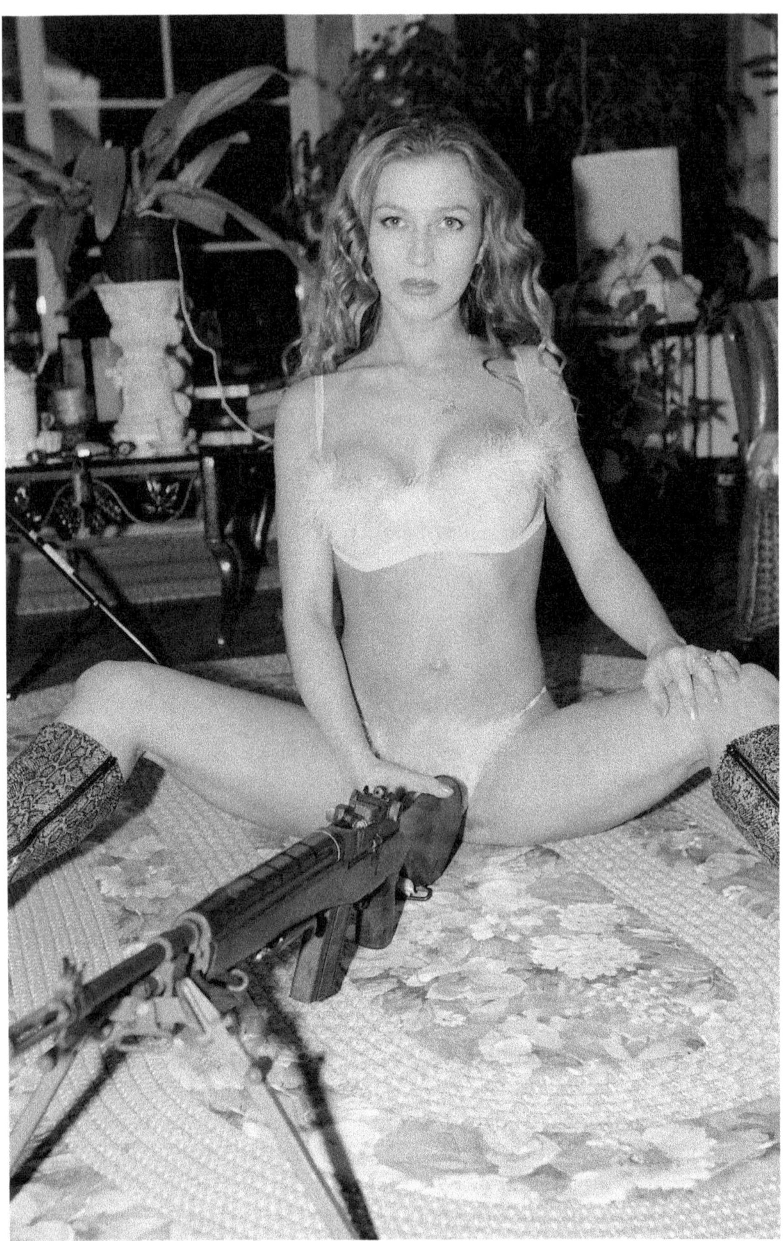

Was I ever wrong, but what can you expect from an eleven-year-old? That M-14 is an M-1, or at least the son of the M-1. The contour of the stock is more streamlined and its flash suppressor gives the rifle more length, which makes it appear trimmer. Moreover, the M 1 appears unwieldy only in pictures. It is a perfectly balanced piece that comes up to the shoulder just so with sights far superior to the Springfield's. It was for its time, as General

Patton called it, the greatest battle implement ever designed, giving the U.S. WWII infantryman firepower far exceeding the bolt actions used by their opponents. Its accuracy was so fine that even today, the M 1 is still winning 1,000 yard matches. The M-14's 7.62 mm cartridge is not European. It's only the metric designation for its .308 cartridge, which was in the late 1950's an American designed cartridge which we rammed down the throat of our Nato allies.

Despite its greatness, the M-1 had several faults. First, its clips were limited to eight rounds. Moreover, once a soldier fired several rounds he couldn't top off the clip. The M-1 uses a clip which the soldier loads into his rifle from the top of the breach. When it's empty, the rifle ejects it into the air with a loud ping which some detractors claim can give the M-1 carrying infantryman's position away. The action is prone to inflicting M-1's thumb on careless shooters-a phenomenon causing one's thumb to be caught in the rifle's mechanism resulting in a severe cut or broken thumb.

The wave of the future had been shown by Germany's late war development of the assault rifle, a weapon with a selector switch that enabled it to be fired either full auto or semi auto utilizing medium power ammunition, which had sufficient stopping power to normally take a man out with one shot but which didn't have the recoil of full power service ammunition. Recoil was modest enough to allow fully automatic fire without having the rifleman's fourth round spray the mosquitos circling above his head. The assault rifle, since it fired a less powerful round could be made lighter and since its ammo was not nearly as long or heavy as 30-06 or similar full power ammunition, a lot more of it could be carried.

In 1947 the Soviet Union's military had adopted the medium powered AK-47 assault rifle as its premiere battle rifle. Meanwhile Great Britain was clamoring a medium powered 28 caliber round as the standard Nato rifle cartridge to be used in a new generation of battle rifles carried by Nato troops contemplating an attack on Western Europe by Russia and its Warsaw Pact allies. But the U.S. armed forces, still enamored with the concept that the United States was a nation of sharpshooters clung to the concept of the full powered 30 caliber long range round.

What we all ended up with was the .308 or 7.62 Nato cartridge. The .308 is basically a shortened 30-06 cartridge. It is somewhat lighter than the 30-06 and more suited to automatic and semi automatic rifle designs, yet it possesses nearly all the power of its parent round. The U.S. as the leading military and economic power of the Western World, succeeded in forcing Great Britain, West Germany, France and other Western European countries to embrace the new cartridge although most of the Western powers would arm their troops with Browning designed FAL battle rifles.

The U.S. which had such a resounding success with its M-1 wound up with an improved M-1, which it designated as the M-14 in 1957. Notable differences between the M-1 and the M-14 include a box magazine that is inserted into the bottom rather than the top of the rifle. The magazine typically holds 20 rounds. It can be topped off after one or several rounds have been fired and is manually ejected when the soldier pushes a magazine release button. Its flash suppressor helps to reduce the fireball produced by firing the weapon at night, which helps the rifleman retain his night vision while minimizing the chance of giving away his position. Early M-14's could also be fired both semi auto and full automatic via a selector switch.

By the early 1960's the M-14 had still not completely replaced the M-1 in the hands of our troops. At this time, the U.S. found itself in a rapidly escalating war in Vietnam. But while the M-14 was replacing the M-1 in the field a new rifle started taking over. Originally intended for Air Force personnel guarding our airfields, the advantages of the lightweight high-powered .22 were not lost on the Pentagon. It could be easily controlled during fully automatic fire and twice as much .223 ammunition could be carried as full powered .308 ammo.

Reliability problems emerged with the new M-16 that were severe enough to cause critics to complain that more American servicemen were being killed by their own weapons than by the enemy. Moreover the high speed .223 cartridge was easily deflected by tall grass, twigs and other obstacles, and at long range the cartridge gave up a lot of accuracy and knockdown power to the .308.

Most of the reliability problems of the M-16 have been solved. However, the M-14 never could be fired effectively on full auto since its recoil was simply too much. Furthermore weighing 9 pounds empty, an M-14 with a fully loaded 20 round clip is a chore to carry. During the Vietnam conflict new M-14's pushed into service were machined to fire semi auto only once top military brass rightfully concluded that fully automatic capable M-14's merely wasted ammunition.

There are still a number of M-14's in our military stockpiles, and although it has been largely replaced by the M-16 and its improved versions, the M-14 is still being used in the field. It is a far more effective long range weapon than its lesser powered counterpart and its bullet is not deflected nearly as much by obstacles. It offers superior penetration while the superior killing power of its much larger 30 caliber bullets over the .223 in a variety of circumstances, particularly at long range cannot be denied.

Last month I picked up my dream rifle, a Springfield M 1 A. It's all business, with its dark walnut wood stock giving it a touch of understated elegance. For me the M-1 Garand and the Springfield M-1 A are both much more fun to shoot than any submachine gun on full auto. With either you can get back on target far faster than you can with a bolt action since all you have to worry about is recovering from the rifle's recoil and pulling the trigger. The M-1 Garand and the Springfield M-1 A are so well balanced that the sights want to line right up on the target like a homing pigeon. You peer through the best peep sights ever designed by man and touch off a round. The gun is instantly ready for a second trigger squeeze but the recoil lifts the sights from the target as you hear the rifle's loud report, and know intuitively that your bullet has arrived downrange with the power of a freight train. It's a challenge to get back on target quickly, but that's what make these things so much fun to shoot. Both the M-1 and the M 1 A are real rifles, meant for connoisseurs who appreciate fine machinery that are capable of performing just about any job required of them--Guns that can shoot well and speak out with authority where a single shot counts. Funny though that Springfield bolt action I worked so hard for all summer when I was twelve, has been relegated to the gun safe while both the M-1 and the M-1 A stand in clear view of my bed. The chunky M-1 I despised so much as a kid, is a very close call to the M-1 A as my favorite rifle. As I told Darien Ross before I took her pictures with the M-1 A-----"If I could own just one rifle, the one you will be modeling with is it. It's my best gun." But not by much. That M-1 Garand's a dream. Just eight shots to the M-1 A's twenty? Who cares unless you are defending yourself against human wave attacks of drug addled aliens.

# Pride of the Gunfighter–the 45 Colt Single Action Army

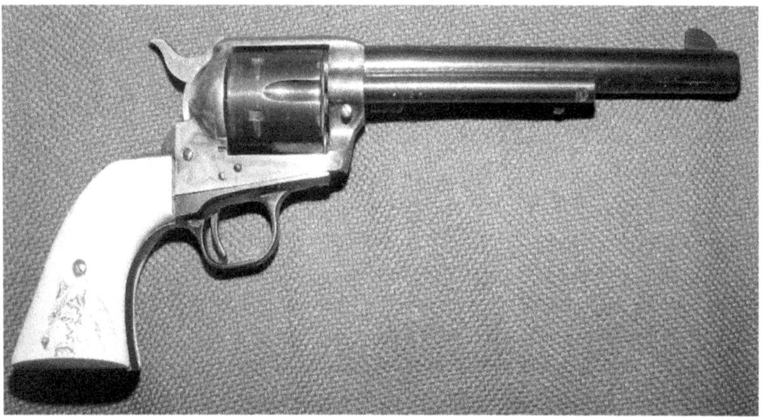

The author's .45 Colt Peacemaker. Note the scrimshawed imitation ivory grips with the Alpha Wolf head which represents his web site at Alpha Productions.

The little boy watches the seasoned gun fighter pull his .45 Colt from his holster, level it, and fire five times, obliterating a white rock each time he fires. The man's speed is awesome. The boy had been admiring the gun fighter's revolver in its leather holster, sneaking looks on the sly. So far its deadly barrel had been hidden from view, concealed in its scabbard with only its pearl grips betraying its lethal purpose. Until now. Each time the man fires the little boy hears a deafening roar breaking the silence in the mountains. The gunfighter and his 45 Colt Single Action Army Peacemaker embody a deadly violence that is quicker and more deadly than the most dangerous predator alive. The.45 Colt carried by the gunfighter in the movie is the Colt .45 Single Action Army. More than any hand gun or any firearm that ever existed or ever will, this is THE GUN, the weapon that has been most closely connected to the individualistic hero of the Old West--or badman-- in movies, legend, and fact.

The Colt 45 Single Action Army rode the hips of men like Wyatt Earp, Doc Holiday, and Pat Garrett. More than a hundred years later I'd be firing over a thousand rounds through my own .45 Colt Single Action Army, each time experiencing a nostalgic sense of a past when personal differences were often settled by the gun.

Ironically most revolver armed Old West cowboys, gamblers, lawmen and desperados didn't start off walking around with metallic cartridge firing Colt 45's or 44's on their hips. Just a few years prior to the Civil War, Samuel Colt developed the cap and ball revolver, the most prolific examples being the 1851 Navy in 36 caliber and the 1860 Army .44's. One had to load each chamber of the cap and ball's cylinder with black powder, ram a ball on top of the charge, and finally insert a percussion cap on a nipple located behind each of the revolver's six chambers, a slow and tedious process. Worse, the cap and ball Colts' ignition systems were often unreliable due to a fired cap's tendency to fall off its nipple into the mechanism of the revolver and jam the weapon. But it would be the 1851 Navy Colt that would be the favorite of the James and Younger brothers for most of their bank robbing careers and the most favored revolver of Wild Bill Hickok, who was widely regarded as the most deadly man with a six shooter of them all.

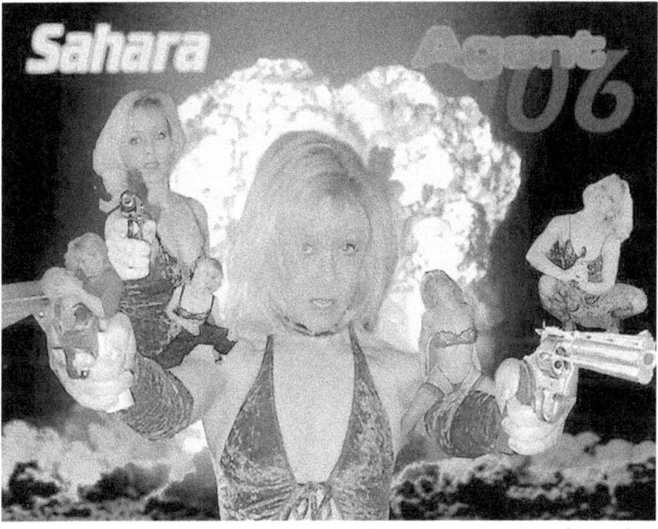


Sahara was agent 006 in one of the madcap internet movies the author and his friends from the St. Louis Metro East clubs used to video for fun in the area's bars. This montage was not done by the author. A Canadian calling himself "Beerman" who used to participate in the author's chat room e-mailed this collage to the author while he was online at the Dollies Playhouse in the Saint Louis Metro East.

It wouldn't be until 1873, when the Single Action Army in 45 Colt became the official sidearm of the U.S. military, that revolvers started using metallic cartridges in which the bullet was crimped into a case containing a charge of black powder. This new revolver, which was also available in calibers other than the .45 Colt, vastly improved both the reliability of a man's personal sidearm and its stopping power, particularly when chambered in 45 Colt, which combined a large .45 caliber bullet weighing 250-260 grains with 40 grains of black powder.

The Colt Single Action Army was to become the most popular sidearm of the Old West although many gun owners preferred their Colts to be chambered in .44-40 caliber simply because they could use the same cartridge in their revolvers they were already using in their lever action rifles, which were unavailable in .45 Colt. By the mid 1880's still a new development in revolver technology led to a few pistol packing Westerners turning in their Single Actions for the new double action revolvers just entering the market. Simply put, a man has to pull the hammer back before pressing the trigger on a single action whereas a double action revolver can be fired by his pulling straight back on the trigger which both cocks and fires the piece. Billy the Kid, for instance, favored the Colt Lightning double action revolver whereas Pat Garrett, the man who killed him, still used the big Colt Single Action 45.

By the 1890's, the U.S. government had replaced the .45 Colt Single Action Army with the new double action .38 long Colt. This worked out real well until soldiers actually had to start using them.  Curtain call for the newfangled revolver came after the conclusion of the Spanish American War during the Philippine Insurrection when American troops were unable to stop fanatical sword wielding Moro tribesmen with their little .38 revolvers. After a few decapitations due to the 38 long Colt’s lack of stopping power, hundreds of .45 Single action Army Colts were pulled out of storage and rushed to the Philippines. It was here that the .45 made its reputation as a reliable man stopper.  Plans were immediately laid to replace all U.S. Army revolvers with a new .45 automatic.

My .45 Colt Single Action Army has imitation ivory grip panels. On one are my initials. I had an artist scrimshaw a picture of an Alpha Wolf on the other. Its sights are fixed, consisting of a groove along the revolver's top strap and a blade for a front sight. My Single Action Army must have been manufactured to a perfectionist's tolerances since it will shoot dimes all day long from twenty-five feet out without my having to make allowances for windage or elevation.

Thousands of Old West buffs compete in Cowboy Action shoots across the U.S. each year. Each contestant is required to compete with a shotgun, a lever action rifle and a single action revolver. All weapons must conform to criteria that qualify that specifies what weapons are Historically authentic enough to be allowed into the competitions. Years ago I entered two Cowboy Action shoots

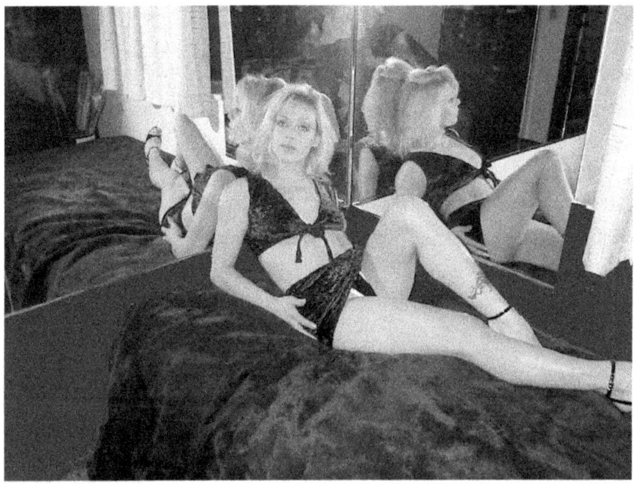

The author's favorite waitress Sahara and the author became fast friends for years. She worked at Visions Gentlemen's Club on St. Louis's East Side, Platinum Club, Hustler, and other clubs, oftentimes as a dancer.

neither of which I was particularly serious about. I could care less about the rifle or shotgun events, but the single action revolver events were a different matter. In these I'd be playing Jack Corbett (in another life time) wanna be Western gunman hero. Most contestants shoot Italian replicas of the Colt Single Action Army or modern Ruger Single Actions that are "Improved versions" of the real thing. A practical reason for going with a look alike is cost, oftentimes as low as $400 versus a minimum entry fee of $1800 for a genuine Colt Single Action Army new in the box from Colt's custom shop. Many contestants shoot 38 caliber single action revolvers because of their lower recoil which gets them back on target quicker. Even competitors firing 45 Colt Single Actions will often opt for reduced loadings that produce less recoil than the modern smokeless powder equivalent of the old classic 40 grains of black powder load.

Me? I didn't care if I won or not so long as I was using the real thing—an authentic Colt 45 Single Action Army shooting the traditional classic loads used by old West gunfighters. Which along with not having the best eyes in the world or shooting 50,000 rounds or so per year is why I could never do better than third place. We'd typically shoot at five heavy steel revolving circular plates, with each of us being allowed only five shots. We'd shoot for best time and each miss would be penalized by more time being added to our scores. I'd generally get four plates out of five at an average speed of one second per shot. The man in first place would often average five hits at an overall time of two ½ seconds.

That is excellent shooting. One has to line his sights up on a steel place the size of a man's head, fire, recover from the gun's recoil, cock the revolver's hammer back, and line up on the next steel plate before pulling the gun's trigger again. But as good as the first place winners were, I've seen a man shoot a single action who's even better. The man's a Central Illinois gun smith. I've seen Bill Ogilvie fire twice from one of his single actions yet only one report could be heard. Fifteen yards downrange, there would be two bullet holes in a fencepost only an inch apart. He had fired two shells faster than a machine gun could deliver its first two rounds.

Finally having to have my own five rotating steel plates to shoot at while I was living at my farm, I built my own gun range and I shot at the steel plates with 9 mms, 22's, 38's, 45 automatics and my 45 Single Action Army. You could hardly hear the 22's strike the heavy plates and the little bullets didn't have enough push to move the plates very far. Shooting 38's or 9 mms would get the plates moving and you could definitely hear them smack the plates but the overall effect was nothing to get excited about. The 45 auto would make the plates sing as it spun them around but the 45 Colt would nail them with even greater authority. And it really wasn't nearly as much fun shooting them with the 45 automatic since all one has to do is to pull the trigger for each shot.

With the 45 Colt Single Action Army you must point, pull the hammer back and shoot. There is no time to get a good sight picture on your targets when you are going for speed. The Colt is a great natural pointer. You just vaguely look down the barrel, pull the hammer back and touch the thing off. The recoil is just enough to let you know you are shooting a powerful round. You just sort of rock and roll with the gun and learn to welcome the revolver's kick like a friend who's letting you know that you can count on him whether you are shooting steel plates, tin cans, rocks, or living creatures. A good Colt Single Action Army's trigger pull is better than you will usually find on a custom target pistol. Its lustrous blued finish is impeccable. And now, here's the true test. Pick up any Colt Single Action Army look alike and slowly pull its hammer back. Now pick up a real Colt. When you pull its hammer back, you will hear a click, then another click, another, and then a final click all at different audible levels. I'm not lying. You will hear the name Colt being metallically spelled out as you cock its hammer back. You won't hear it when you cock the look alikes. There is nothing like it, nothing that takes you back to a time of coffee brewing on the fire, of men riding horses into the night, of horse thieves, train robberies, Indian fights, and cowboys tending the herd. If you think all handguns are created equal after experiencing the Single Action Army in 45 Colt, then you just don't have the old Western frontier or love of finely crafted weapons running in your soul.

# 1861 Springfield

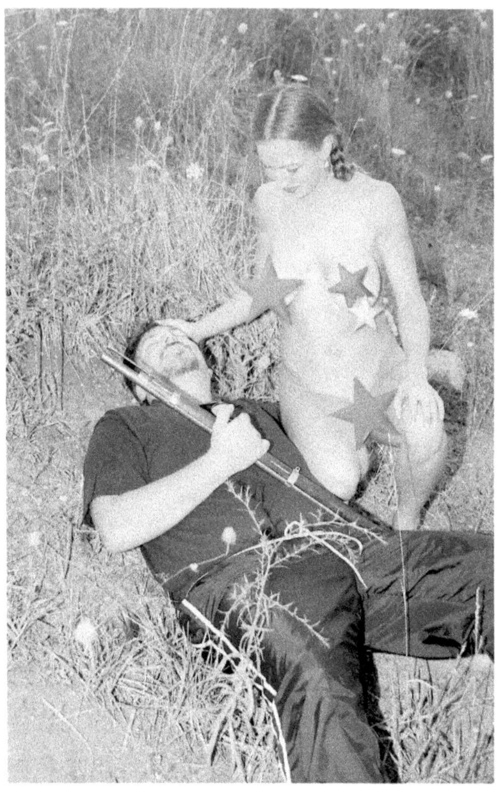

Tornado with Darien Ross and the 1861 Springfield just outside Nude-A-Poppin where the author first met Darien. Although he lived over 400 miles from Jack, Tornado would oftentimes accompany him in his escapades whether they took him to Illinois, Las Vegas, Alabama and later even to Thailand

More Americans were killed during the American Civil War than in all wars before and since. With both North and South totaling just twenty-seven million inhabitants at the war's beginning in 1861, the final tally would reach 600,000 by the war's end in 1865, a figure comparable to the U.S. Armed forces having seven million killed today. Huge advances in war making technology that included the first sinking of a warship by submarine, air surveillance by hot air balloon, the birth of modern trench warfare, improved artillery, and the widespread use of the rifled musket made the Civil War a landmark event of epic proportions not only in terms of weapons development, but also in the scale of carnage such development made possible. Perhaps the most significant of all was the development of the rifled musket, which is best represented by the 1861 Springfield, since it embodied a revolutionary development in small arms that would change infantry tactics forever.

For 150 years the standard weapon of both European and American infantrymen was best exemplified by the British Brown Bess smooth bore musket, a weapon that would undergo minimal change or improvement throughout its long history arming England's infantry. The Brown Bess typically had a smooth bore 69/100ths of an inch in diameter. To load his weapon an infantryman dumped a charge of black powder and ball down its long barrel. Employing a paper cartridge with a musket ball attached he would then bite off one end of the cartridge, pour the powder down the musket's barrel and ram the ball over the powder with a steel ramrod. Since the ball and the inside of the barrel were both smooth, the process of ramming the ball home was easy and quick. But since the ball was less than the diameter of the barrel with nothing in the barrel to stabilize it, the ball would start to tumble once the soldier fired his musket. This tumbling started in the muzzle and continued once it left the barrel, getting progressively worse the farther the ball continued downrange. A soldier armed with the smooth bore musket was lucky to hit a man at seventy-five yards.

Well before the turn of the 19th century, both infantry and cavalry tactics favored well-disciplined units that could quickly close with the enemy after sustaining a "survivable" casualty rate, generally considered to be 15 to 20 percent before troops would become demoralized and lose cohesion. If a sufficient force could survive the initial volleys from both musketry and artillery and turn their sabers or bayonets on the enemy it would be able to drive the now terrified enemy from the field. Considering the tactics of the day in 1776 the mere thought that a rabble of unruly American revolutionaries could successfully stand against well-trained British redcoats was unheard of.

In the early 1800's Napoleon regarded his artillery as the Queen of Battles. Although massed musket fire could not be depended upon to stop a determined attack by well-disciplined troops, artillery represented a much more lethal weapon to attacking troops than the short ranged smooth bore musket. Canister, which consists of a number of small projectiles fired from a cannon, had been in use in various forms ever since artillery had been invented. By the 1800's artillery was being used like gigantic shotguns to effectively mow down the enemy from as far away as 300 yards. Effective long distance shelling with explosive projectiles was to come later which reduced most of the killing by artillery to relatively short distances. But artillery is not nearly as mobile as infantry or especially cavalry, and it was under Napoleon's command that a well armed and numerous Cavalry had its heyday.

All of this would change during the Civil War with the widespread use of the rifled musket. The term rifle comes from grooves cut in barrels called rifling which stabilized projectiles by forcing them to spiral toward a target. Although American colonial troops had used Kentucky rifles to shoot down Redcoats at much greater ranges than were possible with the smooth bore musket, it took too long to load a Kentucky rifle which required a man's getting out a greased patch to wrap around the ball which he would ram down the muzzle after dumping a charge of black powder down the tube. The greased patch served to tighten the fit between the projectile and the rifling of the barrel. Despite legendary exploits by American Revolutionary War riflemen, at least one well-known regiment traded in their Kentucky rifles for Brown Besses before war's end. The technological event that would forever change infantry tactics was Captain Minnie's invention of the Minnie ball during the 1840's while serving in the French Army.

The Minnie "ball" was a soft lead conical shaped projectile with a large cavity molded out of its back. In the 1861 Springfield, which became the standard infantry rifle for the Union at the beginning of the Civil War, the Minnie projectile was 575 thousands of an inch in diameter. Since the bore diameter of the Springfield was 580 thousands of an inch, the projectile could easily be driven down its barrel without the need of a greased patch. When the soldier fired his rifle, the gases from the exploding charge of black powder would force the projectile to expand tightly against the grooves of the Springfield's rifling. The Civil War rifleman got the ease and quickness of loading offered by the smoothbore musket with at least the same accuracy offered previously by the Kentucky rifle regardless of which side he was on.

Rifles similar to the 1861 Springfield found their way to the United States before the Civil War. Union troops were typically armed with the 1861 Springfield and later with the 1863 model, which is identical with the exception of several small cost cutting modifications. Southern troops pretty much grabbed up what they could, many of them initially using smoothbore or rifled muskets using the Minnie projectile that was made before 1861 from a variety of manufacturers. The Enfield rifled musket was shipped to the Confederacy from England while increasing numbers of discarded Yankee Springfields were picked up from the battlefield or got into the hands of Southerners from Northern prisoners of war.

The rifled musket provided the Civil War infantryman a reach out to three hundred yards, roughly four times the range of the smooth bore musket. Cavalry charges against massed lines of infantrymen now became suicidal while artillery that was within canister range (300 yards) of infantry armed with rifled muskets would come well into lethal range of sharp shooting infantrymen. Massed charges of well trained motivated bayonet carrying infantrymen willing to accept a 10 to 20 percent casualty rate to get a chance to close with the enemy were now getting mowed down by riflemen from as far out as 300 yards as well as by canister firing artillery. Even the best troops could not accept casualty figures such as those experienced by the 24th Michigan and 1st Minnesota at Gettysburg of 80 and 81 percent.

The Civil War soldier carried a cartridge box containing forty rounds of paper cartridges. Like the Brown Bess armed soldier who preceded him he'd snatch a cartridge, rip one end off with his teeth, pour the powder down the barrel of his rifle, and ram the attached projectile home with his ramrod. The loading process was completed when he pulled back the rifle's hammer and inserted a percussion cap on its nipple. The percussion cap setup proved to be a much more reliable ignition system for the gun's charge of black powder than the Flintlocks used by the Brown Bess and Kentucky rifles. A trained rifleman could get off three shots a minute. The statistical edge the Civil War rifled musket offered over the smooth bores of the past was staggering.

Consider that an attacking infantryman weighted down with his pack and equipment can cover 75 yards in twenty seconds. The smoothbore musket carrying soldier on the defensive has him in range at 75 yards. By the time he has reloaded the soldier attacking him is only feet away with his bayonet pointed right at his chest just one millisecond from ripping his guts out. But now the same attacking infantryman now has to cover 300 yards to get his bayonet into his enemy's guts. His enemy might get him on his first shot at 300 yards and if he doesn't, he still has time to reload and get three more shots off before his adversary has come within bayonet range.

It is no wonder that massed infantry attacks were often chewed up long before reaching their destination. Malvern Hill, Pickett's charge at Gettysburg, Cold Harbor, along with many other fiascos that combined the spirit of attack tactics of the past with the realities of the awesome lethality of the rifled musket with massed artillery fire ultimately brought both armies, North and South, to the months long stalemate of trenched warfare at St.Petersburg, which ominously foreshadowed the slaughter in the trenches of World War 1 that would occur fifty years later.

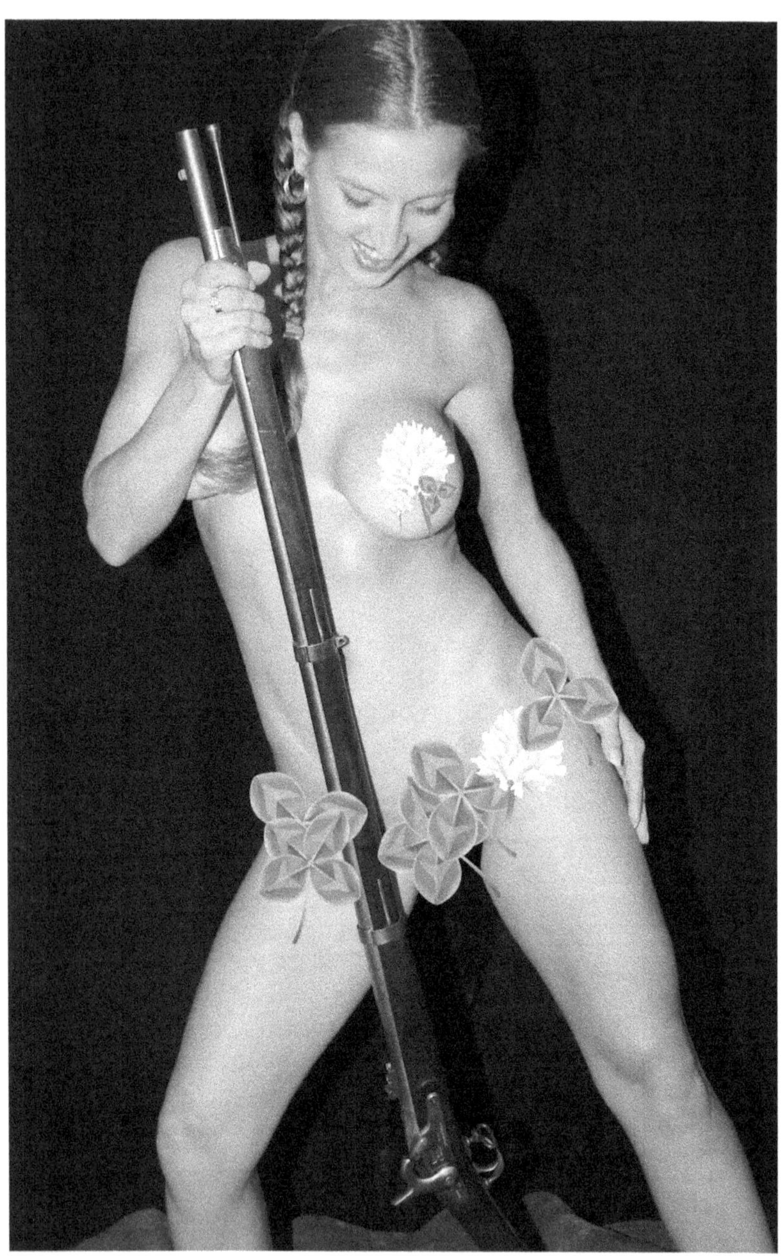

Ever since I was twelve years old, I've wanted an 1861 Springfield. As a young Civil War buff the Civil War fascinated me while the image of the horrific destruction that its 500 grain projectile delivered upon the tissue, bones, and organs of thousands of Civil War soldiers appalled me. I never got one and neither did my dad who had wanted one as much as I did. I finally got the closest thing to it in a very well made Japanese replica that was identical to the 1861 in every respect except that its screws were metric. At my farm I took out a powder measure which I had calibrated to pour out exactly 60 grains of black powder, a can of black powder, a bag full of .577 caliber Minnie balls, and a box of percussion caps. As a kid I had visited many Civil War battlefields and had even slept in Sharpsburg's Bloody Lane which had once filled up to the brim with bodies as my dad slept next to me having nightmares of bugles blaring and men having their arms, legs, and heads being blown off. I loaded my Springfield and just as I had read in the books, the Minnie balls slid down the barrel easily. My mind clouded over as I drifted one hundred and thirty years back into time. The gun kicked back against my shoulder. The large bullet bulled into the target where I had aimed it. I reloaded and fired six more times. It was too much fun–until the seventh slug got wedged halfway down the barrel. I had planned on running a patch down the barrel after my tenth firing; too late now. The residue from unburned black powder had caked the barrel and I couldn't ram the Minnie ball home.

My firing session ground to an immediate halt and I wound up visiting two tractor mechanic friends of mine who managed to drill the barrel clean after leaving bits and pieces of the projectile which fell out. I later asked a couple of Civil War park battlefield historians what Civil War soldiers did to clean their weapons in the heat of battle, but neither gave me a satisfactory answer. It wouldn't matter anyway, for the unprecedented deadliness of the rifled musket, which so suddenly and bloodily restored the preeminence of the infantry over Cavalry during the Civil War, would just as quickly be relegated to obsolescence by the lever action repeating rifle during the same conflict.

# America's gun, the lever action Winchester

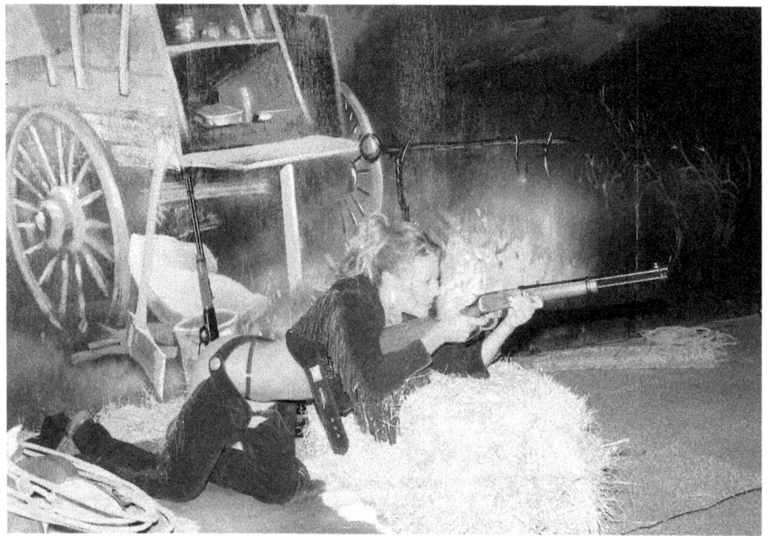

Not only did Louisville's Montana Steel win first place in the Club Maximus M.S. Texas pageant, even though she was exhausted after the 3 night feature competition, she still managed to do the Winchester lever action rifle photo shoot for the author and *Xtreme Magazine*

More than any firearm, the lever action rifle is America's gun, representing American engineering, style, and practicality so much that the name Winchester, is virtually synonymous with rifle. Its fast action, light weight, balance, handiness and good practical accuracy made it an unbeatable tool during the latter half of the 19th century. Although there are rifles and assault rifles that shoot faster, reach out further, and offer superior stopping power, that old style lever action might still be the best all around tool for either self defense or hunting for the 21st century.

The lever action became a practical, reliable killing machine in 1860 when Benjamin Henry designed the Henry rifle for Oliver Winchester. But by the end of the Civil War less than 10,000 Henrys were in the hands of Union troops. Although the rifled musket and the Minnie ball had revolutionized warfare, by the time of the Civil War the difference in lethality between the Henry and the rifled musket was staggering. Firing the 44 rim fire metallic cartridge, ammunition for the Henry was much more reliable than the black powder paper cartridges used during the Civil War by the rifled musket. But what really made it a wonder weapon was its ability to rip off 15 shots as fast as the lever and trigger could be pulled. But those responsible for arms procurement during the War felt that the Henry would be too wasteful of ammunition. Had most Northern troops been armed with the Henry, the prolonged bloodbath would have ended in short order.

The relatively few Henrys used during the Civil War were never issued to units larger than company size. In most cases they were purchased by individual soldiers willing to pay a steep price for the terrific edge the Henry gave them. The Henry evolved into the 1866 Winchester, followed by the 1873 model chambered for the more powerful .44-40 cartridge. 44-40 meant a 44-caliber bullet backed by 40 grains of black powder, the same charge backing the 45 Colt, which became renowned in the 45 Single Action Army revolver as a man stopper. Although the 1873 Winchester would be offered in a variety of chamberings, the 44-40 was the most favored because of its greater stopping power.

Meanwhile, the U.S. military neanderthalish mind set continued to hamstring U.S. troops with inferior weapons. By 1876, eleven years after Lee's surrender at Appomattox, U.S. troops were still armed with the breech loading single shot 45-70 Springfield. The Indians knew better and most Indians who could afford them bought Winchesters. Cattlemen, lawmen, farmers, gun fighters, and townsmen already knew that a Winchester was simply the best thing going for a variety of tasks from hunting game to self defense. And if Montana Steele had lived one hundred and twenty-five years ago, I can guarantee that she would have armed herself with a Winchester. So what does Montana Steele, a feature entertainer from Louisville, Kentucky have to do with all of this? Everything. To dramatize the lever action rifle's greatness I found myself at the right place at the right time. Club Maximus in Wichita Falls, Texas was having its M.S. Texas competition and Montana Steele wound up winning. There could be no better panorama for the lever action's role in American History to be dramatized than Texas, our second largest state, a state that has a History larger than life, evoking names such as The Alamo, the Texas Rangers, and John Wesley Hardin, teemed up with Montana who often uses bails of straw, a saddle, and a lariat for the props she often uses for her shows as a feature entertainer.

I see the new M.S. Texas as the embodiment of the pioneer woman during the later half of the 19th century. A tough, intelligent, resilient, resourceful

21st century woman Montana would have been right in the thick of things during the taming of the Western frontier. Besieged by Indians or cattle thieves, would Montana have reached for her revolver when she had the opportunity to choose her Winchester? Hell no. Even the most vaulted gun fighters of the period chose a rifle or shotgun over their revolvers when the moment of truth arrived. Montana would have had 12 rounds in the magazine which she could fire much more accurately than six rounds through a revolver which is hard to fire accurately under sedate conditions and close to impossible in the nerve-wracking chaos of combat.

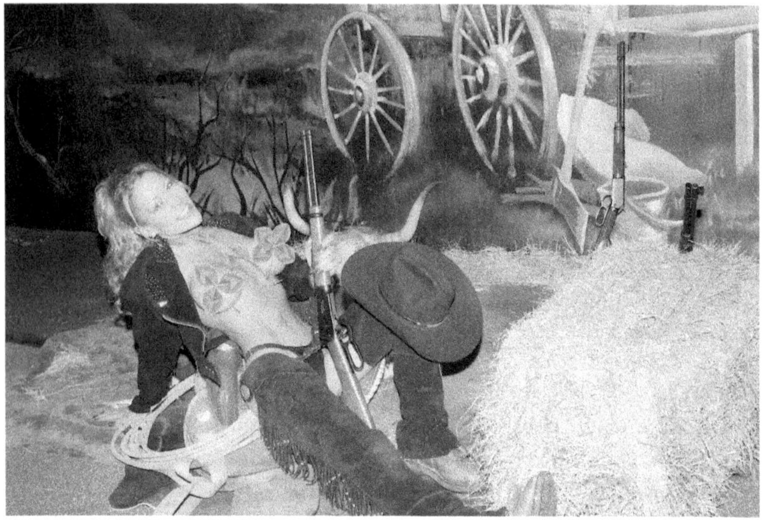

Unfortunately General Custer's 7th Cavalry didn't have the luxury of such choices when the U.S. Army procurement board doomed Custer and five of his companies to annihilation at the Little Big Horn. Although most of the Sioux and Cheyenne warriors were armed with bows and arrows, many of them carried Winchesters, whereas Custer's men were fated to use the much slower firing single shot Springfield 45-70's. But the individualistic Indian warriors didn't have to put up with arms procurement boards. Had Custer's men been armed with Winchesters they might have survived the battle.

By the late 19th century both Winchester and Marlin were offering lever actions in a variety of persuasions. In 1894 Winchester introduced its model 94 in 30-30 as the most flat shooting rifle of its day. More than a hundred years later the 94 in 30-30 is still going strong with over four million model 94 30-30's having been sold and accounting for more deer than any other rifle.

Its critics claim lever actions are not as accurate as bolt actions. In the old days when men were men, women were scarce and the sheep got nervous, a man or a woman had to use a rifle as an everyday tool. This usually meant one all around light weight rifle that could do just about everything reasonably well. Although a powerful single shot rifle was better at long range on very large game, it did not offer acceptable firepower for self defense.

The modern day descendent of the old west frontiersman is today's American farmer. To city folks who think guns should be outlawed be advised that farmers who don't own at least one gun are hard to find. Farmers live in relative isolation and often work alone. When it comes to defending their property and loved ones, they must rely upon themselves. Most farmers are intelligent common sense kind of guys. Therefore they have guns and like their earlier 19th century counterparts it's often a lever action that's behind the seat of their pickups.

I farmed for 22 years. I often shot pigeons off the barn roof because they'd shit all over the place which made me hate pigeons. Then there were those little ground squirrels looking like ugly chipmunks that would destroy two rows of newly planted crops along my drainage ditch banks. I hated them worse than the pigeons. Occasionally there was a ground hog eating thirty foot diameter holes in the middle of my fields and twelve gauge shotguns shooting buckshot couldn't be relied upon to stop one past forty yards. I once shot a neighbor's diseased hog with my Colt Python .357 magnum. There were cats mortally wounded by cars or by farm machinery I dispatched with whatever was handy. I shot possums simply because they were so damn ugly and there were a few skunks that sooner or later would have odorized one of my guests close to my house. I shot such critters with about everything, from 30-06 rifles to a pocket pistol, but the gun that accounted for most of them was my Winchester model 94 in .22-magnum. It killed quickly and cleanly and it was very accurate, light, and handy.

How accurate? Well, you can't hit what you can't see. So just try a little experiment. Take a dime and a penny and pace off 75 feet. Walk back to where you started from and just see how well you can see them. Now see if you can see Abe Lincoln's head on the penny. While I was living on the farm, my neighbor Kermit liked my Winchester 22 mag so well he bought one just like it. When I bought a scope for mine he had me pick one up for him. Then we sighted those scopes in and I laid his Winchester across the hood of my pickup.

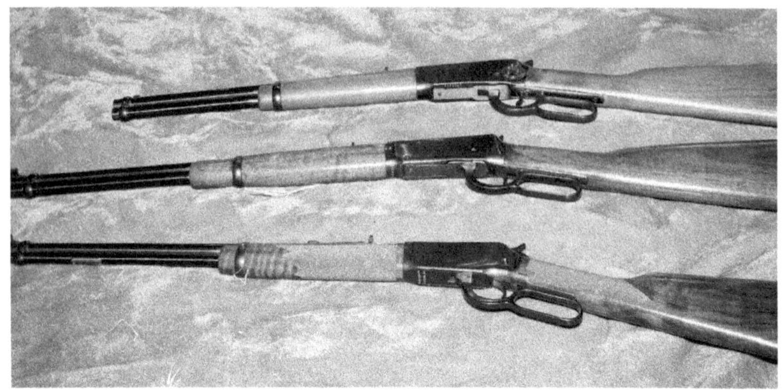

From top to bottom, the author's Winchester model 94 Trapper in .45 long Colt, his pre-1964 94 30-30, and his 9422 M in .22 magnum. The 9422 M came off a separate production line holding it to higher standards for fit and finish, and tolerances. It is no longer made, and even used commands prices of $1000 or more.

"I'm drilling Abe Lincoln's head," I told Kermit.

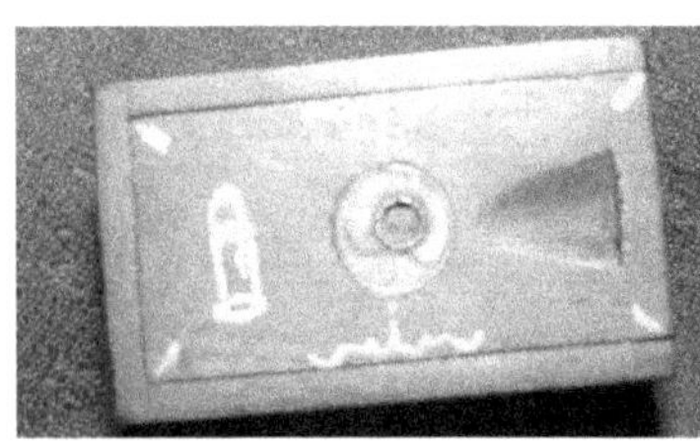

"You can't hit it. I can't even see it.'

I hit ole Abe in the head.

"Lucky shot," said Kermit. "Bet you can't do it again."

So I hit Abe a second time making Kermit eat his words. I must have had that scope on my rifle for only two weeks. The rifle's perfect lines were spoiled by that appendage and it didn't ride as nicely in its boot I had mounted behind the pickup's seat. It didn't handle quite right with the scope. Besides--shooting pigeons off the barn roof just wasn't' a challenge any more which was a lot of fun since you had to shoot high to hit them in the head or neck to avoid perforating the roof. Kermit made two little boxes for .22 magnum ammunition, one for me and one for himself and he embedded the two pennies in their lids.

I don't shoot deer because they are too pretty. Otherwise my favorite Winchester 94 would probably be a 30-30 which is far superior to a .22 magnum on deer. But a few months ago a writer friend of mine was commercial fishing in Alaska. I nearly joined him. Baron told me that he carried a shotgun when he was in Brown Bear territory. Since I had considered joining him, I had thought about what I should bring with me for personal protection. The .454 Casull is the most powerful handgun I own but it would be heavy on the belt. My 45 auto is much lighter. In the remote chance of encountering an enraged bear either would probably penetrate the animal's skull. But could I do it while shaking like a leaf which is probably what would happen? I've thought about what I'd carry for this remote eventuality. It would have to be light and handy since I'd probably never use it and in the event I did, it would have to give me an excellent chance for survival. The answer came to me this morning. It would be my lever action trapper model 94 Winchester in .45 Colt. I'd hand load it to .454 Casull power. With a 16-inch barrel and 34-inch overall length at 6 pounds it's light, short and handy. Holding nine rounds it will fire quickly and much more accurately than any revolver in my nerve wracked hands with 1, 000 pounds of enraged carnivore bearing down on me. Nothing glamorous--just a handy tool that will get the job done. Which is what the lever action rifle has always been, a fine, nicely balanced all around tool that has stood the test of time.

# John Browning's 50 Caliber Machine Gun

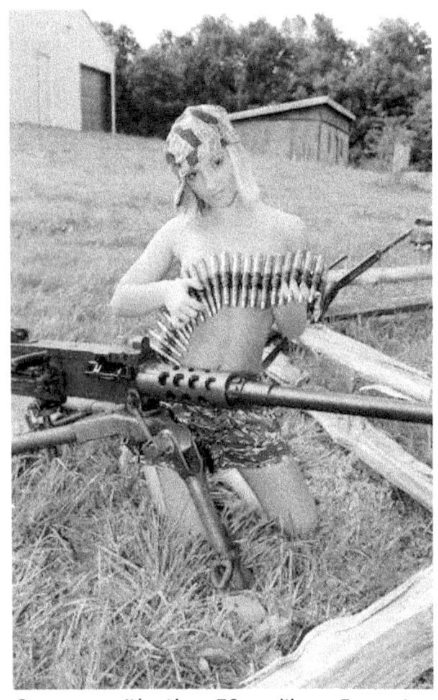

Carmen with the 50 caliber Browning machine gun at the Meyer farm. Carmen danced at Big Daddy's Cabaret in Dixon, Missouri. Later the author would get his scuba PADI certification with Big Daddy and Hawkeye, BD's D.J. and a few months later the trio would go to Thailand and Cambodia together. But the author decided to stay and is now residing in Thailand.

Imagine the prototypal 1827 infantryman's weapon still being used 90 years later in the trench warfare of World War I of 1917. The gun would have been a flint lock muzzle loading smooth bore musket, firing four shots a minute and accurate out to only fifty yards and it would have been competing against machine guns and bolt action repeating high-powered rifles. So at this rate you'd expect a weapon designed during World War I to be just as hopelessly outmoded nearly ninety years later on the 21st century battlefield as the early 18th century Flintlock muzzle loader would have been on the World War I battlefield.

Until you examine the legacy of its designer, John Browning, that is. Browning's 45 automatic pistol that was adopted by the U.S. Armed forces in 1911, now nearly 100 years old, is still the quintessential sidearm of armed professionals worldwide and the finest defensive close quarter combat handgun the world has ever known. The Browning automatic rifle first used during World War I was still giving an excellent account of itself more than fifty years later in Vietnam while etching a permanent spot for itself on the battlefields of World War I and Korea along with its stable mate, the Browning 1919 30-caliber machine gun. Today, practically ninety years later, the heavy 50 caliber machine gun still plays a prominent role in the armed forces of more than twenty nations, including the U.S. If there is any question about John Browning being a man ahead of his time consider that the 50 caliber was much more than a tripod mounted belt fed machine gun used for hosing down enemy soldiers. Browning's 50 caliber machine guns were mounted in the wings and noses of fighter aircraft to be used for shooting down enemy planes and ground targets. It provided the defensive armament for U.S. World War II bombers and it was used as secondary armament for tanks while being mounted in practically every ground vehicle imaginable, used on PT. boats and other naval vessels, and employed in a ground to air anti aircraft role making it one of the most versatile weapons of all time.

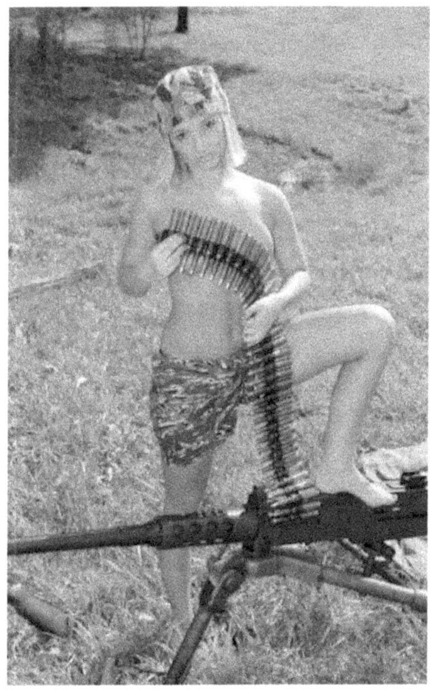

The awesome stopping power of the 50 cal's 700 grain bullet can best be put in perspective by considering that one of the most powerful elephant guns, the .577 Nitro Express, could be relied upon by professional ivory hunters to knock an elephant out with a single shot to the skull whether the brain was hit or not, and that just one bullet from the 50 caliber machine gun churns out twice the muzzle energy of the .577 Nitro Express.

That's more than 13,000 foot pounds of muzzle energy so just imagine what a World War II fighter bomber, the P-47 Thunderbolt, could do with eight 50 cals mounted in its wings. Most of you have probably seen old World War I footage of Thunderbolts and other American fighter planes blasting German trains into matchwood from the locomotive all the way back to the caboose.

Roughly two million 50 caliber machine guns were built during World War II, an almost unbelievable number. Most of those two million 50 cals in sharp contrast to the notion that they were primarily an infantryman's weapon, would be mounted in aircraft, whether they were mounted in groups of six in the noses of P-38 Lightning fighters, six or eight in the wings of long range Mustangs and P-47 fighter bombers or in the turrets and sides of B-17 bombers to name just a few of the deadly combinations used in the air.

For the infantry, the 50 caliber came in two flavors, water and air cooled. Whereas water-cooled models came in at over 200 pounds, air-cooled fifties weighed around 100 pounds for both gun and tripod. So long as one could keep a ready supply of ammunition handy, water-cooled variants could be fired at maximum rates of fire indefinitely. But whether the fifty was water or air cooled, it often proved too cumbersome for rapidly advancing infantry on the offensive. Equally problematical was keeping such troops supplied with ammo given the sheer size and weight of each projectile compared to the much lighter 30-06 chambered for the BAR or 1919 Browning light machine gun.

But in its element, there was nothing quite like it. For example, a favorite tactic employed by American troops to clean out German held villages during World War II was the use of half tracks on which were mounted four 50 caliber machine guns. The quad fifties were then run wide open from one end of the village to the other while shooting into the buildings on both sides. The combination of the speed of a half track running at full-throttle and the deeply penetrating 50 caliber slugs usually got the job done.

But it wasn't really until the 1960's that the big fifty fully started to realize its full potential as a sniper's weapon. A 700-grain 50 caliber bullet can duplicate a much smaller 150-grain 30 caliber bullet's muzzle velocity of close to 3000 feet per second. But the far greater momentum of the much heavier 50 caliber projectile enables it to shoot flatter and buck the wind far better, thus giving the 50 caliber-armed sniper much better range than any sniper armed with a high power rifle of smaller caliber. And just consider the much greater variety in the sniper's new targets of opportunity. With the 50 caliber he can do far more than killing men. He can now use it to wreck an artillery piece or to blow up a mortar position, and by blowing it up we mean to literally blow up the mortar tubes. With the 50 caliber a sniper team can penetrate lightly armored vehicles or take a grounded aircraft out of commission.

One would expect an automatic weapon of such power to shake itself to pieces. But Browning designed a hydraulic buffer that eliminated the problem which could also be used to control the gun's rate of fire. To anyone of less talent than Browning's genius, such a problem would have proved to be nearly insurmountable whereas Browning dealt with it with ease. His fifty caliber machine gun proved to be nearly perfect, a magnificently functioning Swiss Army knife of weapons, equally capable of taking a man out with precision at 1500 yards as it was during World War II of hammering a plane out of the sky in seconds. Great weapons have come and gone during the past ninety years. Yet the 50 caliber Browning machine gun has remained as eloquent deadly testimony to the magnificent inventiveness of John Browning, an American genius far ahead of his time.

# The Kentucky Rifle

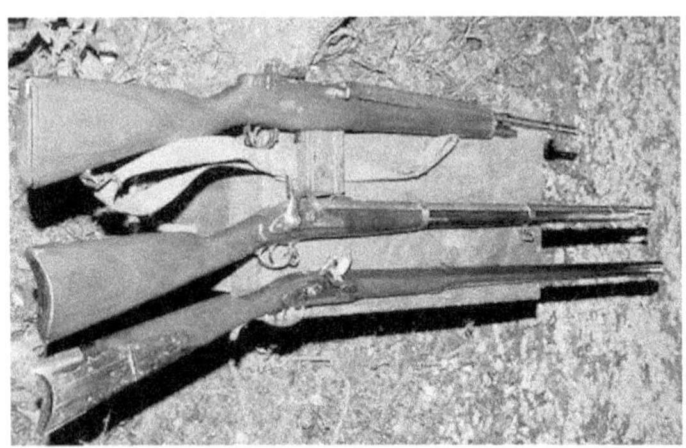

The Kentucky rifle (below) in this photo shoot belonged to a friend of a gun dealer the author met at the Collinsville gun show. The author's Springfield M-1 A at the top. Below it is his 1861 Springfield. The Springfield M-1, unlike Vic Meyer's M-15, does not have a bi-pod nor is it full auto. The model is Amy who the author met at the Lumberyard gentlemen's club in Des Moines, Iowa.

Those were the days–of tales some true and some shrouded in myth, when our nation had first begun, of a land where Indians walked in moccasins and the jackboots of the Hessian soldier and British redcoats stomped. It was a time when men hunted for their dinner and when enemies were both real and imagined, such as Washington Irving's dreaded Headless Horseman, looking for his head that had been taken off by a cannon ball during the Revolution. A man needed his gun, to fight with, to shoot game or marauding wolves, or for self protection. Those were times when men lived close to nature, of our Nation's earliest wars, and when ghosts stalked the land. Between 1760 and 1820 the two firearms taking the front stage as Americans settled into nation building were the British Brown Bess and the Kentucky rifle, which was more accurately called the Pennsylvania rifle. Had our model Amy, from Heart Throbs Entertainment, lived on the early Pennsylvania frontier at the turn of the 18th century, she would have had to choose between these two arms.

The Brown Bess was the shotgun of its day. A long barreled muzzle loader, the Brown Bess employed a flint lock ignition system utilizing a flash pan of powder which ignited when the flint struck and opened the pan on its downward arc once the trigger was pulled. The Brown Bess became the standard for all branches of the British Armed in 1720 and remained the prototypical infantry musket for more than one hundred years. Firing a 75-caliber ball in combat, the Brown Bess's bore was approximately the same diameter of today's twelve gauge. It was the do everything firearm of its time. It could be loaded with a single ball for deer or the battlefield or with small shot for small game.

The ball could easily slide down the barrel since it was undersized and the barrel was smooth. Since the barrel lacked rifling to steady the ball, and the tolerances were loose, the ball would start to wobble on its way to the target. Accurate fire on man sized targets was limited to around sixty yards.

The battle strategy of the day was to close with the enemy as quickly as possible to decide the issue with the bayonet in close quarter fighting. The Brown Bess did not even have a rear sight.

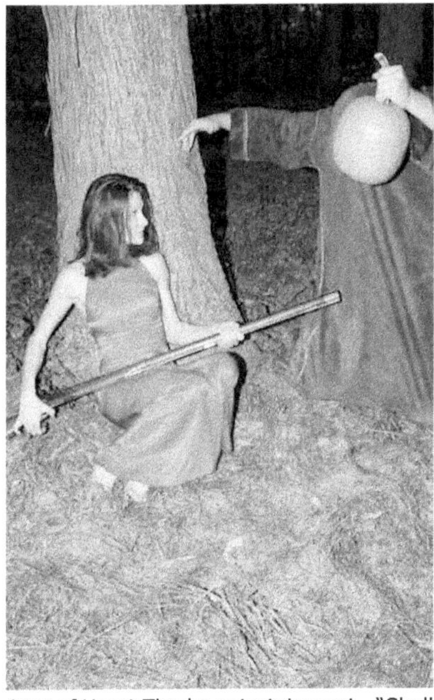

Amy of Heart Throbs entertainment. "Shall I shoot him or just let him have his way with me?"

Outside such settled areas as New York City and Philadelphia was the frontier (when the frontier was as close as upper New York State and Pennsylvania) where a man or family had to live off the land and fight off Indians and other enemies. Deer and small game such as rabbits, squirrels, and wild turkeys abounded. Except for close range the Brown Bess was hopeless. A great need arose for something better suited to the needs of the hunter who often found himself away from civilization for extended periods of time which fostered a whole cottage industry of small shops producing weapons the frontiersmen both needed and demanded.

By the 1730's New World frontiersmen were demanding guns that were far superior to the smooth bore musket. Often out in the woods hundreds of miles from the nearest settlement, the frontiersman required a firearm that was accurate enough to hit the head of a wild turkey to avoid spoiling the meat or hit a rabbit or squirrel out past forty yards, had sufficient knockdown to stop hostile Indians or deer, and which made maximum use out of his limited supply of lead and black powder. By the 1730's what became known as the Pennsylvania or Kentucky rifle, evolved from the hands of the German and Swiss gunsmiths who had recently emigrated to the New World. The bore of the Brown Bess was rifled and typically reduced from 75 caliber to 45 although a man could have his

Pennsylvania from 32 caliber to 50. A hunter who had been able to get 16 75 caliber balls from a pound of lead could now get 48. While the overall length of the new rifles averaged fifty-five inches, their weight was reduced because of trimmer stocks, trigger guards, and barrels.

What emerged was a firearm a man could truly be proud of. Each rifle was virtually handmade reflecting the individual tastes and needs of its owner. As the new rifles evolved so did the patch method of loading which employed a buckskin or a cloth patch greased in tallow that could be rammed down the bore ahead of the ball which provided a tight seal with the rifled bore. Because of this tight seal, the weapon's ball could be molded to a smaller diameter than the rifle's barrel. A good rifleman could now get off a round a minute as he grabbed fresh patches from an ornate patch box that had been fabricated into the stock of the rifle.

The new rifles became known as either the Pennsylvania rifle where they were first made or the Kentucky rifle perhaps to distinguish its overall excellence from other firearms being used on the American Continent by associating it with the frontier, where firearms were required to be the finest implements of survival available. Much of the metal or furniture comprising the Pennsylvania was of brass while its stock was often wound in tarred string which was then burned off to give it an artificial grain. Oil, soot, or varnish completed the gun's finish.

A good Pennsylvania rifle cost half or even an entire man's annual earnings in those days. Lavishing great attention on each masterpiece gun makers often vied with one another to make the most graceful and beautiful rifle possible with its accuracy and skill of the man wielding it being celebrated throughout the entire country in matches where participants shot at a turkey's head and other targets.

During the American Revolution it would often show its prowess, killing British officers at great distances making it the stuff of legend, but it would never be employed in large numbers. By 1850, most of the world's armies would still be using the Brown Bess or smooth bore muskets like it 130 years after the first Pennsylvania emerged from its proud creator's shop. Americans more than any other people in the world have a deep and profound reverence for their firearms. To explain why this is so, I want to leave you with two images. One is of the Hessian soldier, the German mercenary of which there were 30.000 of them, who were virtually forced by their rulers (who got the money) to be transported over to the North American continent in the dark and gloomy holds of British transport ships, who had no choice in either the wars they fought or the weapons they used. The second is of the American frontiersman soldier, cocky and confident of his superior abilities, who dressed as he pleased and carried his

Pennsylvania rifle into battle. Only a few hundred of them ever fought in the revolution during which their fellow soldiers were armed almost identically to their British and German adversaries. Yet their exploits would become so imbued into the American stream of consciousness that the gun would become a symbol of our individuality and our survival as a free people.

# Naked with a Ruger SP-101 and GP-100

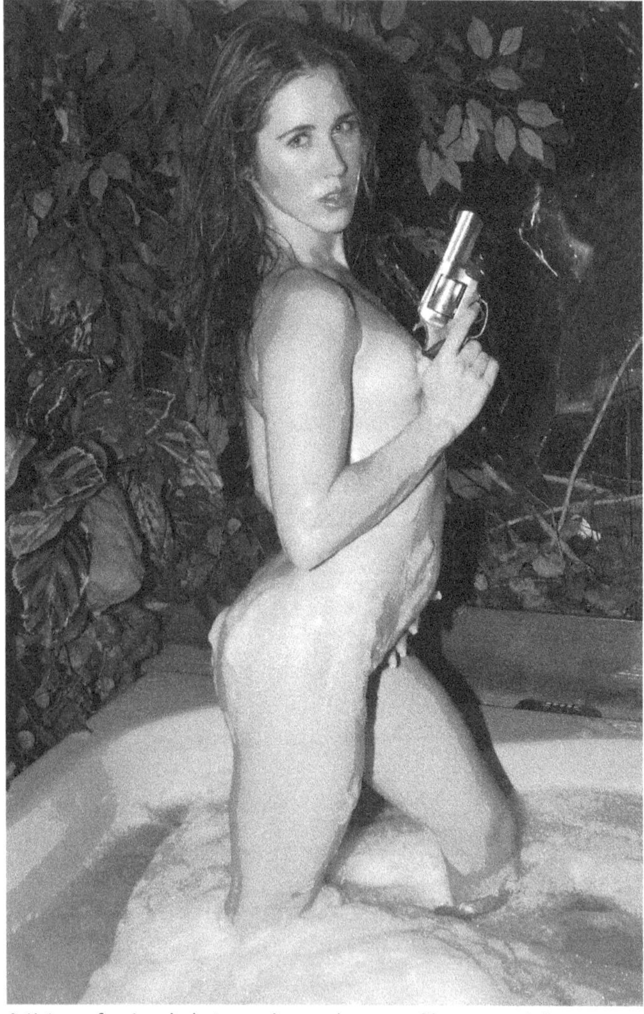

Artist, professional photographer and owner of her own adult entertainment business, Adina Winters lives in Lake Tahoe, Nevada where she snowboards at some of America's most challenging ski resorts, such as Squaw Valley which hosted the 1960 Winter Olympics.

Adina Winters strips to pay her bills when she's not eating up the ski slopes at Lake Tahoe with her hot snowboard. Compared to other topless dancers plying their trade at the gentlemen's clubs in Reno, Adina's physique is matchless due to clean living and lots of exercise as she crunches the slopes at breathtaking speed. She's fearless. Her coordination is superb. She could easily handle any handgun you put in front of her. But which one would be best for her? A pocket pistol, such as a small .32 or .380? Or how about a .44 magnum which can handle just about all critters big or small? While some might recommend a light weight Smith and Wesson or Taurus .38 snubby most true professionals who are worth their salt would probably opt for a 1911 .45 automatic. But for Adina or most of you readers, either a Ruger SP-101 with a 3-inch barrel or its larger and substantially heavier stable mate, Ruger's GP-100 might be even more ideal. Here's why.

Adina is a fascinating woman who has many interests. Among them is photography. She charges other dancers to take them out into the mountains for photo shoots. Now anyone who knows a thing about mountains knows that just about anything can happen. The weather can change suddenly. Temperatures can drop to life endangering levels within hours. You can get snowed in for long periods of time which is exactly what happened to the Donner Party not too far from where Adina lives back in the 1800's when the ill-fated expedition had to resort to cannibalism to survive. It is possible that Adina and the group she is leading can get caught by a winter storm and cut off from civilization for a long enough time for the group to become a modern day Donner tragedy. Obviously, in such dire circumstances a small pocket pistol will not do. A much better piece to pot squirrels with or to down a deer or elk would be a .44 magnum.

But most .44 magnums cannot be carried in a purse or easily concealed about one's body. Adina has to deal with strip club clientele of all types, and this includes some of the biggest perverts in the world. As for the rest of us, twenty-first century America is a dangerous place to live. Relying on a handgun for self-protection that is so large and heavy that one is likely to leave it behind is not what Adina or any of us needs if we are to be limited to just one gun. So this leaves out the truly large handguns--the .44 magnums, most .45 Colt revolvers and even many .357 magnums, all of which would perform admirably if one had to resort to a handgun for hunting both small and large game.

.45 automatics can do the job in the game fields although there are better choices available. And there are much smaller versions of the full size models with three inch barrels that are much lighter and more compact.

But unless one practically grows up with one, they are not nearly as intuitive as a good double action revolver. Let me give you an example. Suppose you were lying in bed at night and suddenly someone burst into your bedroom with nothing but destruction and mayhem of your precious body on his mind. With a 1911 style .45 automatic, you would typically keep it by your bed side or under your pillow cocked and locked. This means that in complete darkness one has to snick off the safety before one is able to fire the weapon. Usually this is done with the thumb. Contrast this need for quickly taking the gun off the safe mode with what one needs to do with a good double action revolver. All you have to do is to pick up the gun and pull the trigger to rid the world of one less bad guy. I'm used to forty-five autos and love them. I've been shooting them since I was ten, but still, I'd be much more facile when the chips are down and I'm surprised as in the situation described with a double action revolver. Believe it or not, most double action revolvers are more finicky than a good 1911 style .45 auto. They do fail. Screws can work loose from the guns recoil. Springs can break and completely disable the handgun. And the mechanism can bind.

And then Ruger introduced its double action revolvers, the odds of having such malfunctions were greatly reduced, provided you bought a Ruger that is. The predecessor of the GP and SP series of revolvers was the Security six. The GPs and SPs were merely an improvement over these. I won't get into the engineering details other than to tell you that the GP-100 is by far the most durable, long-lasting .357 magnum double action revolver on the market. When you pick one up you immediately think of a single block of steel. And although I wouldn't advise it, the revolver seems so strong that you could almost use it for a hammer in a pinch. The GP-100 was designed to digest thousands upon thousands of full house .357 magnum loads without ever causing a problem whereas most revolvers from the competition tend to shoot loose or develop other problems which leads to most gun experts advising owners of these guns to shoot 38's in them most of the time.

This is particularly true with lightweight, short barreled revolvers that chamber both the .357 magnum and the far less powerful Specials. Whereas the GP-100 is a full size revolver firing six rounds, its stable mate, the SP-101, has a much smaller diameter cylinder which has to hold just five rounds. Because of this the size of the entire piece is scaled down. Its five-shot cylinder is narrow, enabling the entire revolver to be relatively slim and flat, which makes it perfect for concealed carry.

I remember carrying mine all night long in Chicago, back in my old married days. My wife and I started in a Thai restaurant, then walked down to the Loop to watch a movie. We then walked back. At one point I felt we were being followed and probably were since we had to go through a bad area of town. But I felt perfectly confident with my SP-101 lying just inside my pants. In spite of my not having a holster it stayed there with its butt just underneath my shirt so that I could easily grab onto it if necessary. I had so much confidence in the gun that I felt I could pull it out, point it at any would be assailant, and scare the living hell out of him as he stared up those cylinder ports at the blue tipped Glaser safety slugs.

Another time I wound up in East St. Louis, on a bad stretch of the road with my red Miata with its top down. A stripper I had been going out with led me down that desolate road. Why? She didn't know what she was doing and was drunk, that's why. I had gotten out of my car which I left parked on the shoulder and sat next to her in a dilapidated pickup she had gotten. Inside the cab the door handle was broken off which meant I would have had to stick my arm out the window and to turn the outside latch to open the car door.

Two guys pulled up alongside the driver's side of the truck--her side. They asked her if she was all right--as if she looked in complete danger having a well-dressed man sitting next to her with his gleaming sports car parked right behind her truck. Then they told her they didn't have any money and asked her to give them some. By this time I had been making mental calculations about how long it would take me to slowly and carefully loop my arm through the truck's window and open the door from the outside. And how many seconds it would take me to get to my Miata and pick up my loaded SP-101 I had on the car's floor.

I could make some sort of excuse for going to my car and by the time they thought about whether it made sense or not I'd have my .357 mag in my hand. There was no question in my mind that if I had to I could stop both guys in an instant before they could shoot me if they had a gun. That little SP-101 simply inspired such confidence. Meanwhile, the girl reached up onto her dash for a couple of bucks which she handed them through her window. Then they drove off. Afterwards I thought about how calm and collected I had been. And only because I had that .357 magnum so close at hand. It was so small I might have been able to palm it enough to bring it back to the pickup without arousing their suspicions. Had I not had it close by I think they would have robbed her, but instead they had noted my calm indifference and didn't carry through with what they were planning to do.

The SP-101 also comes in a 2-inch barrel which is even more Adina Winters concealable. A friend of mine used to have one, but down at the gun range my three-inch model was much easier to shoot well. About this time I had gotten a Colt Detective Special in .38 Special which was even smaller and lighter than my SP-101. I had traded my Ruger in for it and it was now in the gun range's display case on consignment. That Detective Special shot pretty well if I concentrated enough. But if I fired rapidly and instinctively like I would in a lot of self defense encounters it shot pretty much in a horizontal line but grouped a few inches off dead center on the vertical axis of the target. Which is not good since many of the shots would have gone to one side or the other's of a man's chest. I immediately bought my SP-101 back. A couple years later I sold the Detective Special, but I still have the SP-101 which I've now owned for close to twenty years.

At 27 ounces, the Ruger SP-101 seems to be ideally weighted and balanced with that barrel under lug which tends to steady the revolver as it is being fired. It is lightening fast to pull up and get onto the target, much faster than heavier revolvers and pistols. Yet it's so stable that I can get five out of five shots into a small plate sized area when firing rapidly in double action at fifteen feet. This is the kind of revolver old West gun slingers would have dreamed about owning.

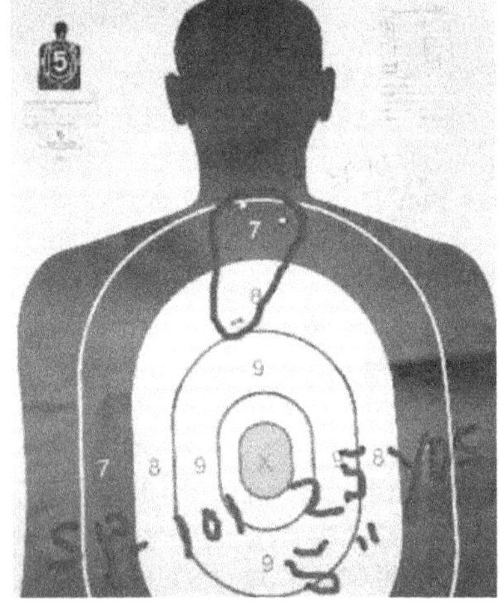


I tried the Sp-101 out at twenty-five yards managing to get five out of five into a five-inch group that would have easily placed them all inside of a man's head. Considering I could hardly see the sights of the pistol (I wear contacts with my right lens being the one for distance. This is my shooting eye which therefore does not focus well on the gun's sights) and that I don't manage to even shoot once a month, this is a remarkable performance out of a revolver that was designed to be a belly gun and backup to one's primary sidearm. Obviously it doesn't have to be a backup to any larger handgun.

Considerably heavier at around 40 ounces, my GP-100 has a four-inch barrel and chambers six rounds. This gives it a little more velocity than the three-inch tube of the SP-101 and should make it easier to get tight groups with. Last month I placed six out of six into a three-inch circle at twenty-five yards with five of those six landing within two inches of each other. Today I didn't do nearly as well, managing just a 5.5 inch group for six, a performance which substantially duplicated that of the SP-101. But at close range, fifteen feet where I could see my sights much better, I put five out of six into a half inch circle.

I was splitting two boxes of full house .357 magnum rounds between my six inch barreled Colt Python, my GP-100 and my SP-101. My GP-100 shot consistently well, right up there with the much more expensive and longer barreled Python.

Shooting 100 rounds of full velocity .357's should be a little wearing. But the Python is a heavy piece and benefits from having rubber Pachmeyer grips. It's always been a soft shooter. Both the GP-100 and SP-101 have grips made of a rubber compound stabilized by two pieces of walnut or black hard plastic in the case of the SP-101. The engineering of these grips is a stroke of genius. The SP-101 should kick a lot harder than it does since it's so light. But the GP-100 is a comfortable revolver to shoot as long as you wear ear protection from the deafening report of the .357 magnum cartridge. The SP-101's grips are nearly identical to those of its bigger brother while both revolvers have a recessed area high up in the grips where the thumb rests. I think Ruger designed this recessed area with the modern day gunfighter clearly in mind. The SP-101 in particular seems to be so stable and such a natural pointer and much of the reason is because of that recessed area. Cops should love either weapon.

When shooting the GP-100 I found myself edging my thumb around in that recessed area, welcoming the impact of the gun' s recoil to hit my hand. This was not the case with the SP-101 which had smaller grips, and which although not uncomfortable the gun's recoil certainly was not welcome.

The .357 magnum is on record the greatest man stopping handgun cartridge one can buy. For what it is worth Evan Marshall and Ed Sanow have compiled a statistical database giving the 125 grain .357 magnum hollow point a 96% rate of one shot stops to the torso on human targets. And now there is a hyper ventilating

180 grain solid point available in .357 magnum which has been exclusively designed as a self defense bullet against bears for those venturing out into Bear Country. This round is loaded so

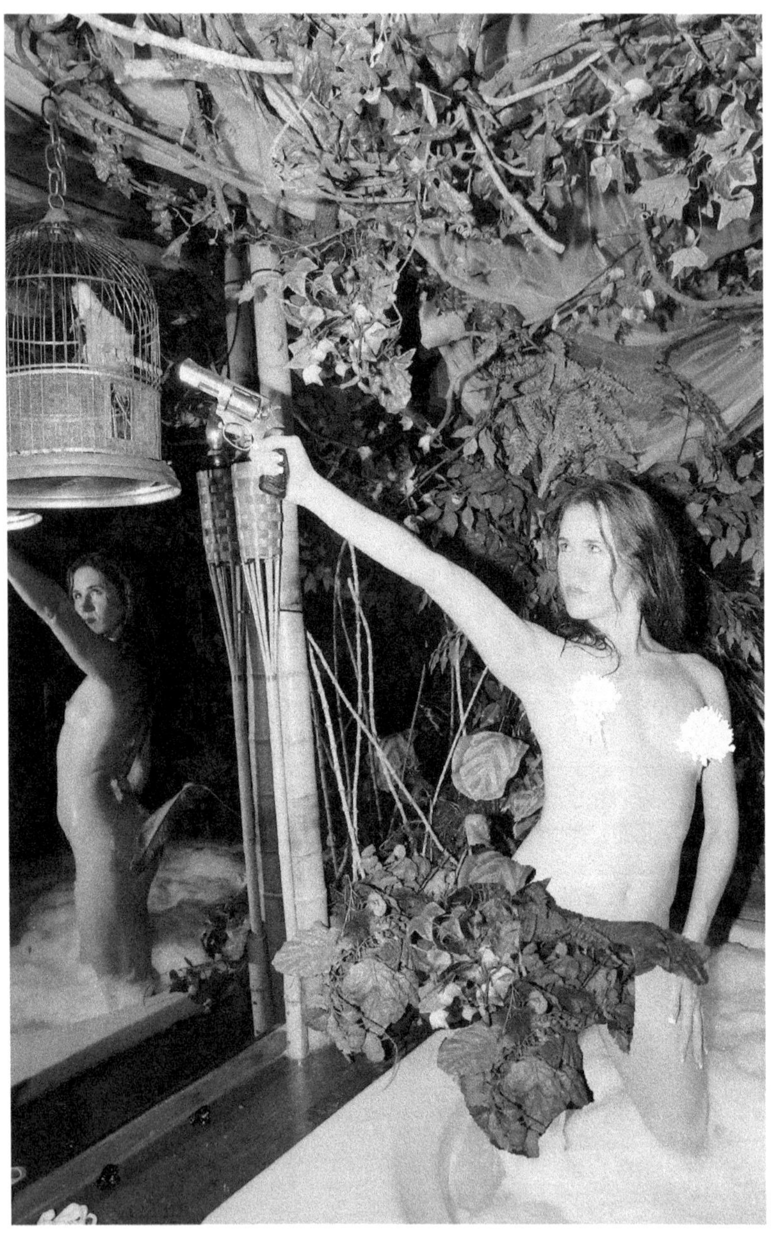

stout that it would no doubt tear up a lot of .357 magnum double action revolvers after just a few rounds were fired.

Now if I had to face an enraged Alaskan Brown Bear weighting up to 1500 pounds, I'd rather be armed with a high-powered rifle, a .454 Casull revolver, or a .44 magnum. But my .454 Casull has a seven 1/2 inch barrel and weighs 54 ounces to the 36 ounces of the GP-100 and the 27 ounces of the SP-101. That's a lot of weight to be hauling around. But whereas the GP-100 is a lot of fun to shoot, even with a couple hundred rounds of full house .357 magnums, the SP-101 is not. And the GP-100 is going to be more accurate at greater ranges day in and day out.

The SP-101 would take up very little room in a back pack and it can be easily carried concealed. At close range it could easily take down a deer, and it inspires, in me at least, a great deal of confidence. Adina could slip one into a fanny pack while out cross country skiing where its light weight would hardly be noticed. For her it would be the ideal ace in the hole survival or self defense piece. Although mechanically there is hardly any difference between the GP-100 and the SP-101 and either one will withstand all the abuse you can throw at it, the SP-101 represents a terrific compromise between a pocket handgun and a full-blown piece one can quickly win fights with or take out hunting if one had to use it to live off the fat of the land. Light weight, easy to maintain, hard hitting, accurate, and the most reliable of all double action revolvers (along with the GP-100), I believe the Ruger SP-101 .357 is the handgun of the century, the most versatile handgun a man or woman can buy, and the last handgun I will ever get rid of.

# The Springfield 03

The doctor's son who lived across the golf course from us pulled the high power rifle out from underneath his father's bed and from that time on–I must have been around ten then–I was in love. The Springfield's rear sight could be adjusted all the way out to 2700 yards, and I already knew a 30-06 solid from it could go through a 30-inch diameter tree at close range. I was looking at the finest World War I rifle to ever hit the battlefront. Surely I could hit enemy soldiers out to 2700 yards with it, and with a rifle this good, who needed artillery? Now if only I could save up enough money for it, I would be set to go for deer, elk, moose, an enraged Kodiak bear, lions and tigers, and even the occasional elephant. All things were possible to a young boy's mind, so right after my 12th birthday I became my father's slave for a summer. I weeded bean fields out at his farms, helped gravel the road to our house in the timber, cleaned out the cistern–did everything he wanted me to do–and by the end of the summer I had fifty bucks.

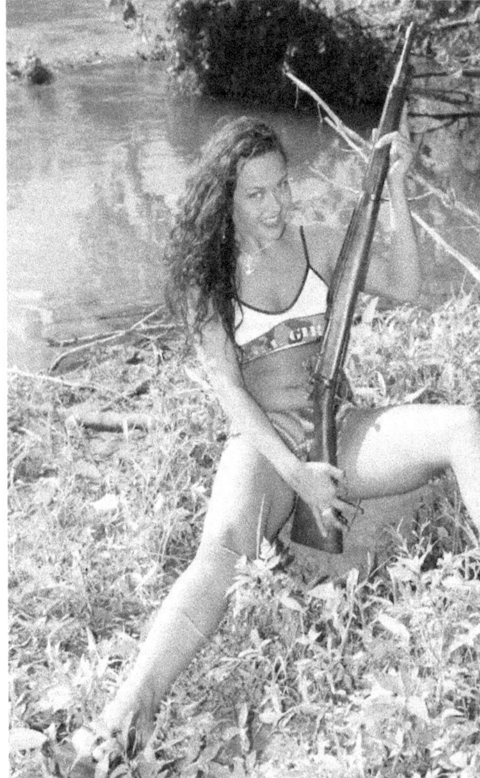

The picture is of Selena, one of Big Daddy's entertainers with the author's Springfield 03-A3 on the banks of the Gasconade River near the club. Both Carmen and Harley were here for the photo shoot. The scenery in this section of Missouri with its high hills, beautiful river and caves is absolutely stunning.

I got my rifle from a cop along with several hundred rounds of 30-06 ammo with each round measuring close to three and a half inches in length. But the rifle didn't say Springfield on it. Instead the name Remington was cut into the receiver along with its serial number, 3,447,301 while the number 43 could clearly be read on the rifle's barrel. Considering it was 1959, this meant that my rifle was just 16 years old and had been made for the Second World War, not World War I. The rifle's rear sight was different from the doctor's Springfield also, and could only be adjusted up to 800 yards. Although I loved the rifle–after all, no one else I knew had the gonads to buy his own .22 at twelve, let alone a powerful piece like this–I felt cheated since I wouldn't ever be hitting the bad guys past 800 yards.

What I had was an 03-A3, which was an improved variant of the Springfield 03. The Springfield became the U.S. standard battle rifle in 1903 for which the 30-06 round was developed in 1906, which today 100 years later has still not been surpassed for all around versatility as an all around big game cartridge. Although the semiautomatic M-1 Garand had theoretically replaced the Springfield bolt action rifle in 1936, by 1941 when the United States entered the Second World War, M-1's could not be produced fast enough by Springfield to arm the millions of American ground troops required to fuel the U.S. war effort. Springfield already overburdened with producing M-1's had wound up licensing its 03 design to Remington, the Smith and Corona typewriter Company, International Harvester, a producer of farm machinery, and other companies. Production was meanwhile simplified with the introduction of new time and cost cutting procedures, the rear sight and stock being prime examples.

In the late 1800's the dramatic increase in firepower provided by Winchester's lever action was topped by Mauser's bolt action repeater, which could not only more easily handle the more powerful smokeless cartridges being introduced by the ammunition companies, but also employ stripper clips that enabled infantrymen to load five cartridges at a time. During the Spanish American War U.S. troops often found themselves badly outgunned by an enemy using 7 mm Mausers against their Krags. Meanwhile, thousands of miles away the British had even tougher times fighting the Boers in South Africa who were also armed with 1893 Mausers.

With the exception of one, perhaps the final evolution of the Mauser is represented by the Mauser model 1898, which armed Germany's armies during WWI before going on to become the standard German battle rifle during WWII in the form of a shortened version, the 98 K. The exception is the 1903 Springfield, which is every bit of a Mauser, so much so that after the cessation of hostilities after World War I, Springfield wound up having to pay royalties to Mauser. But as good as the 1898 was, the Springfield's one notch better, being in most examples slightly more accurate, and particularly in rifles produced between the two world wars, more refined and polished.

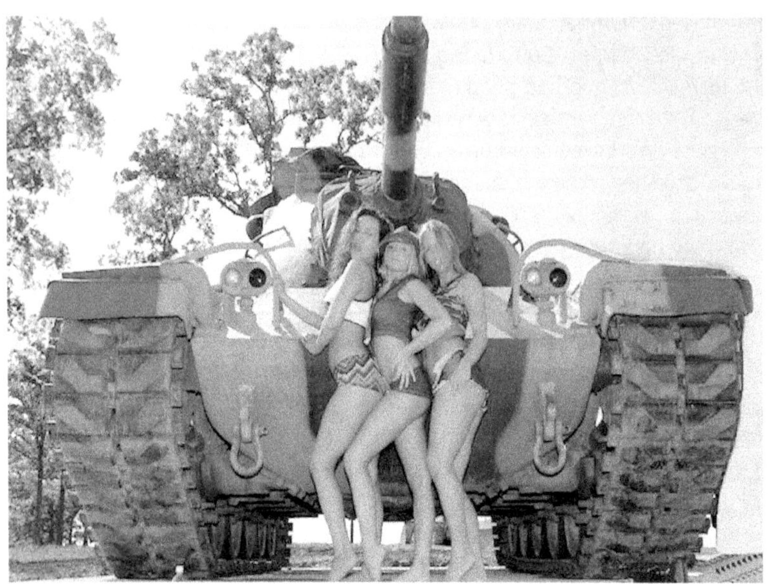

With the tank at Fort Leonard Wood just several Miles from Big Daddy's Cabaret are Selena, Carmen, and Harley. This image would become the cover picture for the *2004 Xtreme Weapons* calendar.

Ironically, the Springfield saw more use in World War II than it did during World War I. The U.S. had entered World War 1 in 1917 and by 1918 it was almost over. When American gun manufacturers were unable to supply our war effort fast enough our armed services turned to an adaptation of the British Enfield rifle, which was re chambered from .303 British to the American 30-06 round. Surprisingly more 1917 Enfields found themselves in the hands of World War I American troops than 03's.

Most Americans probably do not associate the 03 bolt action rifle with World War II. But during the first year of the war in particular most of the hardest fighting was done with 03's, not M-1's. For instance at Guadalcanal, the U.S. Marines who defeated the Japanese were armed with Springfields. It was only when Army troops relieved the Marines that the island saw large numbers of M-1's. And in early 1942, the thousands of American infantry fighting in the Philippines were carrying 03's although in both campaigns Browning automatic rifles, Thompsons, and belt fed machine guns were issued in large numbers to supply additional firepower.

Between the wars, the 03 Springfield and the flat shooting powerful 30-06 cartridge combined to make the bolt action sporter even more popular than the lever action rifle in the game fields. The Springfield action was king, providing the strength from which even more powerful cartridges could be launched while the Springfield's record for accuracy became legendary. Even today, when I work the bolt of my Remington 03 and compare its lightening fast buttery smooth action to those of today's commercial sporters, my 03 comes out way ahead.

Although a sniper's version of the M-1 Garand was developed during WWII, very few actually saw combat. The American WWII sniper found himself using the Springfield A-4, which was simply an 03-A3 with a scope replacing the A3's iron sights. By the early 1950's, most American snipers of the Korean War were using M-1 based sniper's rifles although large numbers of them were still using the A-4. In fact, the Springfield's smoothness and accuracy were so highly prized that American snipers were still using the 03 at the start of the Vietnam War.

With its service record extending more than sixty years, the 03's longevity as a main line weapon for the major worlds armies since 1860 has still not been surpassed. The Springfield 03 was and still is so good that the most versatile and still un-eclipsed cartridge of all time, the 30-06, is still oftentimes called the 30-06 Springfield.

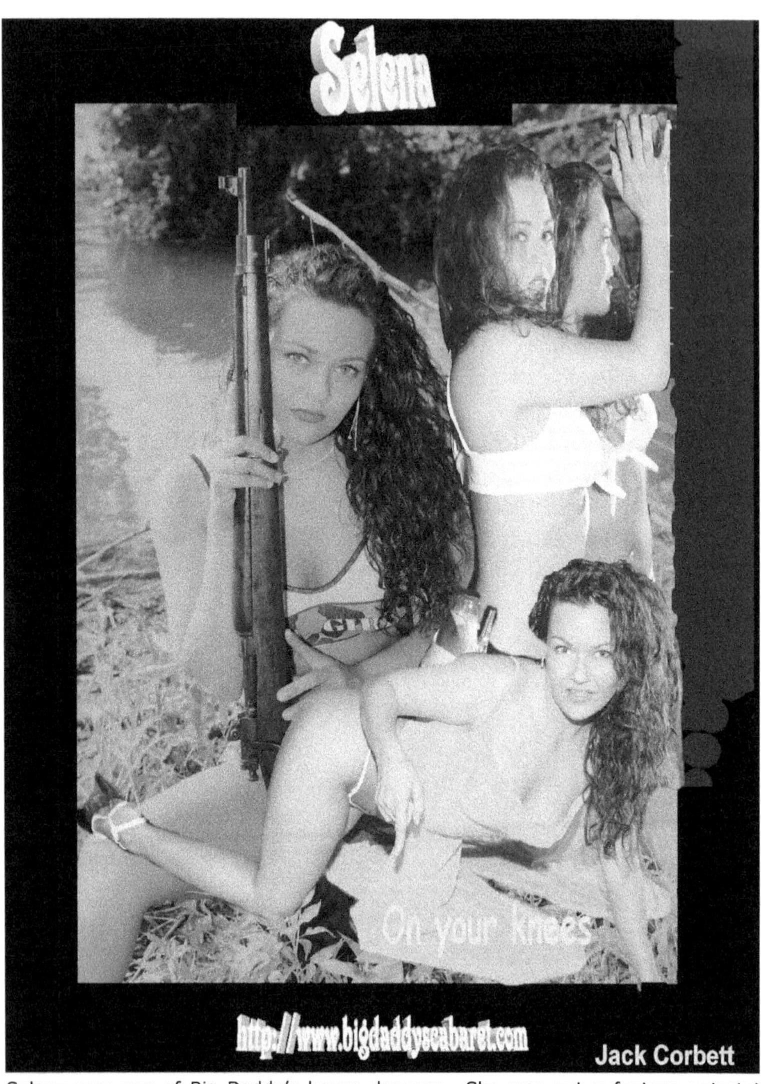


Selena was one of Big Daddy's house dancers. She was not a feature entertainer although she modeled with the 1903 Springfield for the 2004 Xtreme Weapons calendar. To polish up his graphics arts skills, the author created this promo for Selena.

# Paul Mauser's timeless 98 K, the rifle that refuses to die

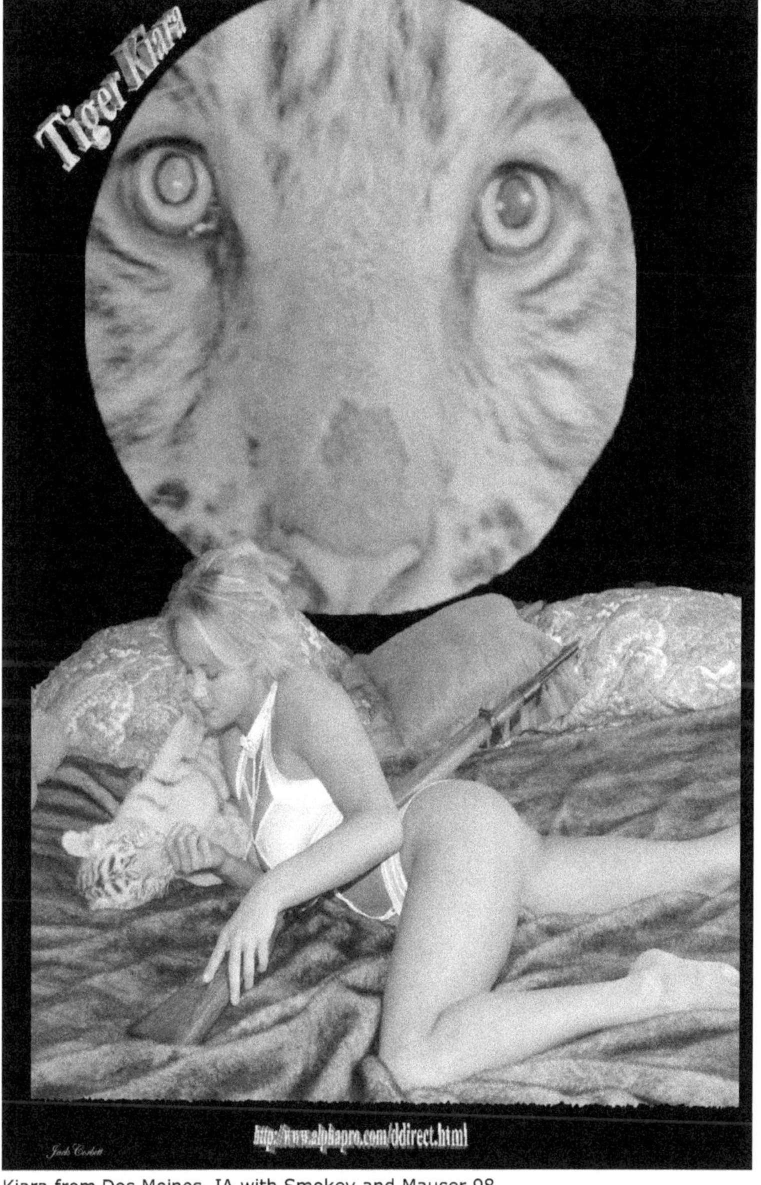


Kiara from Des Moines, IA with Smokey and Mauser 98

The hunter stood in the hot African sun 40 yards away from the Cape Buffalo bull half-hidden in the thick brush of the savannah. Tensely alone, for he had bribed the authorities into allowing him to go for his trophy without a guide, he could feel the sweat streaming down his neck. As he raised his gun he bit his lip and tasted blood. He had seen a picture of a hunter who had failed to make his shot count against a cape buffalo and it wasn't pretty. Where the hunter had taken his shot there remained only a boot with a bloody stump broken off just above the ankle.

Yes, the Cape Buffalo is the most dangerous of all African big game. An enraged buffalo not only endeavors to kill his antagonist, his rage drives him to obliterating the hunter into unrecognizable road kill.

The hunter swallowed hard, taking grim satisfaction in thinking, "At least my rifle's solid: it's a Mauser." Then the Buffalo charged–its huge head lowered with dust flying from its hooves. CRACK the hunter fired--the bullet deflected off the horn--splinters everywhere--he worked the silk smooth action--a second gleaming brass cartridge slid into the chamber as he lowered his aim.

Freeze frame. We have the Buffalo charging down on said hunter who's ready to take his second shot--a shot that he'd counted on and got because he'd chosen the action for his custom rifle carefully. Brave but dicey, the man certainly puts a lot of faith in his shooting ability--which may or may not be well founded but his faith in his rifle was solidly based for at the heart of the custom rifle is the Mauser 98 action. Arguably the best bolt action ever developed-- the standard German Army infantryman's issue during both World Wars-- a rifle that has become a legend-- and this month's *Looking Glass Magazine's* featured firearm of the month.

## A LITTLE EUROPEAN HISTORY

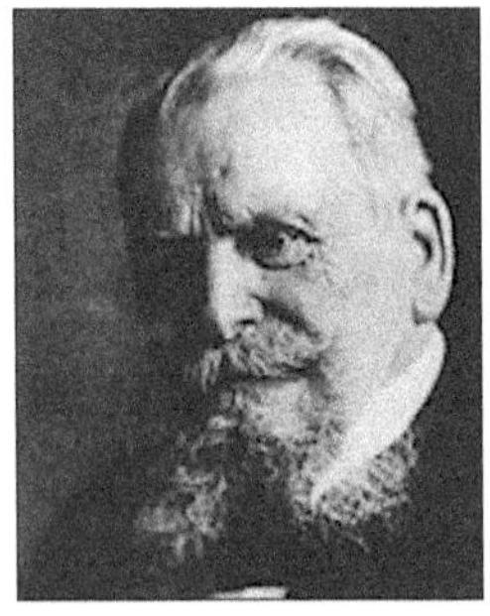

The genius behind the rifle's design was Peter Paul Mauser, born Paul Mauser in Oberndorff, Neckar, in 1838, the son of a royal gunsmith.

Working with his brother Wilhelm Mauser (1834-1882)-- he developed the 11 mm. needle gun that was adopted by the German Army in 1871.

In 1897 Mauser produced his masterpiece, the Mauser Gewehr magazine-rifle. It was Germany's answer to the French Lebel M1888. Peter Paul Mauser died in 1914.

# ACROSS THE ATLANTIC

During this same time period, starting with the 1860's, American arms development had reached its temporary zenith with the Winchester lever action, which had given American Civil War

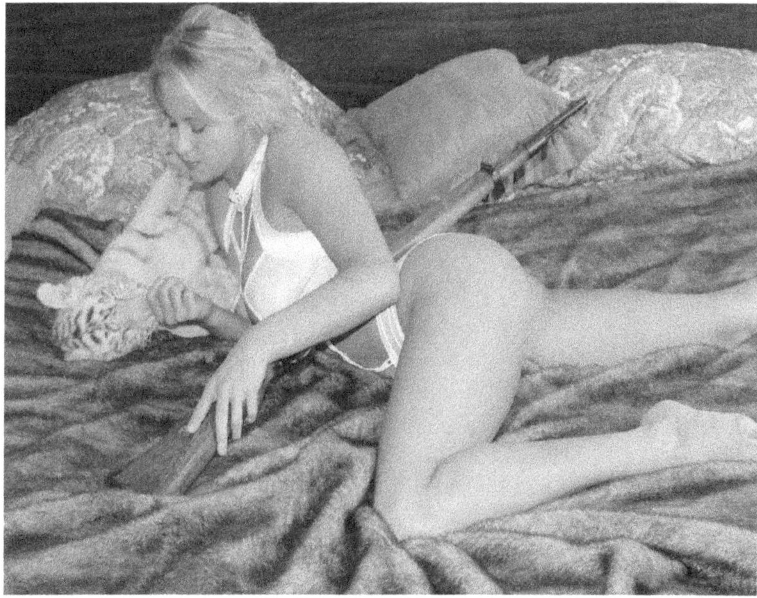

The Anatomy of a photo shoot. The author met Tiger Wayne at Big Daddy's Cabaret during the first S.P.E.W. wrestling championship bout that pitted Iowa's Dirty Heather against Missouri's Killer Kloey. Tiger Wayne had a Bengal Tiger cub upstairs at the club which some of Big Daddy's dancers were cavorting after paying a small fee to Tiger Wayne for taking their pictures. The author convinced Tiger Wayne to bring a Tiger cub to the St. Louis Metro East and paid for the hotel room the photo shoot was to take place in. Then he convinced Kiara to come down from Iowa to model with the Mauser rifle and the Tiger Cub for an Xtreme Weapons article. Meanwhile his friends, Frank and Sherry, the owners of Club 64 in East St. Louis had acquiesced to Tiger Wayne's bringing the Tiger cub into their night club. It would turn out that there would be more than enough fun for all with feature entertainer star Kloey Love in town that Christmas weekend who wanted to put on a special show for Frank and Sherry who had gotted her started in her career as an adult entertainer. And with Ami in St. Louis from Iowa and one of her co-workers from Heart Throbs the stage was set–literally for that night the Tiger took over the topless club.

Union riflemen unprecedented firepower. However, the rapid firing lever action was not widely used by the U.S. military which had instead adopted the much slower firing single shot Springfield 45-70. Unbelievably the military minds responsible for U.S. arms procurement had decided that the lever action's quick firing capabilities would be a waste of ammunition. Long after the death knell of the single shot rifle should have been heard, the U.S. finally adopted the 30-40 Krag bolt action rifle that had been designed by Captain Johannes Krag, director of the Norwegian Arms factory and Erik Jorgensen, another Norwegian.

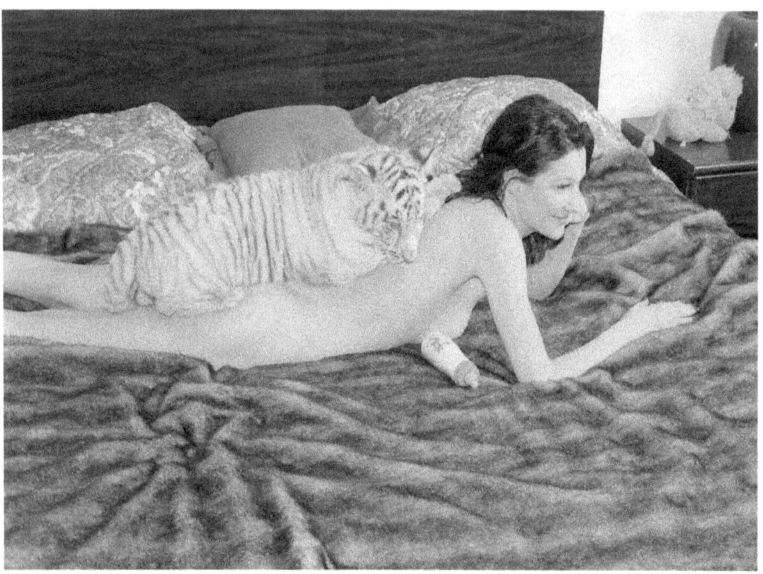

**Amy of the Kentucky rifle photo shoot with Smokey in the hotel room helping out with the photo shoot**

During the Spanish-American War of 1898, the Krag was pitted against Paul Mauser's newest creation, the 1893 Mauser, which utilized a new system of loading by employing a stripper clip that could be conveniently inserted into the rifle's breech and five rounds wiped into the rifle's magazine quickly. The Mauser was significantly faster loading than the Krag and its high velocity 7 mm round out ranged the Krag flat out-- a wake-up call for the U.S. military who found that casualties were more expensive than bullets.

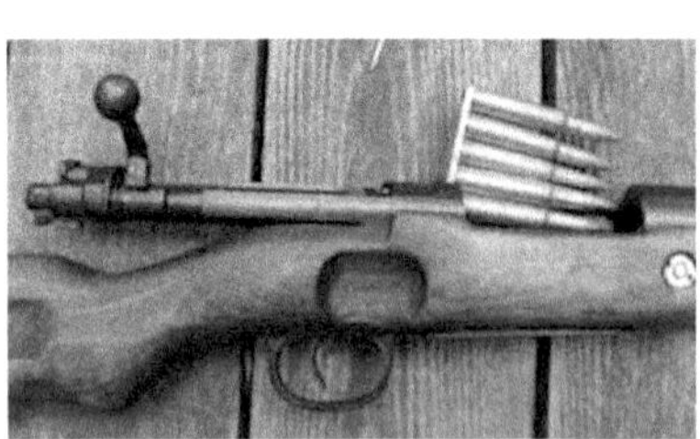

**98 Mauser with stripper clip and 5 cartridges**

The Spanish-American War was a wake up call to the American Arms industry, which immediately started looking for a replacement for the slow loading and out ranged Krag, which would fit in well with the new American military mind-set of the precision sharp shooter ruling the battlefield with his fast-shooting long-range rifle.

The result was the 1903 Springfield, designed around the legendary .30-06 cartridge. Open the bolt of a Springfield '03 and the German 98 Mauser and guess what? Surprise! You can hardly tell the difference. The American Springfield which would soon find itself pitted against the 98 on the battlefields of France had so heavily borrowed from Peter Paul Mauser's creation that after the war the U.S. continued paying royalties to Mauser.

Following the First World War many custom-built rifles were based on the Springfield '03 and the Mauser 98. In general the Mauser 98 action was viewed as stronger than the '03's. The result was that the Mauser became the action of choice for hunters looking for power. But Springfield shocked the shooting world in the 1,000 yard matches at Camp Perry, by compiling a legendary record for accuracy. The period between the world wars became a golden-age for fine rifles. Fine craftsmanship of the Mauser action was highly prized, while labor costs were low. Many of the finest specimens from this golden-age were custom rifles based on the Mauser 98 action.

Both the Mauser 98 and the Springfield '03 are commonly regarded as World War I rifles; yet, both went on to arm millions of soldiers during World War II. In fact, something like 3.5 million Springfields were manufactured during World War II where they appeared in far greater numbers than they ever had in World War I when the common U.S. foot soldier was more apt to be armed with the 1917 Enfield.

## THE GARAND M-1

With its eight shot capacity and rapid loading capabilities from top loading magazines, its ability to fire as fast as the soldier could pull the trigger, its great reliability, and accuracy, the M-1 Garand was truly a revolutionary weapon. It totally outclassed the 98 Mauser and the Springfield with the Garand officially replacing the Springfield in 1936. However, the U.S. found that with the need for millions of U.S. combat troops who would fight both in Europe and the Pacific, production lines could not produce Garands fast enough to keep up with demand. An improved Springfield was developed.

The result was the Springfield 03-A3; a rifle that could do everything the Springfield 03 could do but without as many time-consuming production procedures as earlier models. Formerly milled parts gave way in non-critical instances to being stamped. The intricate rear sight that had been was replaced by a new sight that could be produced much more efficiently.

In the acid test of combat American infantrymen armed with both Springfields and M-1 Garands found themselves slugging it out with their German counterparts, most of whom were using the 98 K Mauser. So which weapons were the best?

First, most infantry units on both sides were armed with a number of weapons. A company of U.S. soldiers would typically be armed with M-1 Garands, the much lighter M-1 carbines, Thompson submachine guns, Browning automatic rifles, and light belt-fed machine guns along with a few bolt action Springfields. A German company would typically have more light machine-guns than its American counterpart and possibly more submachine-guns. But Germany did not have anything like the M-1 Garand, and its attempts to produce a similar weapon ended in failure. In most combat situations neither the Springfield nor the Mauser 98 K could begin to measure up to the M-1 Garand which General Patton called the finest battle implement ever devised.

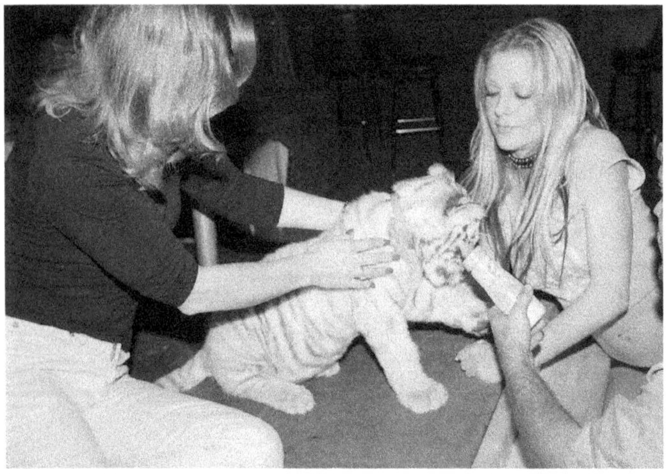

Sherry and Kloey Love on Club 64's stage with Smokey the night they turned the tiger loose in the topless club.

One of the most important parts of any firearm is its sights. I own two Springfield 03 A3's, one M-1 Garand, an M-1 A which is essentially an improved M-1 Garand, and two Mauser 98 K's. From what I've seen on these weapons and on many others I've examined, the M-1 Garand has the absolute finest iron sights ever to be placed on a military rifle. They can easily be picked up in even bad lighting conditions. They are readily seen even by those whose eyesight is no longer the best. The Mauser 98's sights are not even close to being as fast or easy to use. So the German infantryman going against an M-1 Garand armed U.S. soldier was at a clear disadvantage simply because his sights were inferior. When one accounts for the fact that the U.S. soldier could fire his weapon as fast as he could pull the trigger without being distracted by having to manipulate a bolt and that the semi automatic action of his weapon somewhat softened its recoil, the advantages of the M-1 Garand were conclusive.

But the M-1 Garand is nearly a pound heavier than either the Springfield or the Mauser 98 which made it more cumbersome to carry for extended periods of time. And although the Springfield's sights took more time to produce than the more cheaply produced .03-A3's sights, the less expensive sights built during the war were far superior to the sights of the Mauser 98's.

Moreover, the better of my two Springfields is a real tack driver. I bought it when I was 12, and it's been a magic wand, seeming to hit whatever it's aimed at while its action is far smoother than those of most factory produced bolt actions commanding a high price tag.

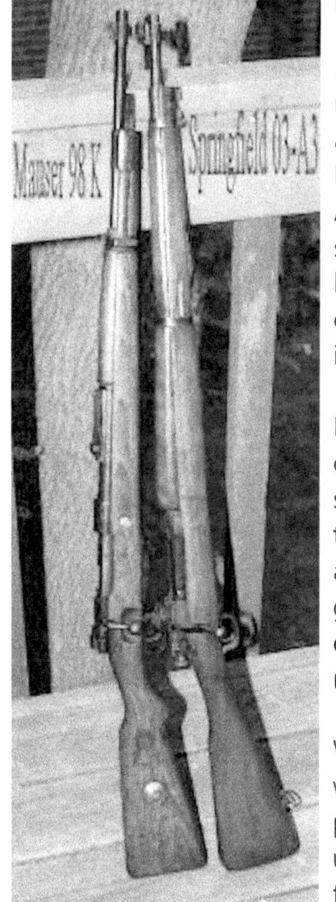


Both of my Mauser 98 K's are Russian capture rifles. I bought one of them at a gun show for around $260, took it home and took it apart. Inside, the action was thick with cosmoline. And the wood stock had been finished with shellac. The Russians wound up capturing literally millions of Mausers--in various states of condition-- some with blood pitting included.

I removed the Cosmoline from the metal parts of that first Mauser, then sanded, stripped, and steel-wooled the shellac finish off its stock. I then refinished the stock using walnut stain and tung oil, oiled the metal parts, and put the gun back together. For the next several evenings I'd use fine steel wool which I used to rub down the stock until it got silky smooth.

What finally emerged was a beautiful piece of weaponry that looks just like it did when the piece was first issued. One thing that I noticed upon disassembling the rifle was the precision fitting. The quality of the machined parts was even a cut above my Springfield. But this was a 1941 model-- and at this point of the war,

Germany's arms program had not been pressured into taking shortcuts that showed in later production.

My second Mauser came from Empire Arms off the Internet. Its price was slightly less than 300 dollars. I like this rifle better than the first. For one thing, its bore is perfect, as bright as a mirror. It seems, however, that it is not quite as finely put together as my 1941 Mauser. Which seems reasonable since it was produced in 1944 and by 1944 German armies were in retreat on every front while German munitions manufactures were feeling the painful crunch of materials shortages.

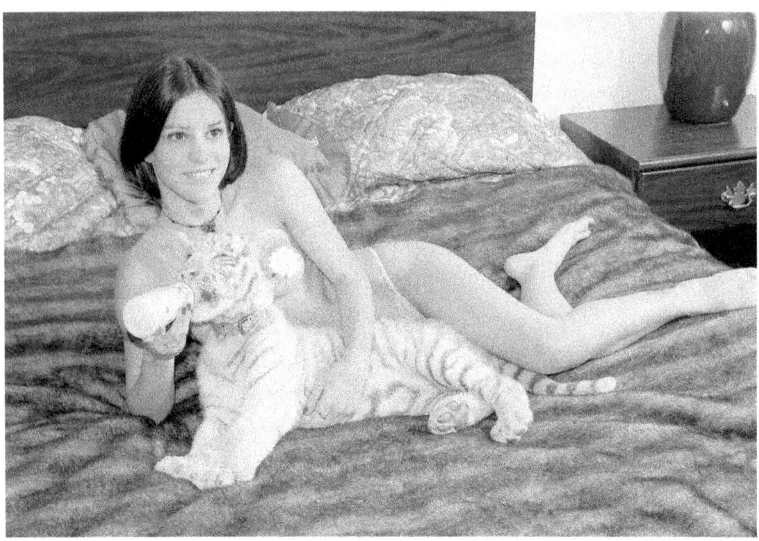

Unless one is willing to spend a couple thousand dollars it is next to impossible to purchase a Mauser 98 in excellent condition with all matching parts. The Russians rebuilt the rifles they captured, without paying much attention to whether the parts matched or not. If for example one rifle had a damaged stock that stock was thrown away while another stock was fitted to the barreled action. The rifle was then re blued, a protective shellac applied to the stock and the metal parts were slathered in cosmoline. The guns were assembled, crated and stored until the Soviet bloc crumpled and the Russian economy had gotten as lethargic as a Missouri mule. Suddenly the Russians were dumping Mausers on the market.

Coming onto the market over the past few years are the Yugoslavian 98 Mausers, which aren't true 98's. These are model 48's. They are close to what the Germans used in World War II but they aren't quite the same animal. Their actions are shorter and parts are not interchangeable between the German and the Yugoslavian 98's. From what I've seen a few hours have to be invested to bring back the luster of the Russian captured 98's whereas little or no work has to be done to the model 48's which are typically in excellent condition right out of the box. But they just don't quite look right. Their lines are blockier and somehow not as streamlined.

And there is nothing quite like ordering a Russian capture German Mauser; seeing it arrive in its box, then putting in a few hours of elbow grease and winding up with an actual combat rifle in nearly immaculate condition. And if that's not enough, surplus ammunition is available for as low as $4.95 per 70 rounds which makes shooting this high power rifle dirt cheap. Buying Russian capture German 98 K rifles is one of the best deals on the firearms market today.

## CUSTOM MAGNUMS

But on the other hand if you've got the bucks--there are spectacular custom magnums based on the Mauser action. There's Roy Weatherby's Magnum rifles for example, that's represented state of the art of modern rifle development for years. And the rifle to covet above all others was the hard-kicking, flat-shooting Weatherby .300 magnum-- an elegant shooter.

A walnut stocked Weatherby in .300 Weatherby Magnum costs around $1,300. Or for the same price the .338 Winchester magnum or .340 Weatherby which churns up something like 5,000 foot pounds of energy is also available. The $1,300 model is conservatively styled. There's also the deluxe model which costs another $800. Then there is a special model called "the Dangerous Game model" that costs a little more than $3,000.

But as impressive as the Weatherbys are, even more impressive are the rifles that have recently been introduced to the market by Empire Rifles. Empire's advertising claims each rifle is handcrafted in the U.S. and "the perfection of the Mauser 98. The rifles start at $3,500 for Empire's Legacy model. Then comes the Empire East Africa model, designed specifically to handle the largest game while firing the most powerful cartridges. A wood stock model starts at close to $7,000. All Empire rifles are guaranteed to shoot into less than one inch at 100 yards. Which has resulted in the object of my lust having recently shifted fromWeatherby to having an Empire's custom 98 Mauser-based rifle that is exquisite to touch and unerring in accuracy and function.

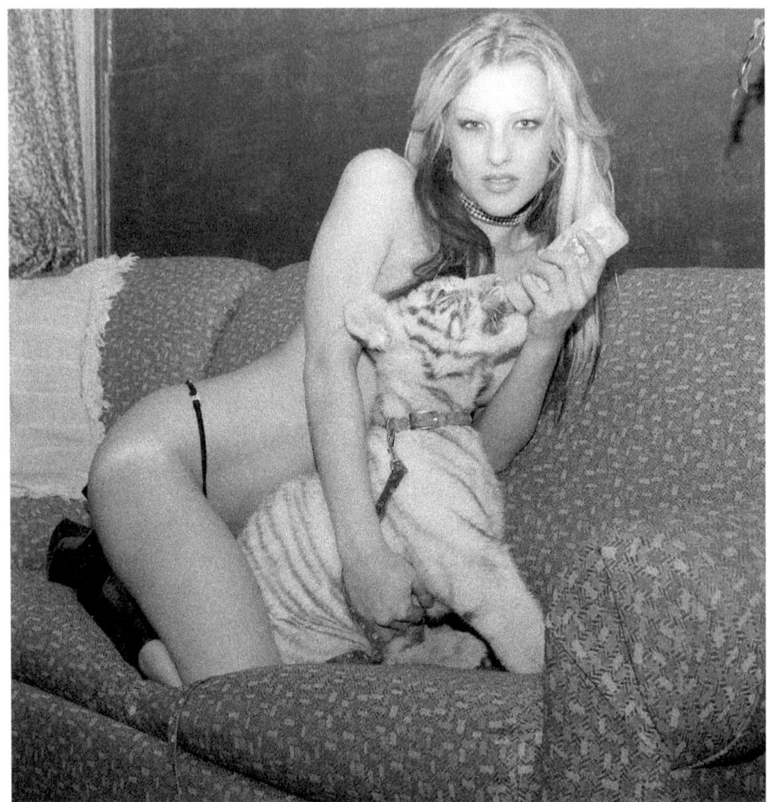

Kloey Love got her start as an adult entertainer at the Platinum Club while Frank and Sherry were managing the club. She would later become one of the top feature entertainers in the United States, but she continued to view the St. Louis Metro East Club scene as her home base, especially those clubs affiliated with the Marcella's

As far as unparalleled function, the 98 Mauser action is and has been world renowned for employing a large claw extractor and a controlled feed system. In a Mauser each cartridge is enclosed by that massive claw and simply forced into the chamber. Upon firing the case is still firmly grasped by the claw extractor which forcibly ejects it from the chamber. And whether based in fact or fiction, the adage is still propagated that nothing short of controlled feed will do for hunting the world's most dangerous game. After all, it only takes one jam when hunting water buffalo to end a hunter's career.

After all, the Mauser 98 action was designed to hunt the most dangerous game on earth--humans. With complete justification the most reliable weaponry is designed while planning for war, not hunting for sport. The Springfield employs a Mauser 98 controlled feed action while a century later Empire Rifles proudly advertises its expensive custom rifles as the "Perfection of the Mauser 98. Meanwhile at the lower-priced spectrum of the big game rifle market is the Czech firm CZ, which offers what appears to be an excellent line of rifles in the $500-$600 range. The CZ uses an unabashed copy of the Mauser 98 action. So while the Mauser 98 had long ago become obsolete on the military front, even back in World War II when German armies fielded millions of them, it represents one of today's most exciting firearms buys and cheapest shooting bargains for a Russian capture 98 K while on the high priced custom rifle market it is still the leader of the pack, more than one hundred years after its introduction. Like John Browning's with his timeless 1911 .45 automatic pistol design, Peter Paul Mauser's genius gave birth to the 98 Mauser, a gun so perfect that even after a century of production nothing else approaches it.

Many thanks to the three sweethearts from Heartthrobs Entertainment for modeling with Smoky, our favorite white tiger, Kloey Love, Tiger Wayne, and Sherry and Frank Marsela of Club 64 for making these some of the most memorable photo shoots ever.

# The 1911 .45 Automatic

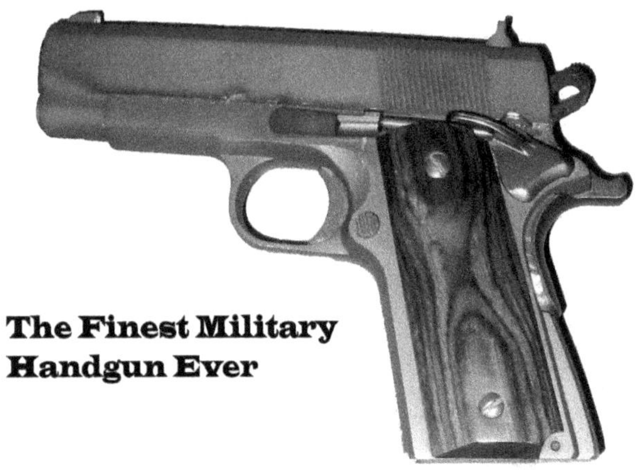


In the 1980's the United States Armed forces replaced the greatest sidearm in military history, the 1911 style .45 automatic with the 9-mm Beretta. The thinking was–1. Since our Nato allies were stuck on 9 mm, we should adopt it also, 2. The .45 auto kicks too much, making it difficult to control, particularly for women recruits, and 3. The Beretta holds 15 rounds versus seven in the .45. Let's examine how absurd this decision was, both from the historical background of the 1911 .45 and the premise that the 9 mm is the more effective round because of the new pistol's greater magazine capacity and its greater controllability due to its lower recoil.

Most Americans are like ostriches, continually sticking their heads in the sand when it comes to learning the lessons of History and how they should be applied to the present. As I mentioned in my last article here, the U.S. military made the fatal error of replacing the Single Action Army Colt .45 Peacemaker with the .38 Long Colt double action revolver in the 1890's. Granted, the double action design was more modern and the new gun could be loaded more rapidly, but the .38 Long Colt repeatedly failed to stop charging Moro tribesmen during the Philippine insurrection at the

close of the Spanish American

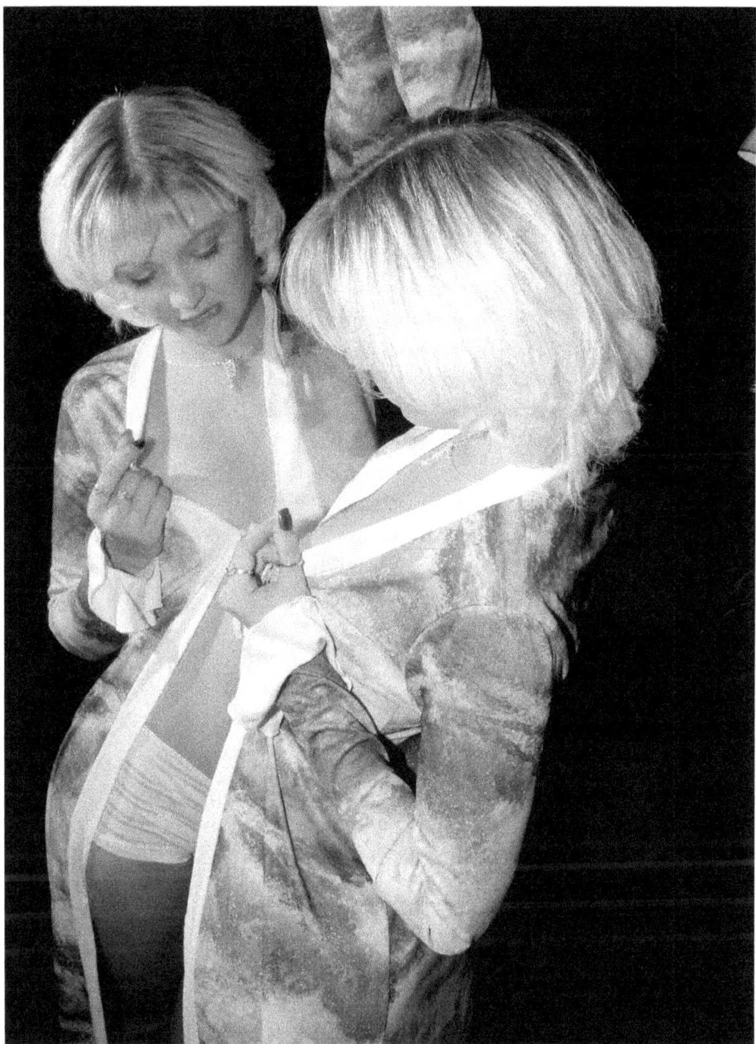

**Skie in front of the author's mirrors at his Collinsville, IL. Apartment**

War, and a number of American infantrymen had to pay the price–literally with their heads. Quantities of .45 Single actions still in storage were rushed to the scene of conflict resulting in American servicemen having a sidearm that could be relied up to stop the enemy

At the turn of the twentieth century, armaments procurement boards across the world clamored for new semi automatic pistol designs, which were just coming into vogue. This was clearly the way to go as the new breed of semi autos could be fired as fast as the trigger was pulled and could be reloaded quickly from fresh clips of ammunition. The problem was most nations are about as clueless about studying History as Americans. Whereas Americans had fresh images in their minds of sword wielding Moros decapitating American soldiers other nations didn't, considering pistols primarily as an officer's badge of rank and settled on 9 mm and even lesser calibers for their armed forces new sidearms. In 1906 the American Armed forces invited gun makers to submit their semi-auto entries for rigorous testing so long as they were of .45 caliber. The winning design would become the standard sidearm of the U.S. miliary.

John Browning, who would develop an unparalleled reputation as a gun designer of belt fed machine guns, the Browning Automatic Rifle (BAR) and many other firearms innovations, supplied the answer in the form of a trim .45 automatic holding seven rounds in the clip. And a manual safety, which could be easily and quickly swiped on and off once the weapon was chambered and cocked. After the final testing in 1910 during which it went for over 6000 successive firings over a three day period without a single malfunction, Browning's entrant was officially accepted as the standard sidearm for the U.S. Armed forces in 1911 and all pistols produced afterwards of this design became known as 1911's regardless of caliber or manufacturer.

If there was ever a test for a handgun's effectiveness in mortal combat that test came during World War I in the vicious close quarters trench warfare between 1914 and 1918. Forty percent of all American infantrymen were armed with the new Browning designed .45 auto whether the pistol was their primary or secondary weapon. Our most dedicated hero of the conflict, Sergeant Alvin York, managed to flank a German machine gun detachment and started to pick off German soldiers with his 1917 Enfield rifle. After shooting more than a dozen soldiers York switched to his .45 auto. The "turkey shoot" continued as Germans dropped one after the other to York's .45. After he killed over 23 men, the whole detachment of 133 men armed with 35 machine guns surrendered to the solitary American.

Ideal for the muddy trenches of World War 1 and the wars that came after, the military 1911 .45 was built with loose tolerances that made it nearly impervious to mud, sand, or dirt. Built to last over 250,000 rounds, typical service testing amounted to randomly selecting one .45 out of each newly delivered batch, firing it 10,000 to 15,000 times without a jam, then putting the weapon back to be delivered with the others of the batch.

The 1911's reputation for great stopping power and reliability continued throughout World War II. Although a rifle or submachine gun was certainly more effective than a pistol in most combat scenarios, there were still many occasions when a soldier was called upon to rely upon his .45 automatic. And when he had to he often had to shoot three or four or more of the enemy and make each shot count. The 1911 continued to supply valuable service as the U.S. military's standard sidearm during the Korean War and throughout the Vietnam conflict.

The .38 Long Colt that failed so dismally to stop Moro tribesmen has a bullet measuring 357 thousands of an inch compared to the 9 mm's 355 thousands of an inch and the 45 auto's close to half an inch in diameter. Sure, the 9-mm bullet travels a lot faster than yesterday's .38 Long Colt, but consider that a fast-moving bullet that travels clear through its target leaves only part of its energy in the target. What makes the 9 mm round a reasonable stopper at all is the fact that it can be made in a hollow point configuration which greatly increases the diameter of the bullet as it expands while traveling through the target and that this expansion limits its penetration, thus concentrating all of its energy to the target. The problem is the Geneva convention prohibits the use of hollow point bullets.

The .45 auto tears big holes into everything that it hits and its heavy bullet tends to move things around a lot. The 9 mm simply doesn't have the size or the horsepower to compare to it. Let's face it, the main task for any military weapon is to stop the enemy. This is a matter of both common sense and historical fact. The big .45 has done this a lot better than the 9 mm.

Obviously, having seven or eight rounds each of which will put a man down with one reasonably placed shot is far better than having 15 rounds in the clip which might take two, three, four, or six bullets to get the job done. Which brings us to the question of user friendliness? That is, is the 1911 45 auto's recoil so severe that it impedes the average recruit's ability to shoot the weapon well and is it comfortable in the hand? Since I have been shooting practically since I've been weaned and have large hands I once again turned to Skie, to represent the average recruit. A former stripper currently working as a waitress at the PTs Sports Cabaret Gentlemen's Club in Sauget, Illinois, at five foot six, just 110 pounds, barely twenty years old and almost completely inexperienced with firearms Skie would be perfect.

She fires two 45 automatics at the local range under my supervision. One is my Springfield .45 compact 1911, the other a Glock .45 auto. One of the attendants running the range is very partial to the Glock since that is what he carries while working as a police officer. Jim feels the 1911 was good in its day but is now a dinosaur compared to the latest and greatest gadgetry out there today. The Glock that Skie takes with her to the firing lane is favored by many police departments and has a 13 shot clip and recoil compensator.

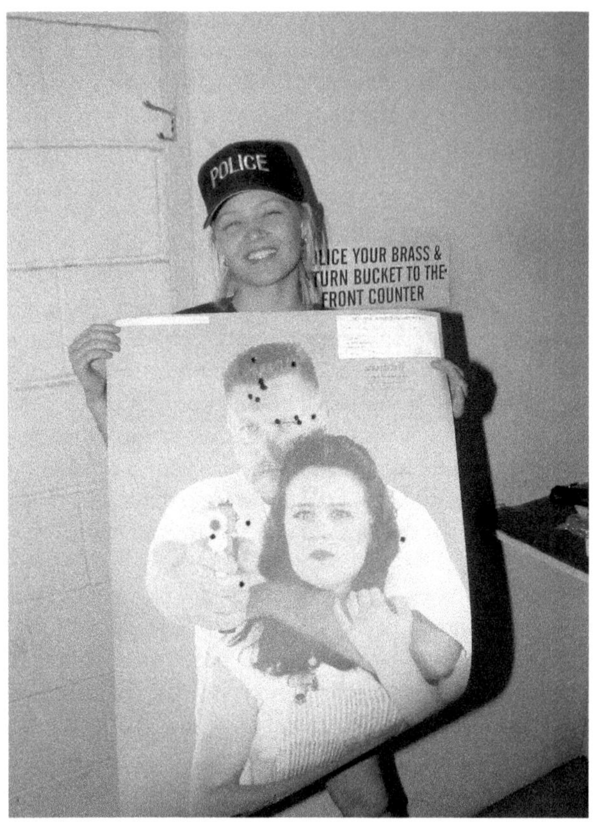


Most of the time Skie shoots at hostage rescue simulation targets at a range of thirty feet. She goes for the terrorist's gun with one of her seven shots, nicking its upper sight, then groups her six remaining shots in a 2.25 inch circle in the middle of the culprit's forehead.

One of her .45 slugs nails the renegade's ear. Regrettably one of her shots grazes the hostage's scalp. But it's her first effort with the .45. And even at that, she groups well enough to have put all her shots into the killing zone of a man's chest at 30 feet. Her groups are more consistent on subsequent targets as she alternates between the Springfield 1911 and the Glock.

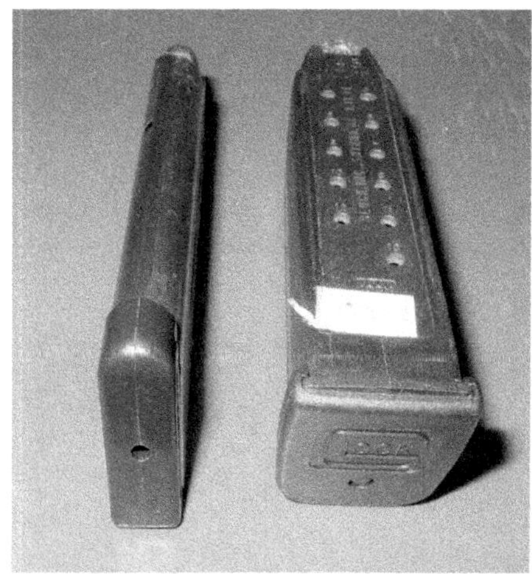

My 1911 Springfield has a single stack magazine, which holds seven rounds whereas the Glock employs a double stack magazine that can hold 13 rounds because it staggers the shells. This makes the clip much wider than the 1911 single stacker and gives the pistol a bulkier feel.

Unlike the 1911, the Glock has no manual safety whatsoever, instead relying upon its proprietary long pull trigger design.

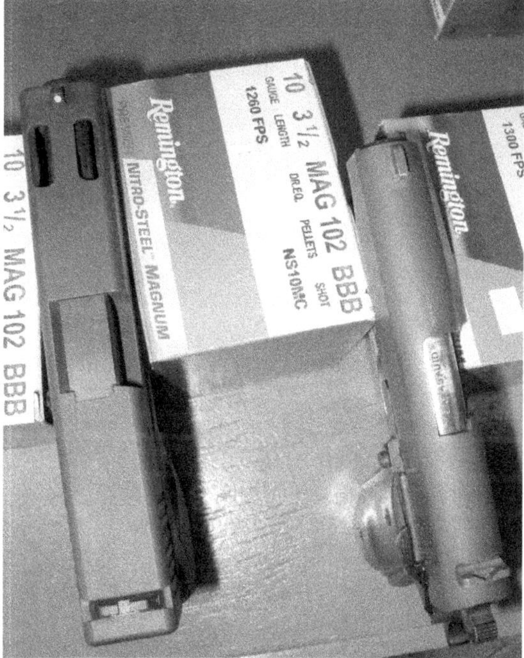


Note how trim the 1911 is compared to the Glock on its left.

Her favorite of the three is my Springfield .45 1911 pistol, because of its trim lines, and slender grips which fit her hand better than the two Glocks. And like the .45 caliber Glock, the 9 mm Beretta which replaced the 1911 in the military has a staggered clip which results in the pistol's having a fat butt. Her shooting the two 45 automatics 100 times and obviously enjoying it once again proves that the .45's recoil is not as unpleasant as its detractors claim it to be. If a slender 110 pound woman new to the sport of shooting can handle a 45so well, obviously the argument for the United States military turning over its 45's for 9 mm's because they kick too much is a wimpish excuse for poor shooting.

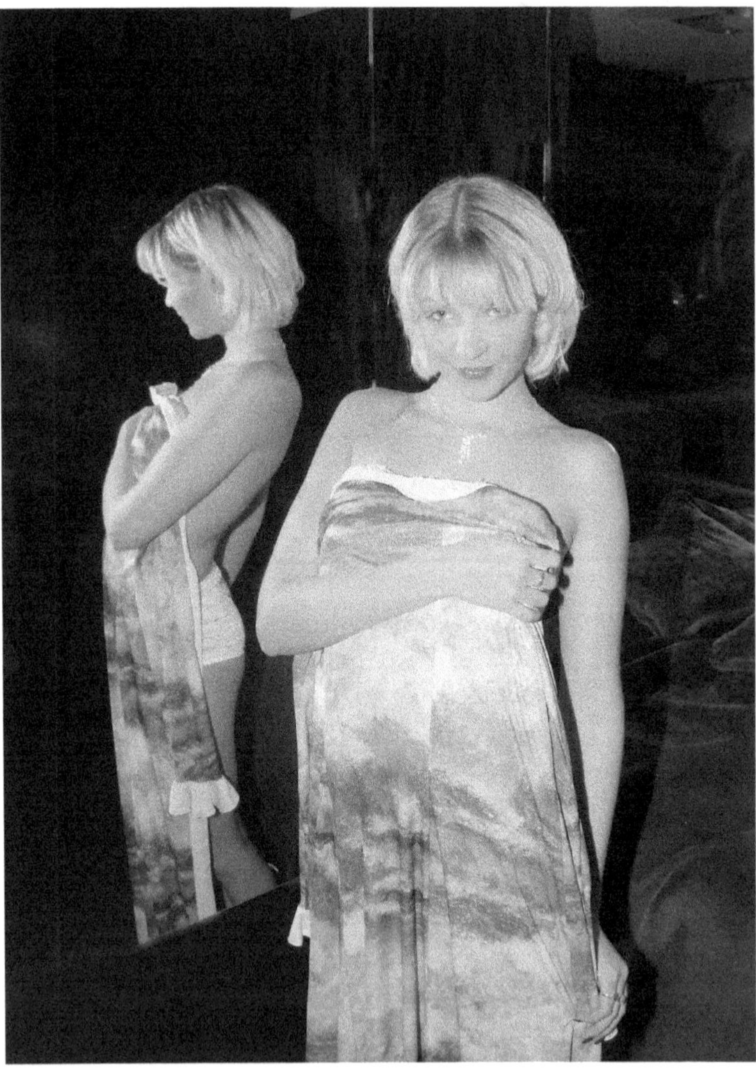

The decision to replace the 1911 .45 auto with the 9 mm is just one more example of this nation's disdain for grasping and applying the lessons of

History. If .38 caliber solid point bullets failed to stop Moro warriors a hundred years ago, what makes the U.S. military think another .38 in the form of the 9 mm will do better? In 1900 our Ordinance Department felt so strongly about the issue that only 45's were allowed in the competition that would determine what would become the new standard sidearm for the U.S. Armed Forces. The 9 mm which was about to become the favored chambering of Europe simply wasn't good enough back in 1900. Although it can be argued that the role of the handgun is no longer as important as it once was, its proper purpose is still to stop a determined adversary, hopefully with one shot rather than as a badge of rank. Two World Wars, Korea, and Vietnam proved that the 1911 .45 Auto is as close to perfection at performing its role as it gets, embodying great stopping power, and the utmost reliability under the harshest conditions, user friendliness, close range accuracy, and portability. The fact that we followed our Nato allies lead by adopting the same 9-mm cartridge they are using proves that we are nothing but a bunch of lemmings who are just as unwilling to learn what History has repeatedly taught us as they are.

# M-1 carbine, was it really a Wimpy Rifle?

Who cares so long as it's topless dancer Jodi from PT's Roxys posing with the M-1 carbine

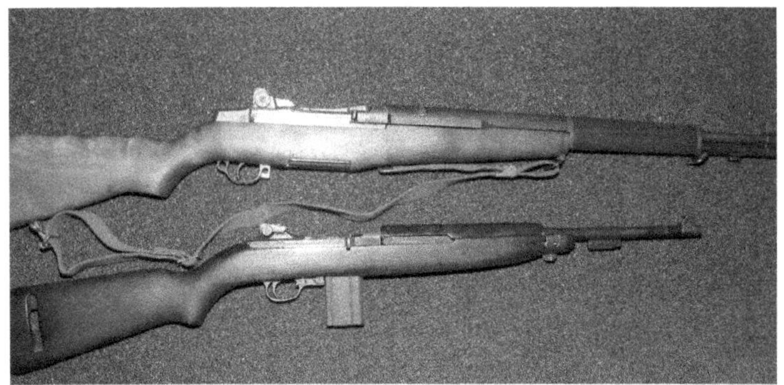

M-1 Garand is on top. M-1 Carbine on the bottom.

Loved by millions of American WWII troops for its extreme light weight, fast handling, and excellent firepower, the M-1 carbine developed a bad reputation for lacking stopping power, range and accuracy. Yet, Audie Murphy, our highest decorated soldier in the war who probably killed more Germans than anyone, heralded it as his favorite weapon. Was it a lemon or a god send?

In warfare troops called upon to serve in the artillery, to man tanks and other vehicles, in the engineers, as mechanics servicing aircraft, trucks and other machines, or in charge of supplying front line troops, often wind up unexpectedly in close quarter combat. By 1940, with Europe once again at war and the U.S. on the brink of the coming bloodbath, the Ordinance Department decided that the M-1 rifle was too long and heavy for such troops and the pistol they carried to be only effective at point blank range. Pistols are very difficult to shoot well, particularly under stress and especially so for the non expert. Weighing more than ten pounds, the Thompson submachine gun was considered to be a handful to lug around and wasteful of ammunition, a factor making it potentially fatal to troops temporarily cut off from fresh supplies of ammunition. Moreover, its .45 caliber slugs plummeted like a rock after a hundred yards. The U.S. Ordinance Department called for a "light rifle project," specifying a five-pound semi automatic rifle firing a thirty caliber 110 to a 125-grain bullet at 2,000 feet per second out of an 18-inch barrel. In a few short months, the Winchester Arms Company developed both the cartridge and a debugged ready for production rifle from original concept to finish. So impressed was Ordinance after witnessing tests of the new weapon that it initiated a production program to replace all .45 pistols and submachine guns with the M-1 carbine.

By war's end more than six million were produced, with the M-1 rifle being the next most prolific small arm at four million copies. The M-1 carbine soon became a much favored weapon by airborne troops, many Marines, and by combatants and noncombatant alike in every branch of the service. But it did not manage to replace the Thompson submachine gun or the .45 pistol simply because even the huge industrial capacity of the U.S. could not satisfy the insatiable demand for weapons. Our troops found themselves fighting side by side with a whole gamut of small arms running from the World War I designed bolt action Springfield to M-1 rifles, forty-five pistols, Thompsons, Browning automatic rifles and belt fed machine guns. Perhaps the M-1 carbine got a bad name in some quarters because it was being compared to nearly every small arm in our arsenal instead of being measured only against the two weapons it was intended to replace, the forty-five pistol and the submachine gun.

First, the M-1 carbine bears little resemblance to the M-1 rifle. The M-1 weighs more than nine pounds and fires a 30-06 150 grain bullet at around 2800 feet per second to the M-1 carbine's 110 grain bullet at 2,000 fps. The M-1's bullet weight and velocity enable it to flatten a man nearly every time and it can do so a long way out there with accuracy equal to the bolt action Springfield which armed most of our Second World War snipers. Such accuracy and power give a soldier confidence that cannot be approached by anything less. Aside from light weight what the M-1 carbine offered the WWII soldier over the M-1 Garand was 15 rounds in the clip to the M-1's eight rounds.

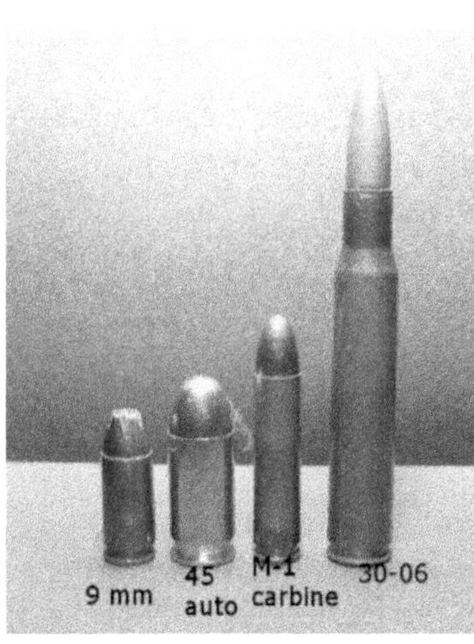

Consider the advantage the M-1 carbine's light weight over the Thompson submachine gun's ten pounds must have had on a fatigued soldier's combat efficiency. Carrying 100 pounds on his body was common for American GI's. While facing exhaustion, lack of sleep, water and food, carrying a five-pound weapon could often prove decisive provided that the weapon was reliable, sufficiently accurate and powerful enough.

## Range and accuracy

My best group with a .45 caliber 1911 semi auto is four inches at twenty-five yards and I can consistently group seven out of seven in a man's head (on a silhouette target) if I really concentrate. My eyes aren't worth a damn anymore. Nevertheless this is far better shooting than most. Shooting eight shot groups with my M-1 rifle I can consistently nail down two inch groups at 25 yards with military iron sights. I finally found a target that had an optimally sized red circle in it which enabled me to put eight shots into 1 inch, comparable to 4 inches at 100 yards.

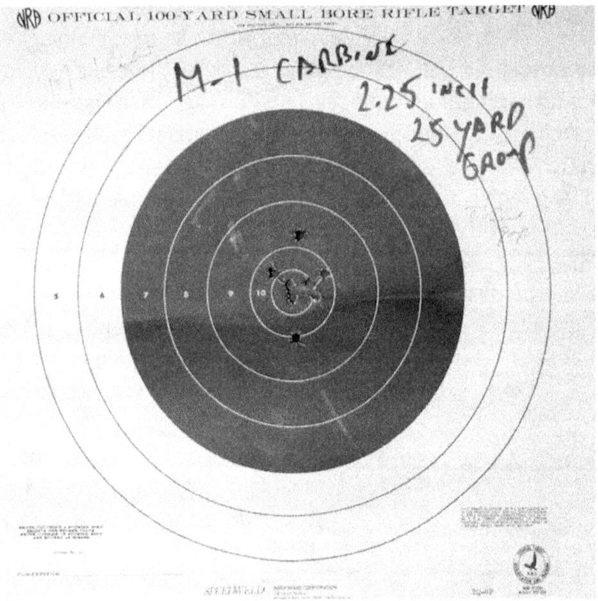


Shooting the "much less accurate" M-1 carbine at twenty-five yards gave me similar two and a quarter inch groups to the M-1's usual two inches. I then fired thirty-three shots in a row into a silhouette's head with the M-1 carbine. Every single shot fell within a three and a quarter inch group----good enough for an instant kill to a man's brain every time. However, 75% of all thirty-three shots fired would go into a one and three-quarter inch circle which equals a 14-inch group at 200 yards.

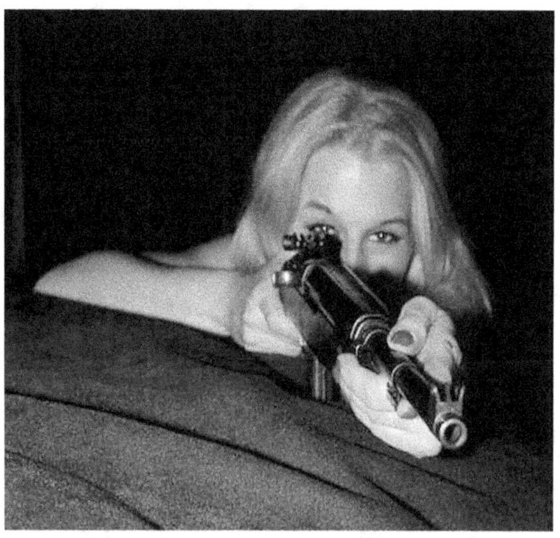

Getting the consistency I got for all thirty-three shots out of the M-1 carbine was much easier than shooting five inch groups with the 45 auto. With the M-1 rifle the limiting factor is my eyes and only by going to a bright easily picked up red circle was I able to cut my group size by half. With a scope I could have done far better. However, in combat soldiers don't have the opportunity to go out and put little red circles on the chests of their human targets. Combat troops are often tired and in nearly all cases, nervous. So out to 200 yards it is not going to make too much difference in a soldier's chances of hitting the enemy whether he uses the M-1 rifle or the M-1 carbine.

## Stopping the enemy in his tracks

The M-1 will do it nearly every time with any kind of reasonably placed hit. But so will the forty-five, if you can hit your adversary. The forty-five does it by making large holes and through the weight of its bullet. The M-1 which only uses a 30-caliber bullet does it by high velocity which does all kinds of strange things to bone, tissue and flesh and by the shock it imparts to the central nervous system.

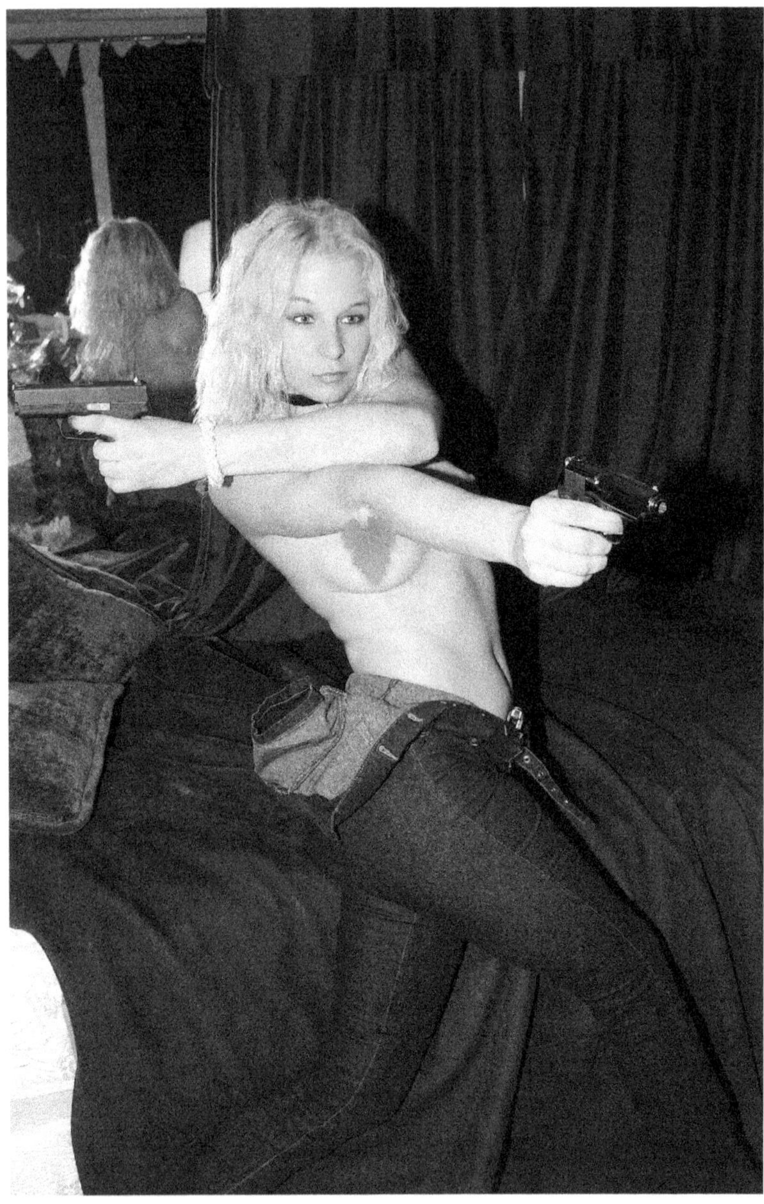

It was only close to the turn of the twentieth century with the advent of smokeless powder that could drive a bullet at 2,000 feet per second and beyond that the U.S. turned to 30 caliber rifles. During the 1960's during the Vietnam War the U.S. military turned to 55 grain .22 caliber bullets at a blistering 3300 feet per second.

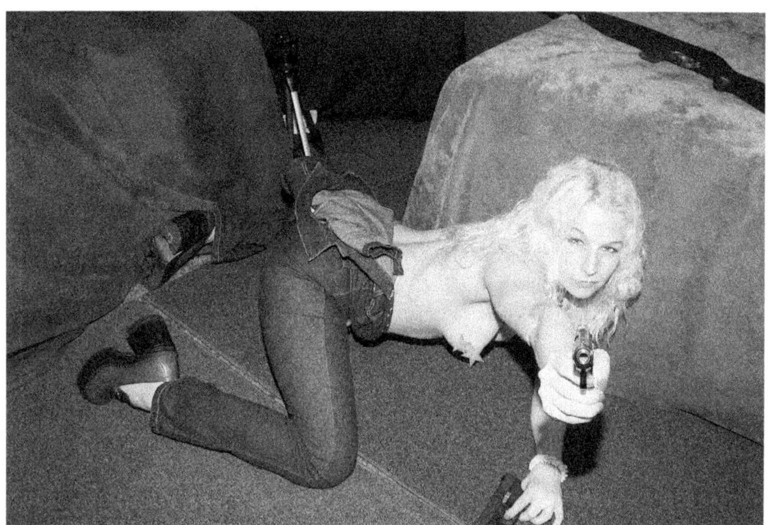

Jodi with the Walther PPK

In the early to mid 1800's it was inconceivable to think that even a thirty-caliber bullet could reliably stop a man. The secret is high velocity hydrostatic shock.

In the 1960's when the .22 caliber M-16 rifle replaced the M-1 carbine the military felt the high velocity .22s were much more devastating than the thirty caliber M-1 carbine's 110 grain bullet. Which brings us to the question of how reliable a man stopper was the M-1 carbine during WWII and the Korean War? Opinions differ drastically on this subject, even among the men who had to use them. One report coming back from the Pacific Theater during World War II has an American soldier wandering off to the latrine. He encounters a samurai sword wielding Japanese solder at a range of thirty yards. The Japanese charges the American, intent on lopping off his head. It takes nine shots from the American's M-1 carbine to send the Japanese off to Samurai Heaven.

This is just one report. Audie Murphy is credited with killing over 250 Germans, many of them with his beloved M-1 carbine. After a mortar round tore up the stock of his M-1 carbine while putting him in the hospital, remembering his rifle's serial number, Audie had it taken out of repair so that he could fix its damaged stock himself with wire.

I immediately got the impression from firing the M-1 carbine that the weapon has considerable power, much more than a .45 caliber slug out of a Thompson or a nine mm out of an Uzi or Sten gun. Until I fired my M-1 which has a lot more kick and which produces one helluva lot more noise. The much heavier and considerably faster 30-06 bullet reminds me when I fire it of a freight train that can level anything in its path. Still, I think 2,000 feet per second from the M-1 carbine's muzzle delivers considerable shock and damage to a human adversary's system, making it a good stopper at close range. However, at 200 yards the same bullet is traveling at less than 1300 feet per second, which is about the speed of a 9 mm at the muzzle whereas the M-1's 30-06 bullet is still traveling at 2200 feet per second at 300 yards. I will suggest that the slightly larger 9 mm bullet, which is not considered a great stopper, delivers greater stopping power at the muzzle than the M-1 carbine will out at 200 yards.

I am convinced that the M-1 carbine got a bad rap when it was compared to the M-1 rifle at longer ranges. Although it could regularly hit a man at 200 yards, it was roughly equal at that range to something on the order of a 38 special in stopping power. The Jap who took seven bullets before being stopped at close range reminds me of a large tomcat I once shot with a 30-06 hollow point. The bullet struck a glancing blow to the cat's abdomen but still managed to blow out its intestines. It knocked the cat down, which promptly got up again to slowly amble off snarling at me with hatred. Tough cat. Tough Jap. Call them Super Cat and Super Jap. Which brings us to the original question--was the M-1 carbine a lemon or a god send? It was no M-1 which seemed to do just about everything well but the M-1 weighs nine pounds. But at a scant five pounds, delivering 15 rounds as fast as a man could pull the trigger with reasonable accuracy, while using far less ammo than a submachine gun, it was revolutionary in design and efficiency. No doubt it was seriously underrated for combat efficiency by those who never had a lot of experience shooting their adversaries with one. Audie Murphy did, and that's why he kept remembering his favorite weapon's serial number.

Note--Many thanks to Jodi (entertainer at PT's Roxys in Brooklyn, Illinois) for a great photo shoot.

# Dirty Heather and the Colt Python .357 magnum

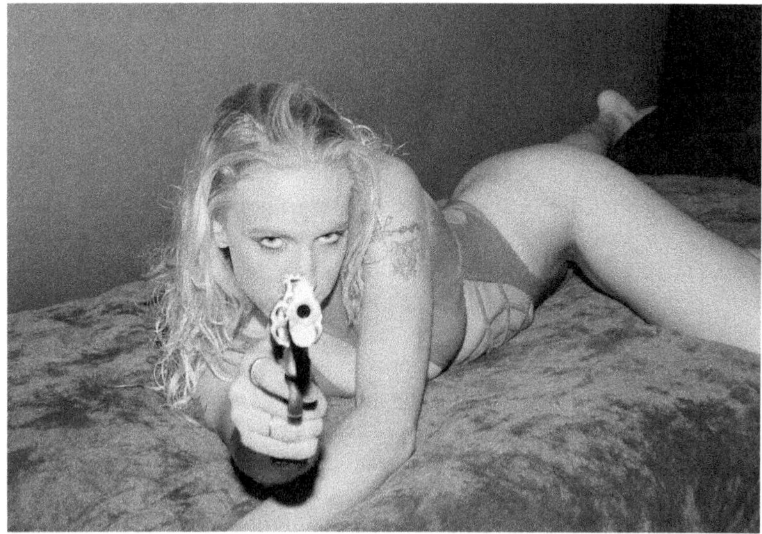

At the author's Collinsville apartment. Heather will later be in the M-19 Browning machine gun article as Machine Gun Heather. And as Dirty Heather, she will represent her home state of Iowa in the first S.P.E.W. (Sexy Professional Exotic Wrestling) match when she wrestles against Killer Cloey at Big Daddy's Cabaret for the U.S. S.P.E.W. wrestling championship.

If a man or woman could have just one handgun for all around protection most gun experts would recommend a double action .357 magnum. Until being overshadowed by the .44 magnum, the .357 had the distinction of being the most powerful handgun on earth gaining perhaps an undeserved reputation for being more than a match for the largest and most dangerous big game on earth.

But as a stopper of predators of the human kind, many leading members of the gun fraternity believe the .357 magnum to be superior to even the big .44. Smith and Wesson's model 29, 44 magnum gained legendary fame and popularity once Clint Eastwood took it to the big screen in his role as Dirty Harry. I've chosen the Colt Python, for this review since even Clint Eastwood, tough and compelling as he was in his role as Harry Callahan, cannot begin to match the peerless, Dirty Heather when she's armed with what is probably the most accurate, smoothest functioning and stylish double action revolver ever made, the Colt Python.

First produced by Smith and Wesson in 1935 as the most powerful handgun on earth, the .357 magnum was originally designed to give lawmen an edge over a new breed of criminal who had emerged during the Depression years. Prohibition saw the rise of the bootleggers, the predecessors of today's organized crime, who fought raging street battles in Chicago and New York for dominance over their rivals. Law enforcement officers often found themselves outgunned by lone psychotic murderers and thieves such as Bonnie and Clyde as well as by tommy-gun carrying bootleggers. This new breed of criminals emerged at the same time as the automobile came into prominence, which gave them unprecedented mobility. The police officer of the era was typically armed with a .38 special revolver firing a bullet only 100 feet per second faster than the .38 long Colt that had failed to stop determined Moro warriors during the Philippine Insurrection just thirty years earlier. Not only did the .38 Special prove to be an undependable man stopper, it also could not be relied upon to penetrate automobile bodies and other barriers protecting the criminals.

The .357 magnum had a slightly longer case than the .38 special and was designed to operate at much higher pressure while firing the same .357 inch diameter projectiles. On paper it developed three times the muzzle energy of the slightly shorter .38 special cartridge. But it also chambered and fired the shorter less powerful round, which is a much cheaper loading that develops significantly less muzzle flash and recoil, which gave the cop the option of loading up with .38 Specials for target practice or .357 magnums for serious business. The .357 magnum soon developed a reputation for being able to perforate engine blocks and automobile bodies and for having superior stopping power. But its recoil and loud muzzle blast was considered to be hard to tolerate which often resulted in poor shooting. Inevitably hunters preferring to take big game with a handgun took their .357 magnums afield until reports came in that the .357 magnum had accounted for the biggest game on the North American continent including Alaska's big bears.

Never mind that the same big game had been handled just as well or just as poorly with pistols such as the .45 Colt. This was a magnum, by God, and it was the only magnum on earth until Smith and Wesson came out twenty years later with its even larger .44 magnum. Until then, the king of the hill magnum to beat all magnums was the Smith and Wesson model 27, a heavy, smooth, finely finished double action revolver which, although it was not the sort of thing one could comfortably carry or conceal, never failed to arouse lust in a true revolver fan's heart.

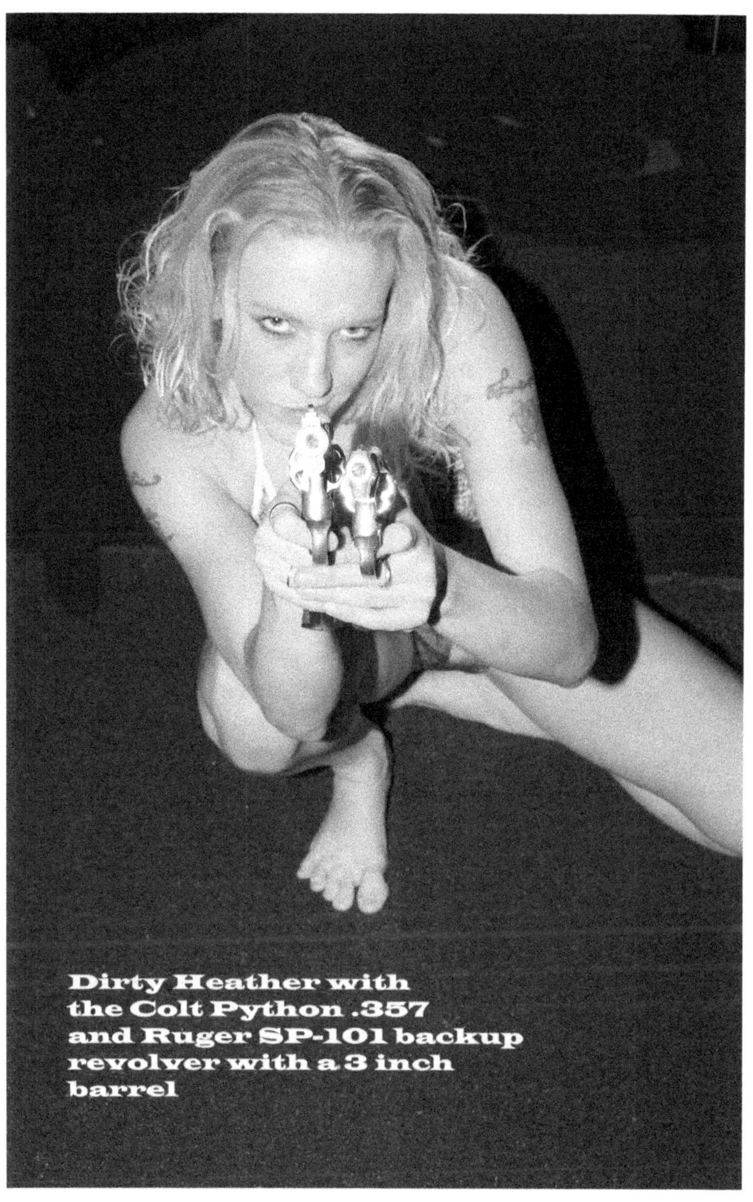

Dirty Heather with the Colt Python .357 and Ruger SP-101 backup revolver with a 3 inch barrel

In 1955 about the time Smith and Wesson was first introducing its new .44 magnum, Colt unleashed what would soon become a true classic, the Python. Name identification with the powerful snake combined with the ventilated rib and overall graceful appearance of the new revolver might have been enough to win it everlasting fame alone, but it's under the hood where the true beauty of the Python lies. Originally intended to be a target revolver in 38 special only, critical parts were custom honed and fitted by hand. The inside of the Python barrel was engineered to taper from the cylinder outward giving them a slightly narrower barrel diameter at the end of the tube than at the breech which gently forced the bullet into the rifling. Since the frame was already substantial enough to handle the pressures of the .357 magnum cartridge Colt decided to chamber the Python in .357 magnum instead of .38 special only. Painstaking attention to detail made the Python twice the price of a good Smith and Wesson, but whereas a typical Smith could be expected to group within two inches at twenty-five yards, a good Python can put six shots into an inch at the same distance. For most this would be a moot point since there are very few shooters who can shoot that well with either gun, but for the purists, the Python's unparalleled fit, finish and accuracy, put it into a class of its own.

Although a .357 magnum doesn't kick nearly as much as a .44 magnum which doesn't kick nearly as hard as a .454 Casull, shooting one is still bound to get the shooter's attention. Recoil is sharp and the gun's bark verges on severe whereas a 45 auto's recoil is gentler and its report is far more muted. Shoot one at night and fire and brimstone shoots out of the barrel in spectacular fashion. Which is a major criticism of the .357 since the fireball unleashed at night tends to destroy the shooter's night vision making accurate follow-up shots difficult. Another major criticism is that the 357's sharp recoil cuts down the shooter's recovery time between shots thus decreasing his firepower in a gunfight. Another negative is that the gun only holds six rounds and reloading is much slower than simply changing clips in a semi-auto such as the 1911 45 auto.

Its adherents claim that it takes just one reasonably placed shot from a .357 to get the job done. After reputedly analyzing the results of thousands of shootings with a number of weapons and calibers, Evan Marshall and Edwin Sanow publicized the results and their analysis in two books, "Handgun Stopping Power" and "Street Stoppers." Their highest rated caliber and bullet is the .357 magnum Federal 125 grain hollow point, good for a 96 percent probability of stopping a man with one shot to the torso. According to their figures not even a .44 magnum or 45 automatic can quite equal it. The .357 magnum 125 grain hollow point gets the job done by high speed. If you read and believe Marshall and Sanow's statistics this relatively small (357 thousandths of an inch) bullet typically blows 80 hundredths of an inch holes into people.

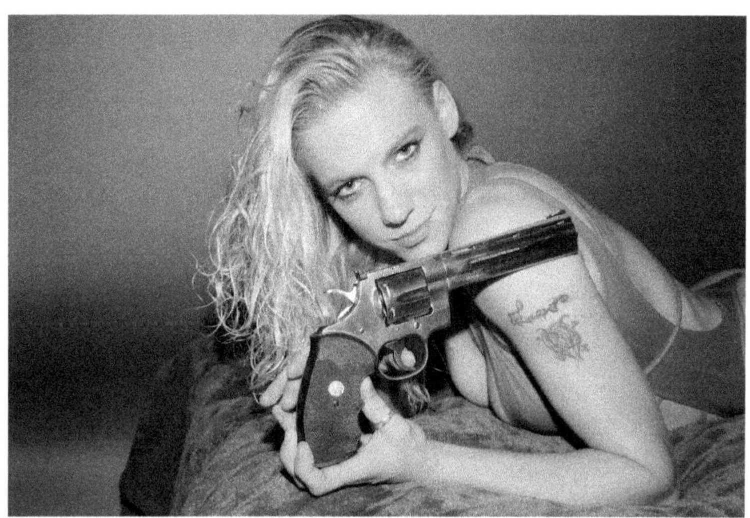

Proponents of the "Large heavy slow moving bullet makes the best stopper theory" such as Colonel Jeff Cooper and Chuck Taylor scoff at the Marshall-Sanow statistical database. Taylor in particular claims that fast moving hollow point bullets such as the .357 magnum Federals are reliable man stoppers only if they expand and that this occurs only half the time. Taylor argues that clothing or other debris often winds up in the hollow point cavity making it impossible for a hollow point bullet to expand and that if one is shooting at large animals that the animals' fur will cause it to fail to expand also. Both men claim that a .45 automatic's large bullet does not need to expand since it's already making a large hole in whatever it hits and that it will reliably stop a man 19 out of 20 times with one solid hit to the torso.

Whether or not the .357 magnum is the top man stopper of them all, there is no question about its versatility. There's a huge selection of bullet types available for it in either .357 persuasion or in .38 Special, from heavy solid bullets such as the 200 grain Corbon that the company claims is just the thing for venturing out into Brown Bear inhabited territory to fast moving 125 grain hollow points to mild kicking 38 wad cutter target loads.

My six inch barreled stainless steel Colt Python is a virtual work of machined steel artistry. I cannot think of a more appealing handgun with its ventilated ribbed barrel, and prominent barrel under lug. Drop the cylinder from the frame to load it and click it back into place, and you are rewarded with a meshing of cylinder to frame that is "just so", a perfect mating of parts. Its low profile adjustable sights with its red ramp front and white outline rear enable quick target acquisition and the ability to focus in at ranges up to 50 yards, even with my bad eyes. I can shoot dimes all day long at twenty-five feet with it. Its trigger pull when firing single action is nice and crisp but it's when one is firing double action that the Python makes a real believer out of the shooter. Its pull is initially long and substantial which is typical of nearly all double-actions. If you flinch anticipating the gun's recoil you are going to notice it long before the gun goes off, and scold yourself for being such a timid idiot. You just pull and suddenly the gun goes off without warning you. Surprise---and that's the way you shoot well, having the gun surprise you when it suddenly erupts. Believe it or not I can shoot the Python better double-action than I can Single Action. Its solid weight and large rubber grips absorb a lot of the gun's recoil, which makes the .357 magnum's bark a lot worse than its bite. And each time it goes off with a full house .357 magnum load its loud crack and prominent muzzle flash inspires confidence that anything that does all of that has got to have what it takes to stop any human opponent.

All other double action revolvers pale in comparison. Let's see--Heather's never been beaten in ten street fights and three professional boxing matches. Tall, slender, and well-proportioned she's assertive when she needs to be, yet reserved when appropriate. She'd be the perfect bodyguard, an alert and sharp navigator to the driver crossing the country, a blonde who's as beautiful as she is powerful. With all due respects to Clint Eastwood and his Smith and Wesson model 29, I think Dirty Heather's got even Dirty Harry beat when she's armed with what is perhaps the finest specimen of the double action revolver maker's art, the Colt Python.

# The Ruger Mini 14 Rifle

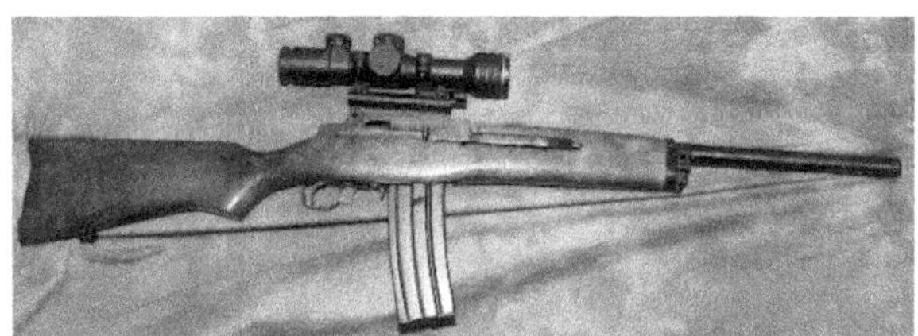

Anyone who knows anything at all about guns is familiar with the mini-14. Chances are he already owns one. Its lines are strikingly similar to the M-14 that had replaced the M-1 as the standard battle rifle for the U.S. Armed Forces and its action borrows heavily from it. But whereas the .308 chambered M-14 weighs in at 9 pounds, the mini comes in at a svelte 6.5 pounds. Light and compact the mini 14 was one of firearms designer genius Bill Ruger's most successful offerings in a long string of successful and brilliantly conceived firearms innovations. Firing the same .223 round as our military's M-16 rifle at more than 3,000 feet per second, the mini 14 can spit rounds out as fast as a man can pull the trigger. Although Ruger supplied five round clips with each gun his company sold, 20 round clips could be ordered from the factory and 30 round clips could easily be found from third party vendors. The rifle could and can still be had for half the price of semi automatic versions of the M-16 sold to the civilian market. The mini-14 was almost too good to be true, and Ruger sold zillions of them.

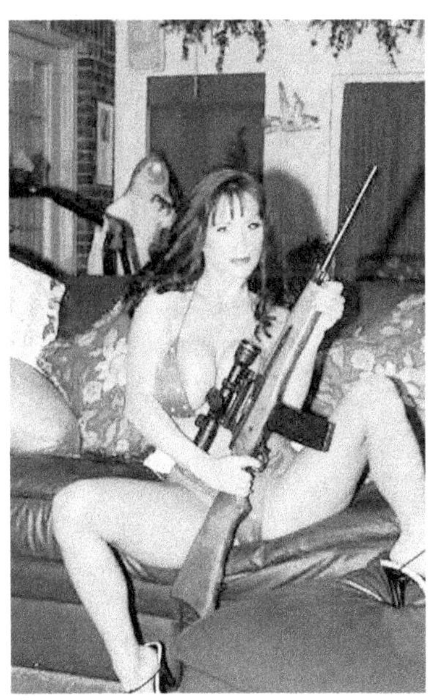

Brittany Love with author's mini-14 at the home of the owner of the Candy Store in Mobile, Alabama where the author was shooting a Pure Talent Feature Showcase.

The model sporting the Mini-14 in this

article is Brittany Love, one of the hottest feature entertainers on the circuit. As good as the mini-14 is, one doesn't just hand Brittany an ordinary Mini-14 and start taking pictures. My mini-14 is that exceptional nearly one of a kind rifle that begs to be paired off with the incomparable Brittany Love.

The mini-14 proved to be so popular with farmers and ranchers that Ruger soon offered its easily scoped ranch model. Shooting flat out to several hundred yards with its light recoiling and hard-hitting 223 round, Mini-14's proved to be the ideal tool for perforating ground hogs, ground squirrels, coyotes and other countryside pests. Although Ruger was selling full auto versions of its mini-14 to swat teams and military organizations worldwide, its semi automatic versions he was selling to U.S. civilians were capable of emptying a thirty-shot clip in less than 10 seconds–firepower not quite up to military specs, but awesome enough for just about anything. Not only was it everyman's good for practically everything pest terminator, it was also perfect for protecting one's loved ones and property against the bad guys because of its high rate of firepower, its small size and its easy on the shoulder recoil. Ruger introduced folding stock variants soon after the introduction of its ranch model. A huge market for Mini 14 accessories that included special stocks, clips, and carrying cases was developed for Ruger's wildly successful do everything rifle. But in spite of the mini-14's success on the world marketplace it never quite caught on as well as it might have supplying military forces for countries across the globe. In contrast to the ubiquitous M-16, one of the reasons was its relative lack of accuracy.

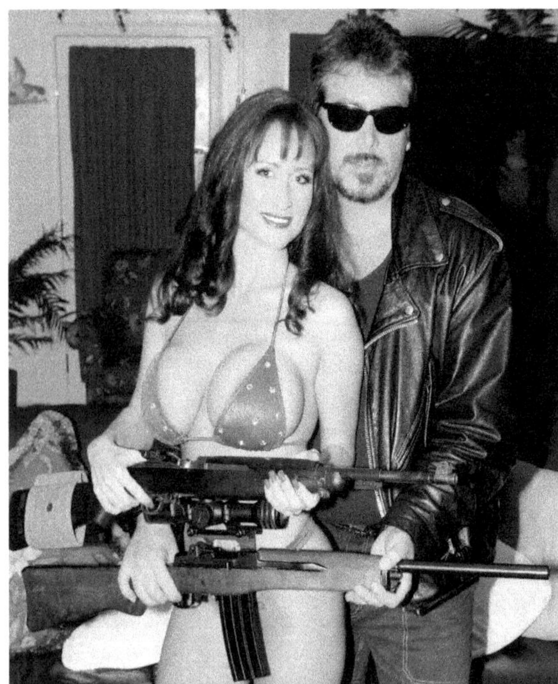

**Brittany Love with author's friend, Mike Skymaster (Tornado) and mini 14.**

Its light weight is both one of the mini-14's outstanding virtues and greatest failings. Its thin barrel's lack of rigidity gives it mediocre accuracy, and it gets worse after several rounds have been fired. The high speed .223 round causes the barrel to overheat which prevents tightly placed groups. Four inch groups from a cold barrel are typical at 100 yards. Considering that a handgun that groups 1 inch at 25 yards is a tack driver, whether this is such a bad thing or not depends upon the requirements of the shooter. Nor does the Ruger's standard peep sights and rough out of the box trigger pull contribute anything close to match accuracy.

Several years ago I wanted a rifle that delivers a high volume of firepower from a round that can stop a man. I had an M-1, an M-14, and an M-16 on my wish list. Each rifle not only could fulfill these two conditions but also represented a significant place in our Nation's military History. I nearly bought the M-16. But being the purist that I am, I also wanted a rifle capable of extreme accuracy. Again, the M-16 qualified. But I already had a mini-14. While doing my weapons research on the Internet I became acquainted with, Accuracy Rifle Systems, a firm out of Odessa, Texas that specializes in accurizing min-14's. From everything I had read, I had learned that the mini-14 was more reliable than the M-16. O reasoned that I could have the best of both worlds if I had a custom rifle made to my specifications.

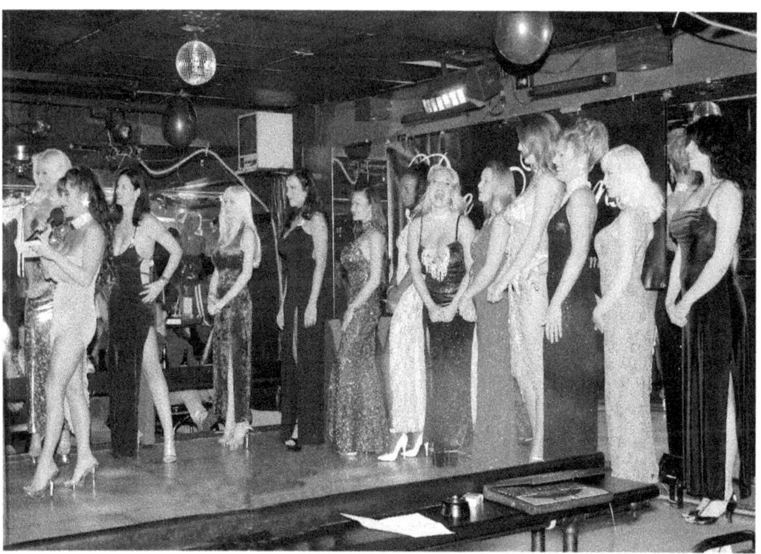

**Brittany Love (lower left corner with the Microphone) as M.C. at the Candy Store Pure Talent Feature Showcase in Mobile, Alabama**

Accuracy Rifle Systems had equipped special units of the Navy Seals during Desert Storm and still do. Units of the IDF–Israeli Defense Forces had bought their weapons from the Texas firm. I asked Tim Lewis, the company's owner, why such elite units would buy his customized rifles when they had the M-16 available. "In Desert Storm," Tim replied, "many of our troops wrapped their M-16's in panty hose to keep the sand out of them. You never see pictures of our soldiers landing on Omaha Beach during World War II with anything protecting their M-1's from the sand and dust, do you? The mini-14's action is very similar to the M-1's."

He had a point. Accuracy Rifle System's web site suggested that the German-made Lothar Walther bull barrels it fitted to mini 14's would guarantee sub 1 inch groups at 100 yards out of a mini-14 and that one half inch groups were not uncommon given the right load.

My mind flashed to all kinds of improbable fantasies. "I'm a sniper trying to shoot the head off of a chipmunk at 300 yards. Or surrounded by thirty drug addled aliens armed with machetes wanting to take my Mazda Miata sports car away from me."

“Let's see, a very reliable mini-14, stoked with a thirty round clip, capable of firing into half an inch at 100 yards as fast as I can pull the rifle's trigger should be just what I need. And hardly anyone else is going to have anything quite like it. It's just the thing that will impress all the babes down at the beach."

Back to reality, and I'm on the phone again with Tim Lewis. "What rate of twist do you want your barrel to have?" he asked. "Do you want it to stabilize a 62-grain bullet? If you shoot those, I want to suggest a one in 9 inch twist to the barrel's rifling."

"I'm only going to shoot 55 grain bullets," I replied. So I ordered a 20 inch German barrel with a 12-inch twist.

"I need a scope. I'm thinking of a Leopold 1 by 5 X variable. Something like that. What do you think?"

"Good scope. One of the scopes I use for hunting coyotes at night is the ATN. It's manufactured in Russia and assembled here in the U.S.," Tim suggested. “It's got a red-illuminated reticle which makes it deadly on coyotes at night."

"Well, I'll never shoot a coyote," I told Tim. "When I farmed, those coyotes were the only things interested in watching me at night when I was driving my tractor. But I like the idea behind the scope. And I want a nice trigger job."

I sent my mini 14 in. Two weeks later I got it back. It now looked stubby with its new thick German bull barrel and with its scope and mount it now weighed about as much as an M-1.

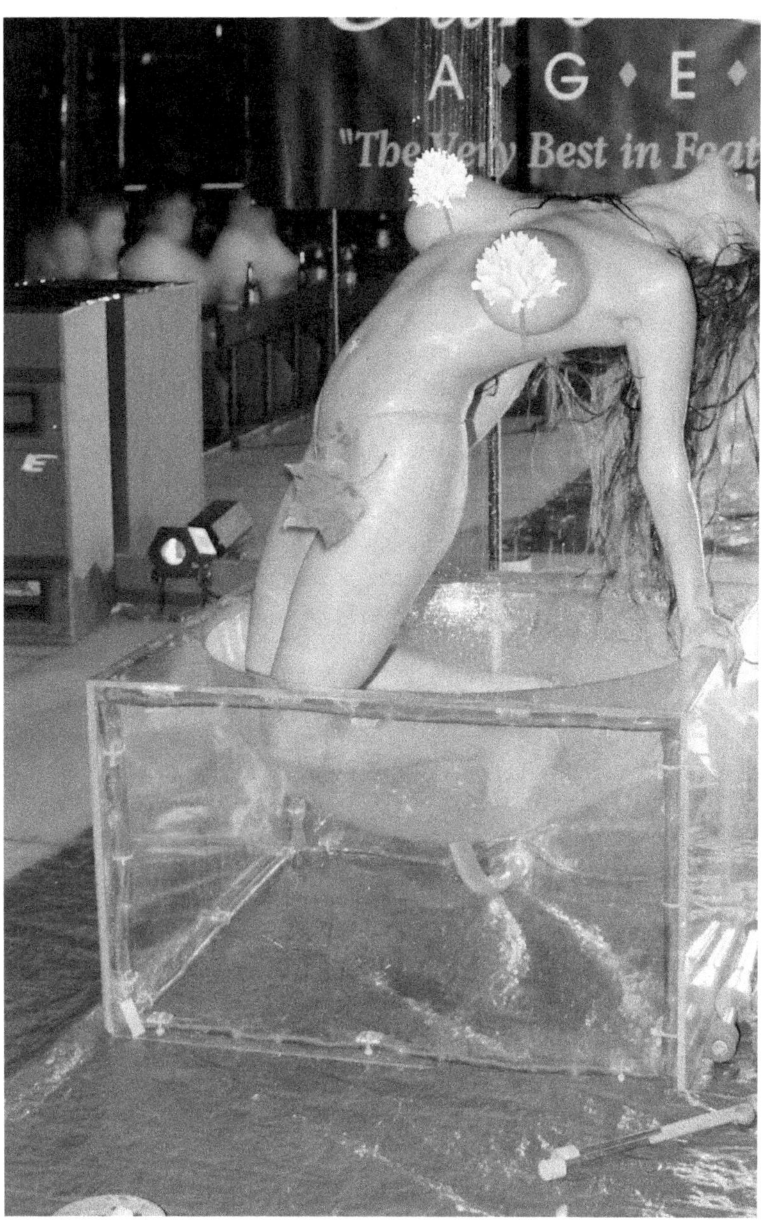


Brittany doing one of her shows at the Candy Store

The scope is the ATN 5 X 33 L professional. Note that this is called "professional," not "hunter," "tracker" or "big game." It has a built in range finder, with a series of parallel hash marks one uses on a six-foot target. Although one can use a deer in the standing position to estimate range, the .223 is not considered a deer cartridge. It was designed to be a man killer. One simply finds two hash marks while looking through the scope at a six foot man, then reads off the range in 100 yard to 500 yard increments. The shooter then turns a dial on the scope to the range indicated which moves the scope's reticle to account for bullet drop. Say a man is standing 500 yards away. The 500 yard indicators will bracket him within the two horizontal hash marks from head to toe. Turning the dial to 500 yards allows the marksman to center the scope's cross hairs on any part of his adversary, say his nose. If the shooter does his job, the bullet will hit exactly where he's aiming at.

The scope's reticle, or cross hairs are permanently etched into the glass lense. ANT claims this setup is 7000 times stronger than traditional scope reticles which utilize fine wires mounted in the tube. When firing at night, the sniper can turn a rheostat to 10 different positions governing the red light's intensity. Note how I changed my wording from shooter to sniper because that's exactly who this setup is intended for. The scope's built in rangefinder is governed for a 55 grain .223 bullet employing a cam that adjusts the reticle for the range one's firing from.

It's a custom rig incorporating the best technology from the finest American and Russian minds in the shooting business starting with Bill Ruger who built the mini-14 for the average farmer or rancher wanting a handy rifle that combines good power with a high rate of fire. The scope's from Russia, the land that gave the world the T-34 tank, the AK-47, Rachmaninoff, Tolstoy, and Dostoevski. Since we don't give the Russians enough credit, largely because we once viewed them as the people who'd blow us off the map, I will. The Russians design some damn good stuff and this scope's just the thing to take out people hunting when the spirit moves you, or hunting mice at night. But it takes a platform capable of superior accuracy to put all this together. The guru who makes all the right parts work together so well is Tim Lewis of Accuracy Rifle Systems. Which pairs off so well with Brittany Love, who blends incredible photogenic appeal, scintillating dancing ability, and a penetrating intellect into one beautiful package.

# SKS—a lot of bang for the buck from the former evil empire

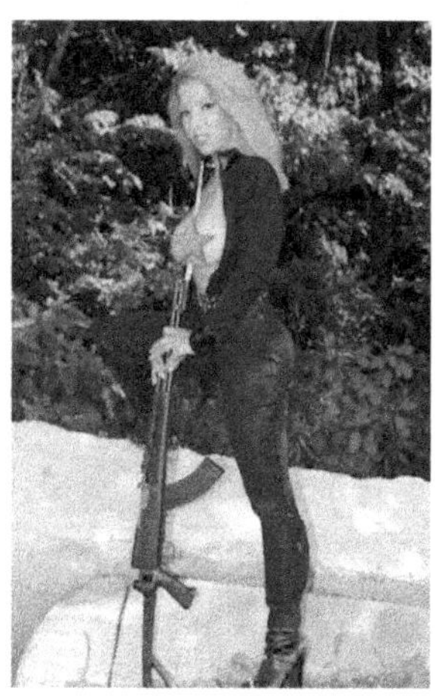

A few years ago one could buy an SKS rifle and several hundred rounds of ammunition for a hundred bucks. This was just a taste of what was to come from the former Evil Empire–cheap utilitarian weapons that would include rifles, pistols, shotguns, scopes, and night vision sighting devices from Russia, our former Cold War antagonist. Aside from the fact that today a man can buy 1000 rounds of 7:62-39 mm ammo, which is very inexpensive stuff to fire from 30-30 power level SKS's and AK-47's, just what is the historical role played by the SKS and how does it compare to other military rifles of the same time period to shoot?

During the Second World War, most Soviet troops were armed with short ranged submachine guns and bolt action 1891 model Moisin Nagants along with smaller quantities of Tolkarev semi automatic rifles firing the full powered 7:62-51 mm round originally intended for the Moisin Nagant. The Tolkarev, however, proved far inferior to the American M-1 on the battlefield, which pretty much left the Russians with the choice of very short range firepower or the long range capable but slow firing bolt action.

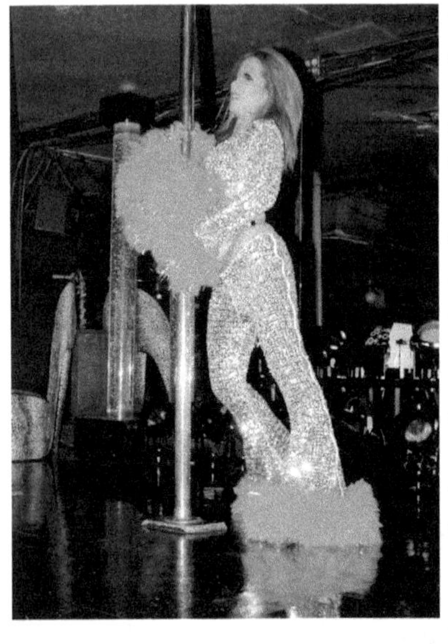

The Soviet answer to the M-1 Garand was Soviet Weapons Designer Sergei Simonov's SKS which went into full production in 1949. It was similar to the M-1 since it has a 10 shot internal magazine that can be recharged with stripper clips whereas the M-1 uses 8 round clips that load into the top of the rifle's action. But whereas the M-1 uses full power 30-06 ammunition that can easily drop a man at ranges of up to a thousand yards, the SKS fully embraced the new concept of the medium range assault rifle cartridge first introduced by the Germans in the waning months of WWII. This cartridge would later be used in the AK-47 that would enter production in Soviet factories a scant two years after production started of the SKS.

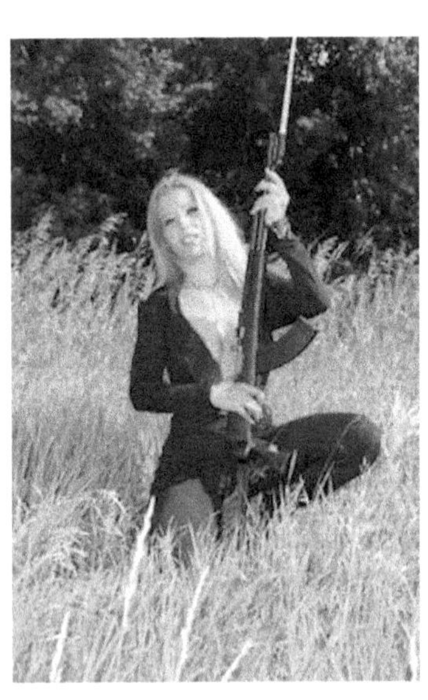

Had American troops ever gone to war against the Soviets in Europe during the early 1950's, we would have pitted our M-1's against Soviet SKS's. By the mid 1950's with the AK-47 having replaced the SKS as Russia's battle rifle, Russia had its arms engineers help the Chinese set up arms production for the SKS in China. Less than ten years later, American soldiers would be fighting a new enemy in Vietnam, who would be armed with both the SKS and the AK-47. Meanwhile other Communist nations started producing their own versions of first the SKS, then the AK-47.

In general, Americans who have purchased SKS rifles like them. Accuracy is reportedly anywhere from marginal to good, although hardly anyone will argue that the SKS wins any long range accuracy awards. Depending on the country of origin, construction and the quality of its metal parts and stock runs from indifferent to excellent with most Russian specimens being the most highly touted. Yugoslavian versions are also well regarded for their quality, but are significantly heavier than SKS's from other former Communist block nations. Since I would be shooting pictures of Lollitops, a well regarded and very popular feature entertainer you can book through Universal Talent, only one of the best specimens would do-- a well put together Chinese SKS with a synthetic stock that was loaned to me by my favorite arms supplier, Vic Meyer.

Ironically although I still have it (until Saturday when I return it to its owner) I would never shoot it. Leaving it at home I went to the gun range with my Hungarian AK-47 and a new .357 magnum I wanted try out. Unbelievably one of the guys shooting downrange from me just happened to be firing two SKS's. Before I even told him I was doing a gun article on the SKS he offered to let me shoot both of them.

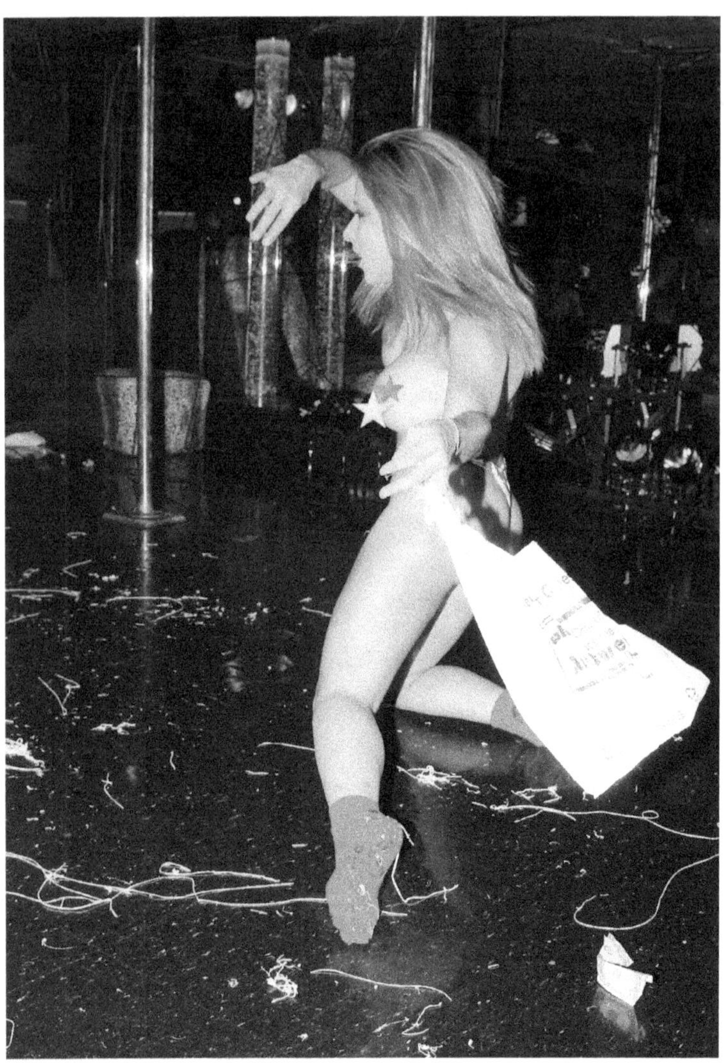

Lolly Tops competing at the M.S. Texas pageant. The feature entertainers would compete by doing their shows for three straight nights. Montana Steele would win this time

Lollytops competing for M.S. Texas at Club Maximus, Wichita Falls, TX

The first, his favorite of the two, was a shortened paratrooper version of the full size rifle. Pulling the rifle's trigger reminded me of trying to open a can with a Kabar knife. The full size rifle he handed me next was much easier on the trigger, something akin to lifting a barbell with one finger. My impression from firing the rifle was that it had good power with minimal recoil. The gun's owner assured me that neither weapon had ever jammed and that he liked shooting both of them very much. I later found out that the paratrooper model had never been manufactured to be the battle rifle for any nation but had been produced only for the export market.

I then turned to my AK-47, which looks much cooler than any Uzi with its black Dragunov style synthetic stock, jet black finish, and flash suppressor. At twenty-five yards I proceeded to put 25 rounds all into the black, shredding the center of the target. For a still relatively inexpensive rifle, its trigger was simply magnificent in comparison to the two SKS rifles.

Disappointed with my shooting experiences with the SKS, I returned home, and went over the weapon I had borrowed from my friend. Its fit and finish were clearly superior to the two I had just fired. I tried its trigger and found it to be infinitely superior. An interesting feature of the SKS is a clever integral bayonet that folds under the rifles for end out of the way, which can be instantly pulled into position for proper impalement of one's enemies.

The SKS never was designed to have nearly the range of either the M-1 or the M-14–M-1 A. However, like the AK-47, it was designed to fire a new generation of medium powered ammunition, deadly out to several hundred yards but not much more. However, a soldier could carry a lot more of it. Although later models of SKS's could use much larger capacity magazines such as the AK-47's, such magazines are reportedly not nearly as reliable and are best left in their original configuration. A fair assessment of the SKS is that it was an evolutionary weapon whose capabilities were roughly equal to but still inferior to the M-1 that would soon give way to one of the finest weapons of the twentieth century–the AK-47.

# Double Barreled Pleasure and Pain

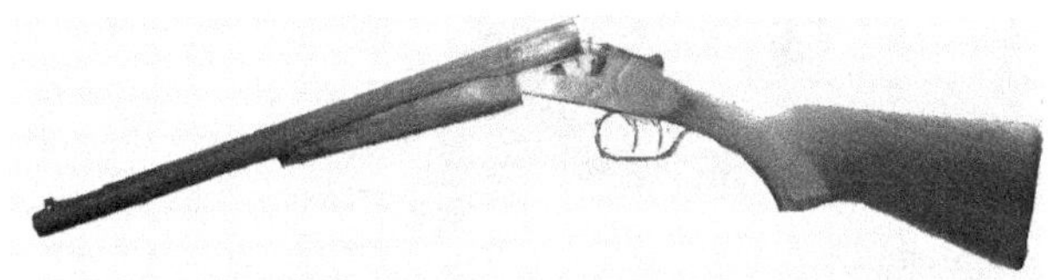

The pain was still there high in my cheek the morning after shooting Baikal's double barreled Bounty Hunter. This had been no trap shooter's 12 gauge meant for shooting strings of twenty clay birds, so I had paid the gun's price of very high recoil for extreme potency in a small package. After paying my bill at the gun range I had asked the guys working behind the counter–"If you were in Africa and couldn't return to the U.S. for a week what gun would you want if you suddenly realized there was a man-eating lion loose and your odds of surviving the week weren't good?"

One of the men replied: "A scatter gun but I might take a high-powered rifle if I could get a long range shot off at him which would take him out as a threat."

"But if the lion didn't show himself except at night, then the only clear choice would be the shotgun," I replied, to which everyone agreed.

Although strictly a short range weapon, the shotgun was often favored over more modern rifled arms by the Confederate Cavalry during the Civil War, was used as a trench broom during World War I, and was still being used for short range jungle fighting in Vietnam. It was preferred by Old West gunmen over the six shooter when things really got tough, and it is the most commonly used backup weapon to a cop's handgun. The gun carried by Pleasure in the pictures on these pages is the Russian made Baikal Bounty Hunter, a side by side double barrel with improved cylinder chokes targeted for Cowboy Action competitions in which the contestants wear 19th century Western garb and shoot revolvers, shotguns and rifles that are authentic to the Old West. Paine, Pleasure's mother, the other half of the blonde feature entertainer duo, is carrying a Winchester 94 trapper in .45 long Colt, a rifle roughly equivalent to the Winchester 1873s and 1892s chambered for the .44-40.

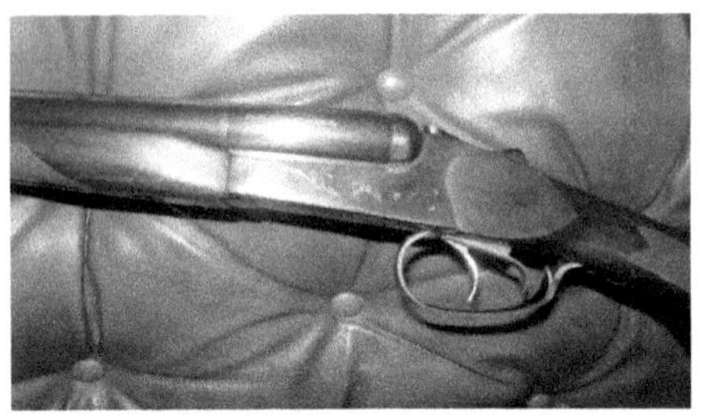

One of the reasons why the Baikal 12 gauge double barreled Bounty Hunter recoils so ferociously is because it weighs just 6.3 pounds and its lack of a recoil pad. It is an extremely compact very attractive shotgun with 20 inch twin barrels set in a svelte yet striking dark walnut stock. When shooting it at the range I fired only the heavy two 3/4th inch magnum double O buckshot or rifled slugs since I would be evaluating it as a self defense weapon against either humans or the largest and most dangerous animals that walk this earth rather than as a small game getter. To summarize its short range killing power, "Anything that hurts me this much to shoot it, has got to be able to stop anything that lives with one shot."

I started off with rifled slugs, doubting my ability to hit anything with it. Unlike slug guns used for hunting deer, which employ a wide range of sights, my Baikal only had a simple bead on the end of its twin barrels for sighting. I had always thought of short barreled side by sides as being useful only for spraying shot at one's enemies at close range but then I reminded myself about the Southern cavalrymen using shotguns in the Civil War and how infantrymen had used smoothbore muskets with no more than a small post on the end of their barrels for sights for well over a century.

Shooting rifled slugs at 25 yards, eight shots all landed within 14 inches of each other. However, five shots were within 3 inches of each other in the exact center of the chest of a man-sized silhouette target. The three outermost shots struck the silhouette in the shoulder, arm, and side. Keep in mind, however, that rifled slugs weigh something like 400 grains, are nearly twice as heavy as typical .44 magnum bullets, and that they are traveling substantially faster, while poking entrance holes that are nearly twice the size.

Although many shotguns employ sights and shoot much more accurately than side by sides such as the Baikal, one has to keep in mind what one is using such weapons for. Any of the hits registered with the slugs at 25 yards would have taken

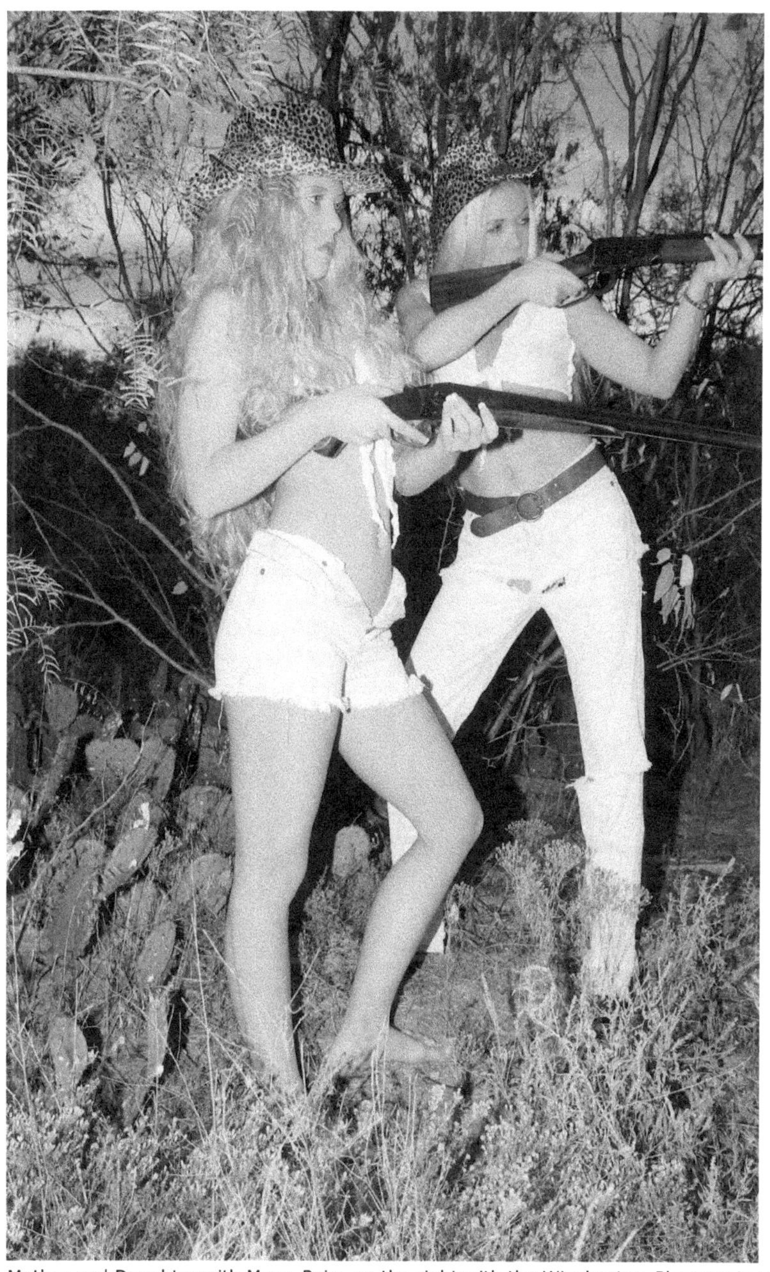

Mother and Daughter with Mom, Pain, on the right with the Winchester, Pleasure is on the left with the shotgun.

most men out of combat with five of them causing instant death. But for self defense  against either man or beast, 25 with 12 yards or less being a much more likely scenario. At such ranges even my most poorly aimed shots would have struck in the chest area.

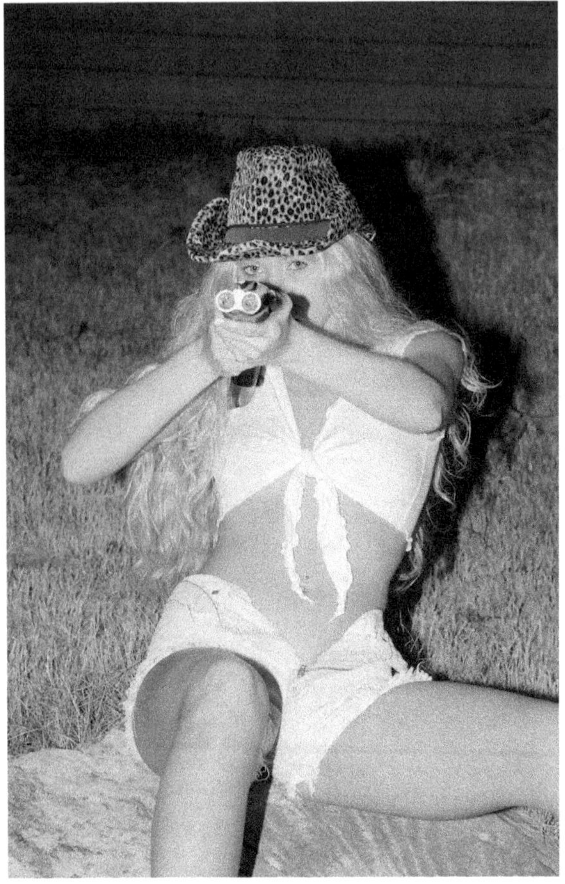

Then I tried the double O buck shot. There are 12 pellets in front of four drams of powder in the loads I used. I shot my first silhouette target at 25 yards aiming my first barrel at its head. With OO buck each pellet is about the size of a 32-caliber pistol bullet. One pellet went into each shoulder. Three more went into various portions of its chest with the rest of the pellets landing on either side of the silhouette's head. I emptied the second barrel into the target's lower chest. One pellet struck where the heart would have been with three more hits in the lungs or less vital areas of the chest. Four pellets stuck various area's of the figure's periphery. The average distance between each pellet for both barrels was three inches.

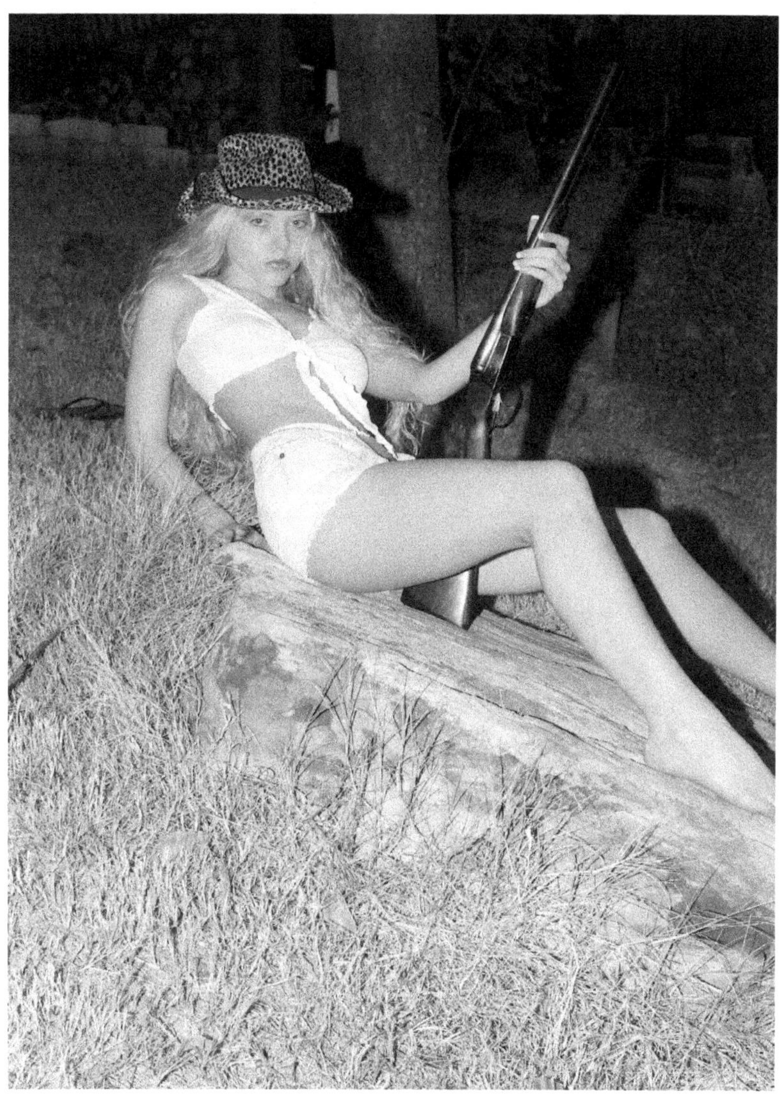

I next shot at fifty feet. Pellets for both barrels wound up an average of one ½ to 2 inches of each other. Three pellets from one barrel either struck the heart or grazed it. Moving closer still, at thirty feet all twelve pellets grouped in a five-inch circle with nine of the twelve striking the upper portion of the silhouette's head.

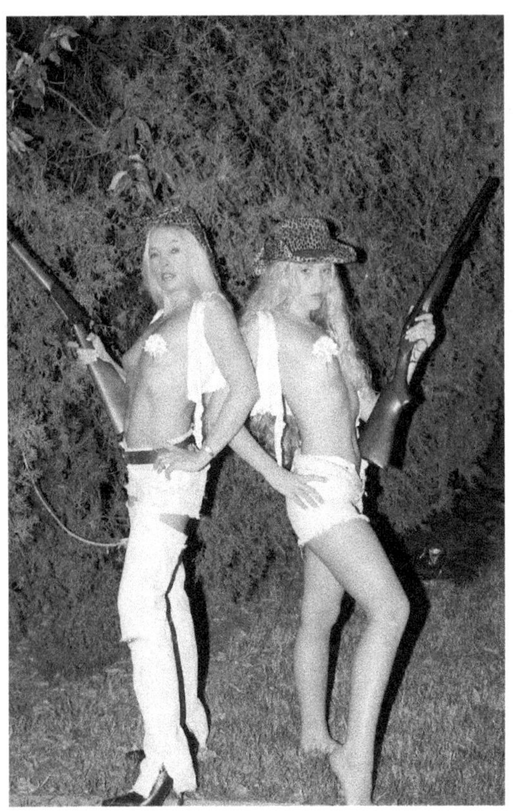

The Baikal Bounty Hunter like its Old West side by side forebears, is a very powerful piece of short range ordinance. It is so well balanced, lightweight and handy that it nearly punishes the shooter behind it as much as whatever's in front of its twin barrels. One gets only two shots at a time with it, but these can be delivered one after the other without conscious thought as soon as one has recovered from its considerable recoil. Within this two shot limitation probably nothing probably equals its killing power at close range or gives one a better chance out of emerging from a mix-up with monsters of either the two or four legged kind. I got my Baikal for around two hundred and forty bucks, and wind up praising the Russians every time I look at it for delivering so much pleasure and pain out of what could very well be the deal of the century.

Many thanks to Pleasure and Pain who you can visit at
http://www.alphapro.com/fame/painepleasure.htm

# The 30 caliber Browning Machine Gun

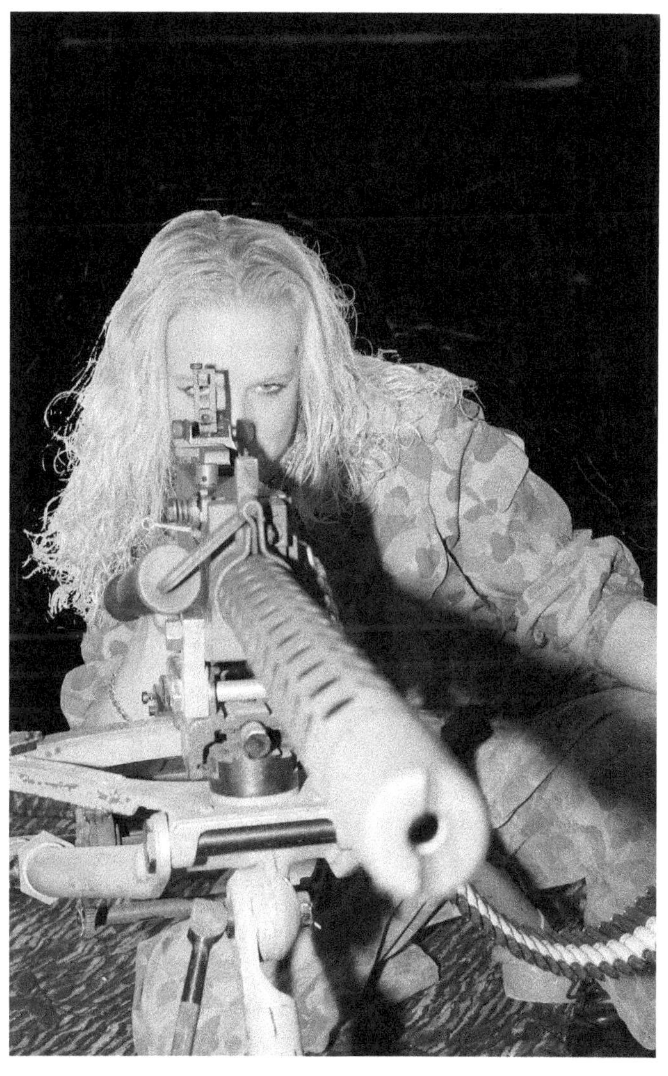

Man's search for the ultimate hose down weapon--that is, the perfect machine gun for spraying his enemies into dough boy oblivion, is challenging because firepower and portability oftentimes needed to be encompassed in the same weapon. We are not talking about submachine guns typically firing pistol cartridges, usually 9 mm or 45 auto, good only for short-range work and which lack penetration and accuracy. It's the tripod or bi-pod mounted weapon of the "Machine gun nest" firing high power rifle ammunition which merits discussion here, and the 1919 Browning 30 caliber machine gun, in particular, which World War II, Korean, and Vietnam War Soldiers relied upon to kill their enemies.

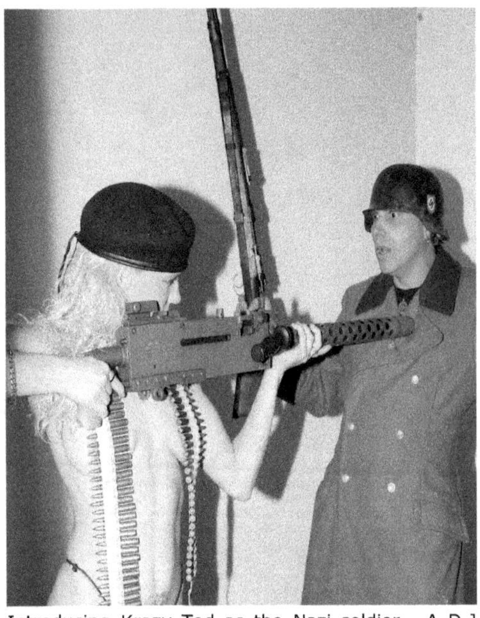

Introducing Krazy Ted as the Nazi soldier. A D.J friend of Heather's at Club Sapphires in Iowa, Krazy Ted would later write a column for the author's Looking Glass Magazine .

The heavy machine gun practically immobilized the battlefield in World War 1 while killing millions of soldiers, which made infantry attacks an invitation to suicide. During the waning months of the Great War, a firearms genius, named John Browning, came to the rescue with a new weapon both he and the top American military brass hoped would give attacking infantrymen a fighting chance. The Browning Automatic Rifle, or BAR, fired from a twenty round magazine in either semi auto or full automatic mode at up to 500 rounds a minute, vastly bolstering the firepower of attacking infantrymen most of whom were armed with bolt action repeating rifles. Originally weighing in at 16 pounds, the BAR could easily be carried and fired by one man from the shoulder. Each attacking squad composed of roughly eight U.S. infantrymen would have one BAR man. The rest would have bolt-action rifles. As the squad rapidly advanced on enemy trenches, the BAR man would unleash torrents of heavy hitting 30-06 ammo at the enemy position that would force the enemy's heads down while reducing his effectiveness to fire accurately at the attacking Americans.

The brilliantly conceived BAR performed its assigned task admirably. However, the war ended just a few months after the BARs made their first battlefield appearance. Twenty years later the role of the BAR was to change to a do everything light machine gun during World War II. "Improved versions" of the BAR sported an attached bi-pod and other weight increasing accouterments which increased its weight from its original 16 pounds to more than twenty.

World War I was the first war in which troops experienced both the onslaught of tanks and the grim reaper's death dealing machine gun. While John Browning was still busy perfecting his BAR, a need was perceived for arming tanks with reasonably compact light weight machine guns. The machine guns of the day were heavy contraptions using water cooling jackets to keep their barrels from turning into melted junk. They were ideal in the static trench warfare of the time when major gains could be measured in a few feet at the cost of thousands of lives since the very effective cooling systems could keep machine guns firing continuously without having their barrels overheat. But they were too ungainly to be mounted in a tank.

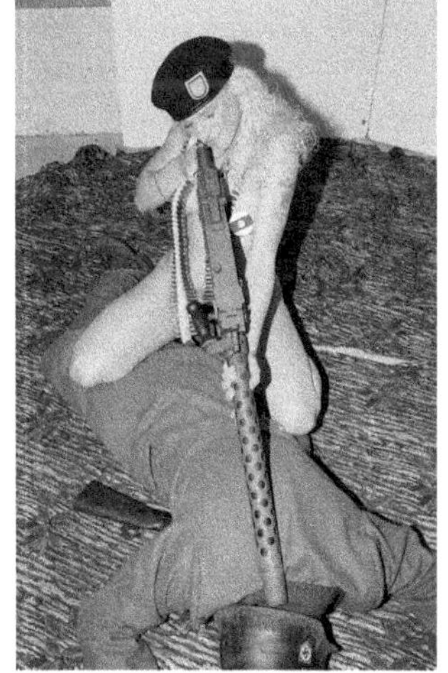

Browning's new machine gun arrived off the drawing boards a little too late to play a role in World War I, which ended in 1918. Designated as the model 1919 it would later play a considerable role in both War II and Korea.

The United States entered WWII in 1941 armed with the Springfield 1903 as its primary infantryman's rifle although the semi automatic M-1 would rapidly replace most of them. But unlike WWI, World War II would prove primarily to be a war of maneuver. Because American troops usually wound up on the attack, the 30 caliber heavy machine gun weighing in at

41 pounds with its 52-pound tripod was simply too heavy and difficult to set up quickly for troops always on the move.

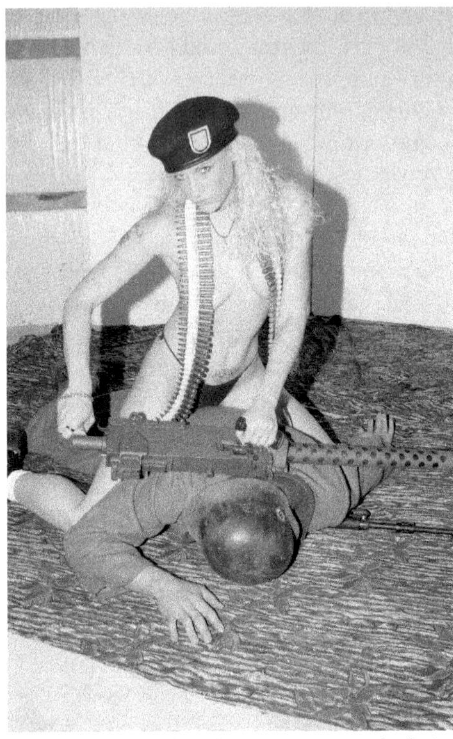

Krazy Ted would also play a prominent role during the first S.P.E.W. (Sexy Professional Exotic Wrestling) match that pitted Dirty Heather, the Iowa female champion against Killer Kloey Missouri's top wrestler Ted would be sliced in the ring with a razor that according to rumor had been wielded by Big Daddy himself, the club owner.

American troops were probably the best-armed troops during the conflict. The M-1 firing full power 30-06 ammunition that could penetrate most trees and which was accurate up to 1,000 yards while firing from its eight round clip as fast as a man could pull the trigger was by bar the best all around battle implement of the conflict since it could do just about everything well. Adding a substantial increment in fire power was the Bar Man, but as good as the Browning automatic rifle was, it did have two major faults.

First--you could only get twenty rounds off before having to change magazines. Second, after changing enough magazines the fast firing BAR's barrel would overheat since the BAR did not have a fast replacement barrel feature. These two problems kept the Bar from being the weapon it could have become for keeping up a sustained rate of fire.

The 1919 was soon to fulfill the role of providing the sustained firepower the BAR could not deliver. The 1919 light machine gun employed a ventilated shroud around its barrel to facilitate air cooling. It weighed 31 pounds while its tripod added a scant 15 pounds, for a total weight of 46 pounds versus the water-cooled machine gun's 93. No--you could not fire the thing all day such as you could with the water cooled heavy machine gun. But by limiting yourself to bursts at an average sustained rate of sixty rounds a minute, you could keep your enemy under cover for half an hour or even more without overheating the weapon's barrel.

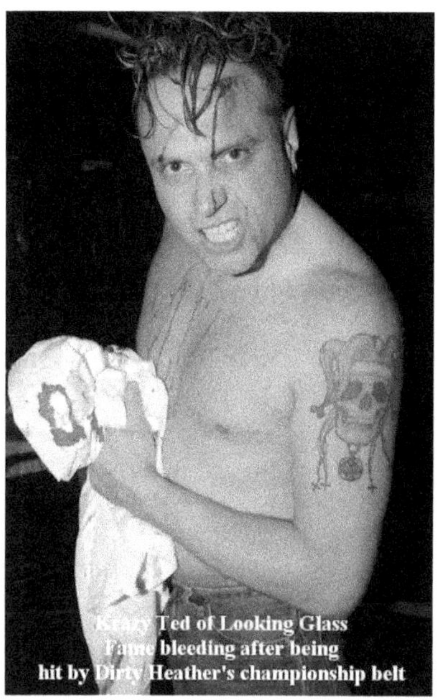

Krazy Ted of Looking Glass Fame bleeding after being hit by Dirty Heather's championship belt

The weapon fired from 250 round belts which could be linked together when needed.

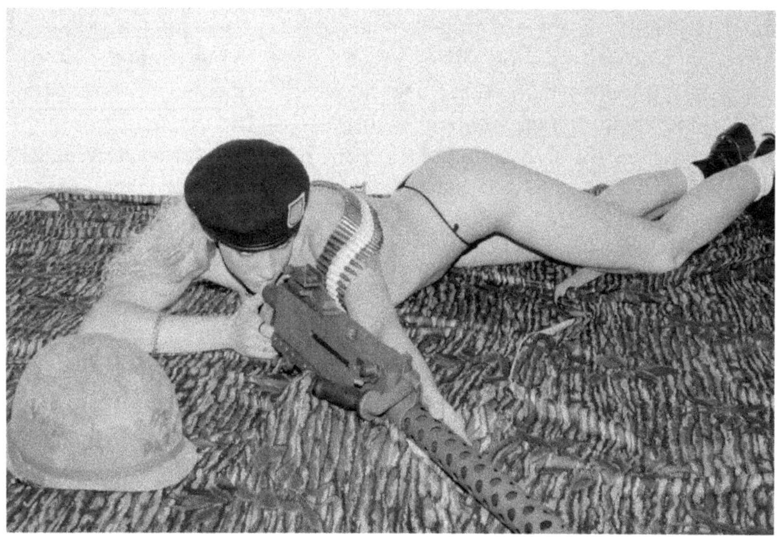

The 30 caliber 1919 Browning proved to be a versatile piece of equipment that was mounted in tanks, armored cars, jeeps, and other vehicles to

provide the infantryman a boost in firepower that greatly exceeded the BAR's.

But as good as it was, there was one infantryman's weapon that was even better.

Unfortunately it belonged to the other side. The MG-42 machine gun weighed less than 25 pounds, bi pod included, which made it almost as light as the BAR. Made out of pressed and stamped parts and plastics, it could be easily and cheaply produced. The thing would work reliably in any climate, was accurate, and best of all, it fired normally at 1200 rounds a minute, and oftentimes could hit rates up to 1500 rounds a minute.

Imagine lying behind your machine gun. The enemy patrol approaches. Ten men deliberately scattering themselves to avoid being mowed down in tight formation approach. You rip off a burst but your machine gun fires 600 rounds per minute or 10 rounds a second. You hit several of the enemy, having gotten off fifteen rounds in the first 1.5 seconds. By this time the rest of the enemy has hit the deck and is firing back at you. That's if you are firing the 1919 Browning.

Try it again, this time with the MG-42. Firing at 1200 rpm you hear a sound like ripping canvas, getting thirty rounds off in the first second and a half. Which means you are going to kill twice as many of the enemy before they've hit the ground. If you are good that is.

But just imagine keeping enough ammunition on hand for that MG-42. Moreover, at that terrific rate of fire, you are going to overheat your barrel with just 250 rounds. If you don't have access to a good supply of ammo, you could get into trouble fast. You might wish you had that 1919 Browning which conserves ammo a lot better while still being able to deliver a good rate of fire at reasonable sustainable levels. It all depends on what you are doing with that machine gun. If you are just providing covering fire, the Browning is probably a lot better.

Unless you are German. Face it, the German bolt action 98 Mauser supplying most German infantrymen isn't in the same league with the American M-1 rifle. Sure, there are a few submachine guns carried by your fellow soldiers, but except for close in combat they are nowhere close to the M-1. The fly in the ointment is German tactical doctrine differed dramatically from American tactics which stressed a balanced unit that employed M-1 rifles, BAR's, 1919 Browning machine guns, Thompson's and M-1 carbines.

The Germans based their tactical doctrine on the machine gun. And later in the war there was one dominant machine gun, the MG-42, which handled the roles of light, medium and heavy machine gun, with minor accessories added to the weapon depending on what role it was playing at the time such as optical sights, bi-pod or tripod, etc. Per every 1,000 men the Germans had a lot more MG-42's than we had Browning 1919's. The Germans employed their best and steadiest soldier to be the MG-42's gunner. He was extremely well trained in its use, being much more of a specialist than our troops who had to be reasonably skilled with a variety of weapons. German tactics stressed a unit getting its MG-42 firing as fast as possible with the other soldiers keeping it in ammunition while protecting it with their small arms. Meanwhile the gunner was taught how to carefully ration his ammunition by controlling his bursts.

You could easily switch barrels on an MG-42. German infantry often had as many as four to five barrels for each machine gun and a skilled gunner could swap a cold barrel for the red-hot barrel he had been using within six seconds. The skill of the German gunners and the quick-change barrel feature made sustained fire with the MG-42 possible.

After the Korean War, the U.S. settled on a new machine gun, the M-60. Although it borrowed heavily from the MG-42, like the MG-42 it had a rapid interchangeable barrel feature and weighed less than twenty-five pounds, there are some notable differences. A major departure is its relatively slow rate of fire, 600 rounds a minute, similar to that of the 1919 Browning. Meanwhile the Germans are still using the MG-42, practically unaltered, except it's now chambered in 7.62 Nato. Although we are still using the Browning 50 caliber machine gun originally designed at the end of WWI, the U.S., like the Germans in WWII have for the most part settled on one machine gun for its infantry, the M-60, to handle a variety of combat assignments.

Although it lacked the MG-42's light weight and terrific rate of fire, the 1919 Browning machine gun was a reliable and formidable agent of death in its own right. But had I been transported back into time to World War II or the Korean War, I would have wanted Heather to be serving with me on its crew. Sure, the MG-42 might have been a little better, but I don't think there would have been that much difference in the two machine guns' ability to perform their assigned combat roles to make a decisive difference.

# Tec 9 shoot out at Peter's Corral

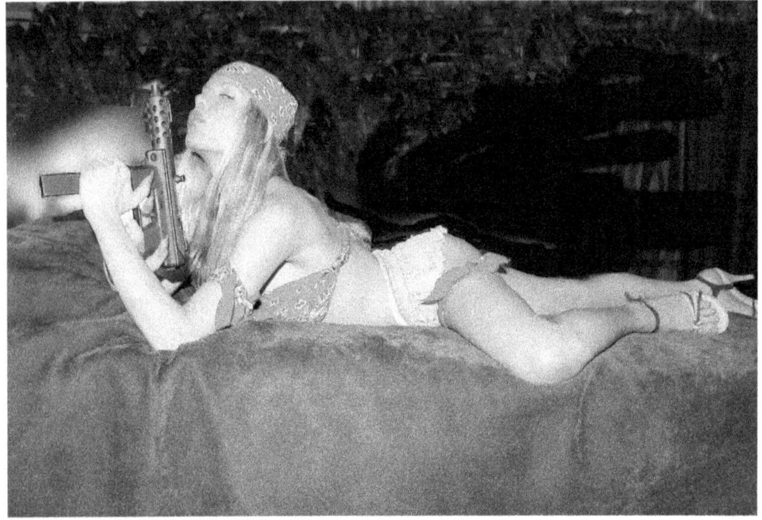

It's feature entertainer Leah Layne with Vic Meyer's Tec 9 the author borrowed for an upcoming Xtreme Weapons article. A former winner of the Miss Nude Illinois Pageant at Big Al's , Leah would do several articles for Jack and *Xtreme* and referee the Dirty Heather vs. Killer Kloey S.P.E.W. wrestling match at Big Daddy's Cabaret.

This story starring feature entertainer and a mythologized Peter the Great is a review of the fully automatic TEC 9 assault pistol--as originally published by the author in *Xtreme Magazine*.

No one knows exactly how Peter the Great came back from the dead to save the United States from disaster. The country's health care system had been ruined because of the lawyers after every insurance company had gotten out of the health insurance business and nearly every established health care provider had been driven out of business because of the astronomical cost of malpractice litigation unleashed upon them by rapacious lawyers. Hardly anyone wanted to start a business any more for fear of being sued for wrongful dismissal of an employee or personal injury on the job. In his long reign as the Russian Tsar in the late 17th and early 18th centuries Peter had transformed Russia from being one of the most backward nations to one of the most preeminent nations in Europe. Peter had been the prototypal benevolent despot, building Russia a modern navy and powerful army, gaining Russia ports on the Baltic and Black Seas, defeating Sweden's Charles XII, stopping the unbeatable Ottoman Turks from conquering Europe, and putting the Greek Orthodox Church in its place by wresting power from the Church and putting it into the hands of the Tsar. Some say Peter came from God, but wherever he came from, whenever his voice commanded, people obeyed.

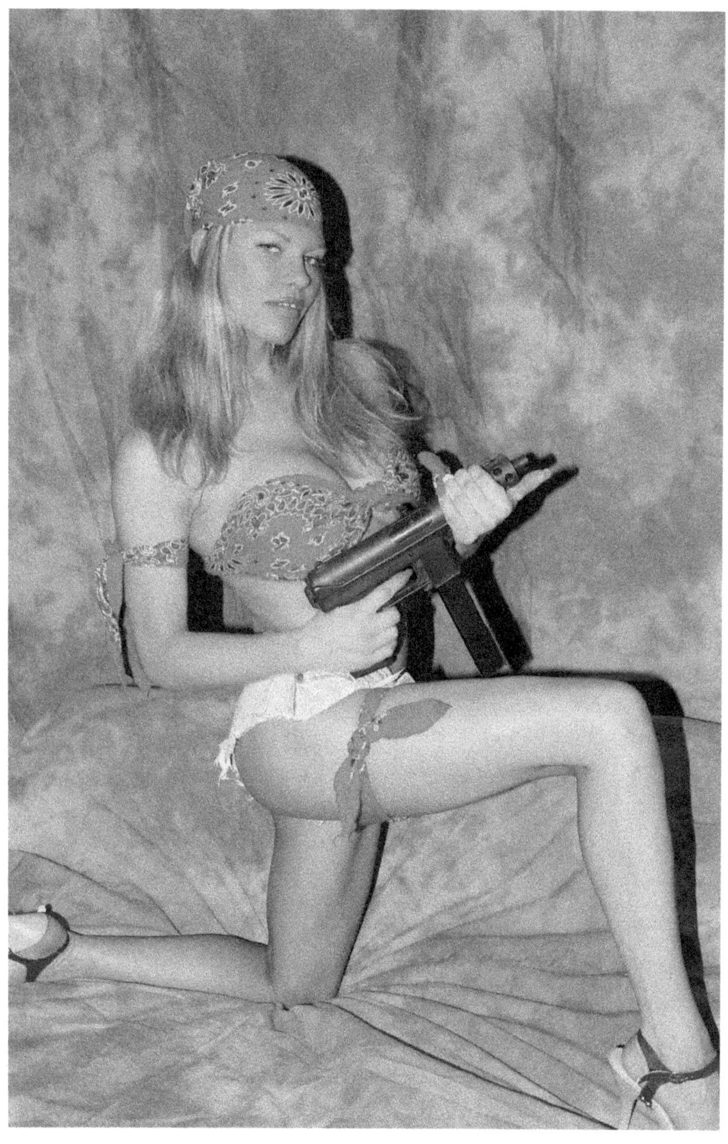

Seated before Peter was a group of lawyers and gun control advocates who had sued gun manufacturers in Civil Court in Camden, New Jersey for punitive and treble damages they claimed had been incurred by the County and citizens of Camden. This was Peter's first case. The defendants were on trial for their lives for wrongfully trying the Tec-9 and other "Bad" guns in the United States District Court for the District of New Jersey.

Peter slumped in his chair as he addressed everyone in the courtroom: "The defendants introduced into this courtroom the following action which sought to deprive all citizens of this county of any firearm they didn't approve of. I read from their legal brief":

## Nature of Action

"This is a civil action for injunctive relief and compensatory, punitive and treble damages for harm caused to the County of Camden and its citizens by the defendants, each of whom individually or collectively, have (a) created a public nuisance by causing certain firearms to be present or to be used in Camden County in a manner which has interfered with the County's, and the Country's citizens', enjoyment of life and property; (b) placed in the possession of County residents, employees, or visitors, firearms which are not suitably fit or safe for their intended purpose because of defective designs and inadequate warnings; (c) breached their contract with the intended and foreseeable users of certain firearms; (d) caused bodily injury and death, and the fear of bodily injury and death to Camden County citizens and guests; and (e) interfered with the economic advantages which would have been available to the County of Camden and its citizens had the County not been forced to expend its resources to address the harms caused by various firearms introduced into the County of Camden."

## The Proceedings

Peter rose to his full seven-foot height from the Bench: "This is my first of many cases. You are on trial because you are a bunch of arrogant, rapacious crooks who have put your own selfish interests above those of the country and have practically ruined this great nation. Specifically I am charging you with calling up on legal charges innocent victims for the sole purpose of lining your own pockets and the coffers of Camden County. Your fate will be determined by this court's decision on the innocence or guilt of the Tec-9, a so-called assault weapon manufactured by Kel-Tec which you put on trial for the sole purpose of disarming American citizens and extorting money from the manufacturer along with other manufacturer's of guns you called evil weapons.

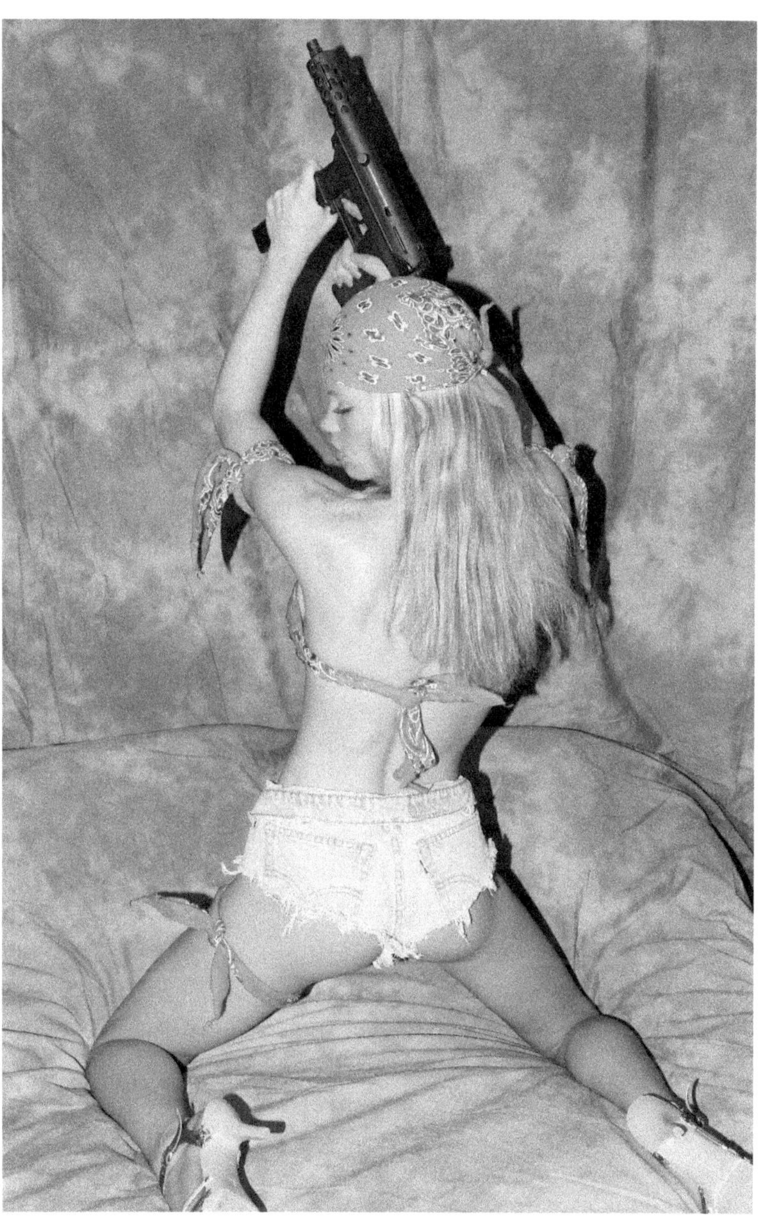

For my first witness I present Leah Layne, who was among other things Miss Nude of Illinois in 1999."

Carlos Bullshit (acting as counsel for his follow defendants): "Your honor, I object on the grounds that Leah Layne is a feature entertainer, dances nude on the stage, and is hardly an expert who can even begin to testify in a case such as this one."

Peter: "Bullshit. Sit down. Leah Layne served four years in the United States Navy before she had to start stripping to make ends meet, got an honorable discharge and on numerous occasions fired different weapons. Her qualifications far exceed yours or those of your fellow lawyers on trial here whose qualifications extend only to advanced techniques in twisting the meaning of words, extortion, chicanery, lying and treachery." Then turning to Leah who had now seated herself comfortably in the witness box. "Tell us a little about the Tec-9."

Leah Layne: "It's a small gun weighing less than 3 pounds. It's chambered for 9 mm, a round that has not gained a very good reputation for stopping power. It normally uses a 32 round clip and has a 5-inch barrel. It can get a lot of rounds out in a hurry as fast as one can pull its trigger but you can also do that with a lot of other weapons."

Peter: "How would you rate the effectiveness of this weapon compared to other types of weapons?"

Leah Layne: "It is relatively small and can be concealed by a person wearing, say, an overcoat, but it is not nearly as concealable as a good 45 automatic or a .357 magnum even with their longer barrel lengths. The 9 mm doesn't stop an adversary nearly as well as these cartridges or many others. The Tec-9 has crude sights and a coarse trigger pull which makes it hard to shoot well. It sold for around $200 which made it very affordable. Its earlier versions were fairly easy to convert to full auto, which made them into small submachine guns. Even so, it was the kind of thing that is only useful for short ranges–say up to 15 yards or so and for spraying a room full of people in a hurry. But you can accomplish the same thing and do it better with a 12-gauge shotgun"

Peter: "Why is that?"

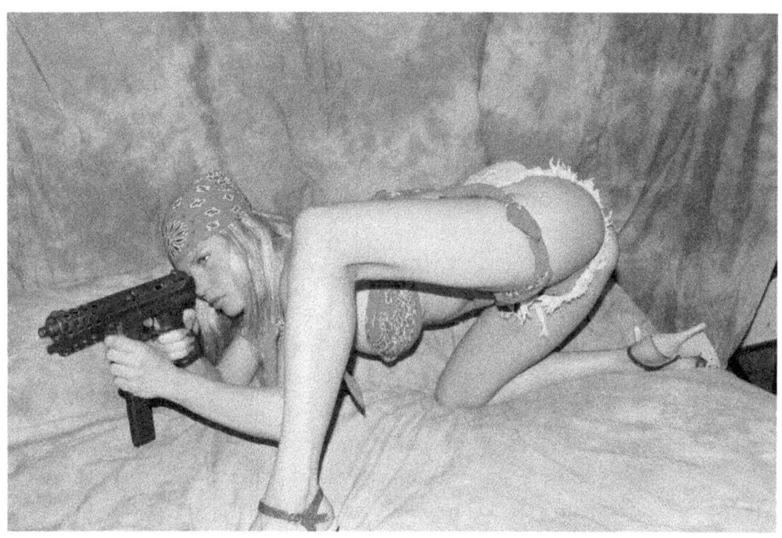

Leah Layne: "Suppose you got an eight shot pump or automatic with an 18 to 20-inch barrel both of which are legal. You can cut a man practically in half with one up to 25 yards and have an excellent chance of hitting him. You can identity up to eight armed men attacking you and put one load of buckshot into each one of them. With a fully automatic Tech Nine, one tends to put his bullets into just a couple of people with the rest of them going into the air. And you can always use a hacksaw to saw a shotgun's barrel down which makes it just as conceivable as the Tec-9. "

Peter approached the witness stand and put a rifle in front of Leah.

Peter: "And what do you think of this weapon compared to the Tec-9?"

Leah Layne: "That is an M-14 which supplied much of our military throughout the first half of the Vietnam War. It fires a .308 high-powered rifle cartridge from a twenty round clip. The M-14 and its civilian variants known as the Springfield M-1 A will fire as fast as you can pull the trigger. It is very powerful, nearly always putting a man down with just one shot and it is extremely accurate. If you are good enough with one, you can hit people from a thousand yards off. In most circumstances, it is far deadlier than a Tec-9."

Approaching the witness stand, Peter replaced the M-14 with a 1911 style 45 automatic, a Tech-9 and a ten shot Browning Hi Power in 9 mm.

Peter: "And how would you compare these weapons, Leah? Which would you choose?"

Leah Layne: "The 45 automatic hands down. It is the choice of professionals world wide. It is the fastest in action, has the best stopping power, and the greatest accuracy. Most of the pros winning combat style shooting matches choose the model 1911 45 auto. The Browning Hi-Power has had wide acceptance with many countries as a military sidearm but it is not nearly as good as the .45."

Peter: "Then why was the Tec-9 so popular if it isn't nearly as deadly as the .45?"

Leah Layne: "Because it looks cool. Look, during the 1980's it was popularized in the t.v. series, *Miami Vice*. It fires from a 32 round clip so it makes a lot of noise and looks good on t.v. or in the movies. A lot of drug dealers liked them because it looks intimidating. It's the sort of thing that appeals to an eleven-year-old kid, drug dealer or drug dealer wanna-bee all of whom have the same mentality and it's pretty cheap but no self respecting FBI agent, Navy Seal or cop would prefer it to a lot of other weapons."

Peter addressing Carlos Bullshit: "Not only did you charge Kel-Tech with making dangerous weapons available to criminals, you also charged Browning, Ruger, Smith and Wesson and many other companies. In your indictment of Browning you and your people pleaded: "Defendant Browning markets the High-Power model, a 9-mm semiautomatic pistol which has a ten-bullet magazine capacity, yet has a barrel length of only 4.75 inches, an overall length of 7.75 inches, is only one 3/8 inches wide and only 5 inches in height." This powerful firearm is still small enough to be concealed inside a waistband and under a shirt."

Peter smirked as he continued. "Yet here you sought to try Kel-Tec and its Sub 9 9 mm rifle for having a barrel that is too long. Your legal brief states: *According to Kel-Tech's own description, the Sub 9 will deliver much higher muzzle energy and penetrating than the relatively short barreled pistol. Further the Sub 9 has greatly extended range compared to a hand-held firearm or shot gun firearm*. Is it true that you and your colleagues charged fifteen other handguns with similar misdeeds such as having a barrel that was either too long or too short, being able to fire double action, being a semi auto and therefore firing faster than a revolver, or being small enough to be tucked in a man's belt and concealed by his coat?"

Carlos Bullshit: "No. We didn't."

Peter: "Liar. I find you guilty of contempt of court. I read all 28 pages of the original transcript which degrades all rational thought and common sense. I also find you and your fellow lawyers and gun control advocates of wrongfully bringing to court innocent victims starting with the Tec-9, the Browning High Power, the Glock 17, Smith and Wesson Chief's special and other guns. How can you bring charges up against an inanimate object? Guns don't kill. People do. And look at all the criminals you got off? And as we have seen from Leah's testimony, you and your co defendants have tried to label guns as either good or bad weapons as you saw fit. Guns you call "Good weapons," such as the shotgun, M-14 and the 45 auto are the most deadly, while what you called the bad weapons such as the Tec-9 and Browning Hi power are not nearly as lethal as those you call good. This whole document amounts to a trainload of pure shit and you charged the taxpayers of Camden County for it by the wheel barrel at lawyers' inflated prices. You are a disgrace to the human race."

Carlos Bullshit: "But your honor."

Peter: "Shut up. I also find you and the others guilty of treason. You have sought to disarm U.S. citizens by suing the gun manufacturers in your proceedings. The whole proceedings lined your pockets at more than a hundred dollars an hour. You sought to take all guns away from Americans on the basis that they were semi automatic, were too heavy or too light, too inexpensibly produced, or were too powerful. Thus you wilfully tried to overturn the U.S. Constitution which guarantees Americans the right to own and bear arms just to line your own pockets as if you knew more than our Founding Fathers. I condemn you to a shootout in Peter's corral which is an 80-acre field. You and your co. defendants will be armed with Tec-9's while your adversaries will be armed with M-14 semi automatic rifles. You will soon see which are the deadliest weapons."

Carlos Bullshit: "But we will be hunted down and massacred. We will have a chance only if we get real close to the riflemen."

Peter: "Okay. I'll give you more of a chance. Half of your adversaries will be FBI agents armed with 1911 style .45 automatics."

Carlos Bullshit: "You will still be sending us to our deaths. Those FBI agents are very skilled with those 45's."

Peter: "Then you should have thought of that as you were trying to self-legislate which guns Americans can own and which ones they can't with the ultimate goal of taking all guns away from Americans. Your time would have been better spent learning to shoot at the gun range."

I have changed the names of the lawyers initiating the court action in Camden County against the gun manufacturers to protect the guilty. The rest is pure fiction on what could happen in a more just world. Those wanting more information on this sorry episode are invited to view the 28 page document at http://www.vpc.org/graphics/camcount.pdf

# M16–How many more soldiers will our own battle rifle kill?

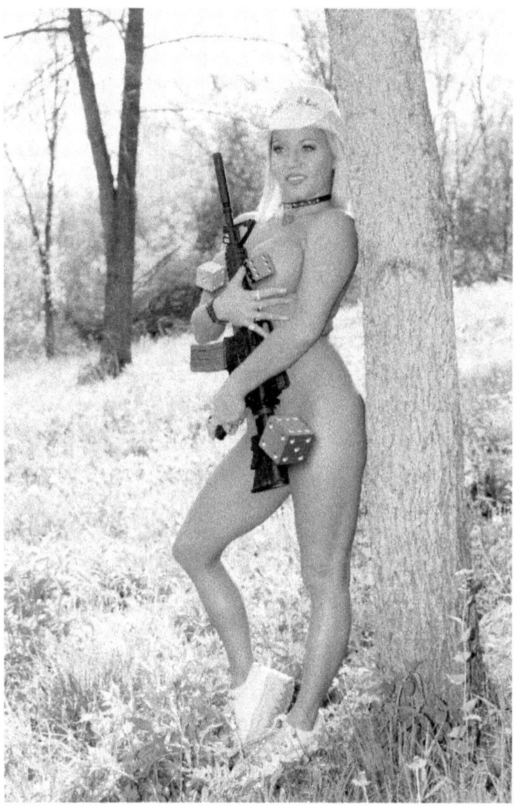

`Pure Talent Carrie Bare. There were two models for the M-16. Arriana a Del was the first, and it was Arianna who appeared in the Xtreme Magazine article.Later when Xtreme teamed up with the author and Vic Meyer to produce the 2004 Xtreme Weapons calendar , it was Carrie Bare who did the shoot for the calendar. Jack wrote two articles about Carrie for Xtreme while shooting the pictures on the state extensively at night clubs throughout the U.S. from Las Vegas, Baltimore, Philadelphia, Des Moines. Mobile, etc.

In the early 1960's reports came back from Vietnam of a revolutionary rifle firing a high speed .22 caliber bullet, weighing just 55 grains, a pipsqueak round compared to the 168 grain .308 Nato round used by the M14 rifle that had recently replaced the M1 Garand as the U.S. mainline infantryman's rifle. Typical of these reports was an incident of a Communist soldier being hit in the head, his arm and through his torso. His head and arm were both taken clean off by two 3300 feet per second .223 bullets with a third leaving an exit wound over five inches in diameter. The rifle, later to be designated as the M-16, weighed just six and a half pounds, was built out of plastics and lightweight metals, and looked like something from another planet.

Still serving as the standard battle rifle for the U.S. military more than thirty-five years later, the M16, in all its variations has served more than fifty nations across the globe, making it the second most prolific rifle in modern History, being eclipsed only by the AK47. One of the most controversial small arms in History, after initially surviving serious questions about its reliability, reports initially out of Somalia and now filtering in from Afghanistan attest that the weapon that had proved so devastatingly lethal in Vietnam is now having problems stopping the enemy. The M-16 certainly has been a pivotal weapon deserving its place in firearms History. But is it as effective as Arianna a Del, the young feature entertainer from Louisville, Kentucky carrying it? Whereas Arianna's pictures prove conclusively how dazzlingly and tantalizingly effective she is, this article's about the M-16.

Combat during the Vietnam war was usually fought at close range. Oftentimes the combatants couldn't see beyond a few yards in the country's thick rain forests and jungles. Although not quite as heavy as the M-1 it replaced, the M-14 our main battle rifle of the early 1960's that was essentially an improved M-1, still weighed more than eight pounds unloaded. An infantryman typically carried between 100 and 150 rounds of full powered .308 ammunition. Although the M-14 was a great rifle, having great accuracy and stopping power at long distances, most men could not control the M-14's recoil on full auto whereas it was easy to manage the much lighter recoiling 223 cartridge of the M16. Of even greater importance to the American soldier in Vietnam was he could now carry a rifle and three or four hundred rounds of ammunition for the same weight exacted by an M-14 and one hundred-fifty rounds of .308 cartridges. The huge advantage of being able to carry more than twice as much ammunition cannot be overemphasized.

In 1965 units of the first cavalry helicopter troops lost more than 250 men killed in action to a vastly numerically superior enemy. U.S. servicemen

found themselves cut off in the confusing whirlwind of combat in the Ia Drang Valley, and often
ran out of ammunition although they carried what normally would have been considered ample ammo for their M-16's. Such an event was even more commonplace fifteen years earlier when American troops often ran out of ammunition when they were cut off by human waves of Chinese Communist troops during the Korean War.

It wasn't long after the battle in the Ia Drang that serious problems concerning the reliability of the M16 arose. A Congressional investigation was launched by Representative Ichord of Missouri. Although initial tests showed that the M-16 was a reliable weapon the army had changed from the IMR powder, it had originally been tested with to ball powder. The ball powder was found to gum up the gas mechanism of the M-16 and other critical parts. Furthermore, although the army was well aware that chrome lining the barrels and chambers of weapons such as the M-16 would help ensure reliability, it did not specify that those M-16 barrels and chambers had to be chrome lined. Many soldiers were not issued cleaning kits for their rifles nor were they trained how to maintain them. No one knows how many U.S. servicemen died while trying to get their jammed M-16's back into action, but once the findings of Ichord's investigation were made public, cleaning kits were issued to the troops, daily maintenance of M-16's was stressed, rifles were reissued with chrome lined bores and chambers, and the powder formulation of all cartridges was changed.

But still more concern arose with recent reports out of Somalia and now filtering in from Afghanistan attested that the weapon that had proved so devastatingly lethal in Vietnam is now having problems stopping the enemy.

For the most part the M-16 became a reliable rifle once its early teething problems were resolved. It was easy to shoot and developed a reputation for terrific accuracy. At ranges of a hundred to two hundred yards, it developed a good reputation as a man stopper although its killing and stopping power fell off rapidly to the M-14's .308 full powered ammunition at longer ranges. One of its major drawbacks was its small high speed bullet was easily deflected by jungle foliage and other obstacles and penetration was not equal to an AK-47 and well behind that of a .308.

Modern small arms bullets now use a spitzer or sharp-pointed bullet. Military ammunition because of humane reasons imposed by the Geneva convention cannot be of soft-nosed or hollow point design. A spitzer bullet becomes unstable once it hits anything solid since the front of the bullet is a lot narrower than its base. Ultimately the bullet will turn 90 degrees and travel sideways, a phenomenon that can be proven by dropping a spitzer bullet on the floor. This is called yawing. The only thing stopping it from yawing in mid flight is the rifling of the bore inducing it to spin, which forces the bullet to travel with its point toward the target.

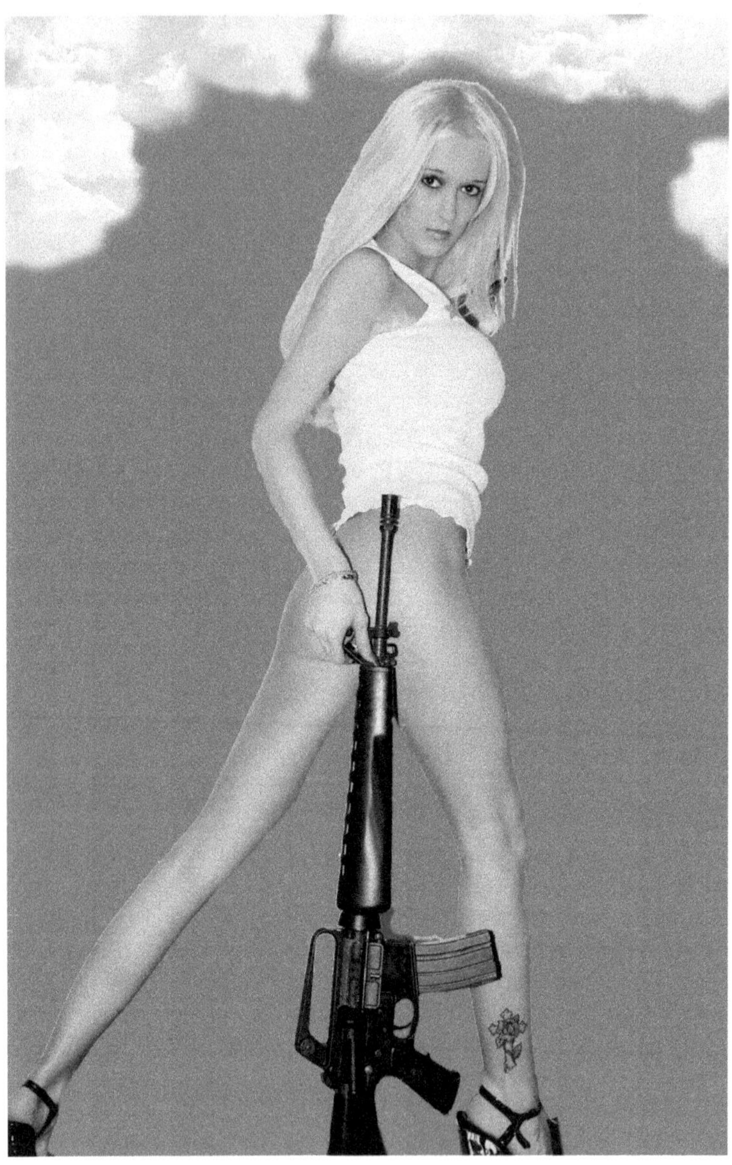

Arianna a /del with the M-16 rifle at Vic Meyer's farm

During the Vietnam era, M-16 rifle barrels were bored with a slow twist to their rifling. A lightweight 55 grain .223 bullet driven at high speed from a barrel imparting a slow twist to the bullet causes the bullet to be inherently unstable which is both a good and a bad thing. Although the bullet spins fast enough in flight to be accurate at close to medium range, once it hits anything, it starts yawing. Which is why the .223 developed such a horrific reputation for tearing huge chunks out of the human body at close to medium range since it starts to upset after penetrating just several inches of tissue, bones and vital organs.

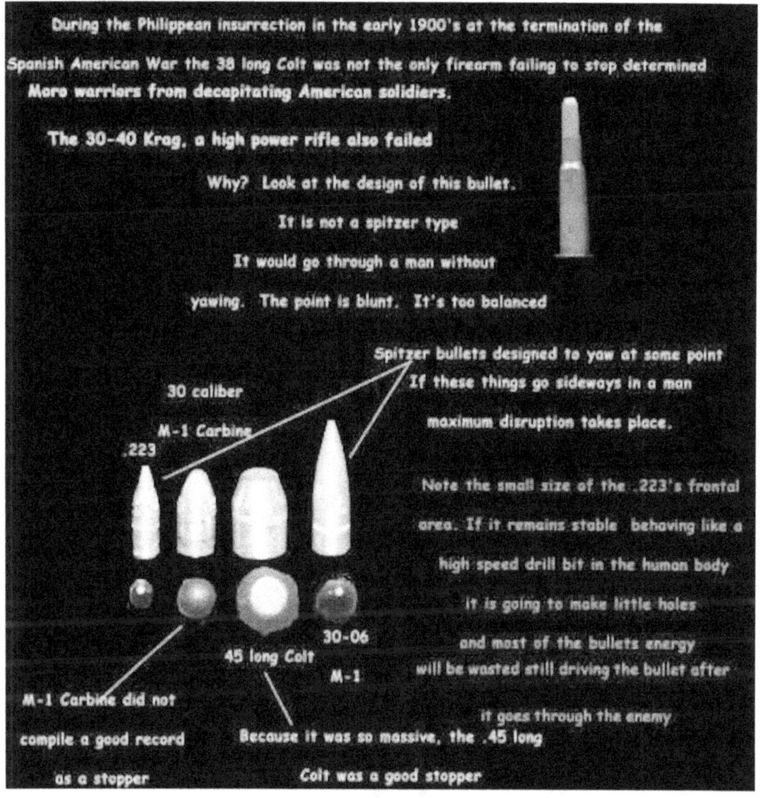


During the late 1970's, the American military reevaluated the M-16 and its .223 bullet, deciding that its inherent instability was detrimental to adequate penetration. The Armed Services perceived the main threat to our security to still be the Soviet Union and its Warsaw Pact satellites in Eastern Europe. The Russians were introducing new armored vests that could defeat the unstable poorly penetrating .223 bullet as fired from its present inventory of M-16 rifles so the M-16's lack of good penetration, particularly at long range, became a real issue. Barrels were introduced on new models bored with a rate of twist that would spin a bullet one revolution for each 7 inches

of barrel length

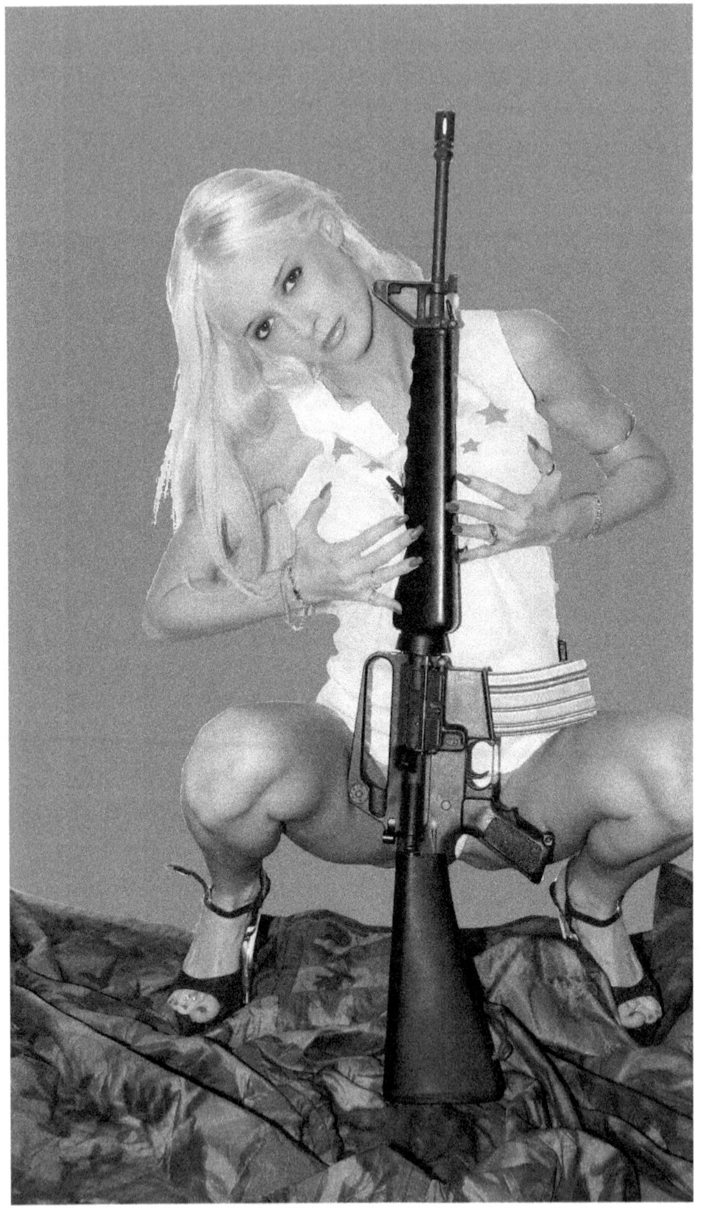

whereas the M-16's we used early in Vietnam War had rifling with a one to 14 twist (one revolution for each 14 inches of barrel length). A new bullet was introduced, substantially heavier at 62 grains to the original bullet's 55 grains. The bullet being longer and heavier was much more stable. One can compare the rifle–ammunition combo to a high speed drill that drives its bit inexorably in a straight line through whatever's in front of it. The new combination of barrel and bullet promised much better penetration and much greater resistance to deflection after hitting obstacles.

I once shot a possum six times with a .223 from my mini 14 and the critter just kept walking away from me. I went back into the house for my .357 magnum Python and killed it with just one shot. The reason why the possum hardly noticed the small fast moving 22 caliber bullets zipping through it was the bullets had already penetrated through the small animal before they had a chance to start tumbling. The possum's body was simply not thick enough to cause enough resistance to destabilize the bullets. Hollow or soft pointed bullets would have told a different story however. Meanwhile both the Russians and Chinese have given up their 30 caliber chambered Ak-47's for new assault rifles firing high speed .22 bullets that were inspired by the .223 developed for the U.S. Military. Obviously the Russians and Chinese were more impressed by this cartridge than the possum I shot. The Russians introduced a particularly fiendish innovation to its new bullet. There is a hollow cavity in the Russian bullet's point. When the bullet hits anything solid the base of the bullet slams into the cavity causing the bullet to destabilize or yaw right after initial penetration.

Three major powers recognized the great advantages they'd gain by giving up their 30 caliber weapons for .22 caliber lightweight bullets–the ability for carrying a lot more ammunition and better controllability on full auto being two of them. The problem is the lethal combination of a high speed .223 bullet and the slow twist rifling of the Vietnam era M-16 barrel that caused the barely stabilized bullet to turn schizophrenic once it struck its target, was sacrificed for a rifle–bullet system conceived to fight an enemy who no longer exists. The threat of armored vest wearing Russian and other Warsaw Pact infantry overrunning Europe died with the fall of the Iron Curtain. Without question a full powered 30-06 or .308 would give far superior stopping power and penetration over the .223 in a greater variety of combat situations. But one would have to give up the ability to fire on full-auto, carry a far heavier rifle, and not be able to carry nearly as much ammunition. The current generation of heavier and far more stable .223 bullets spinning rapidly out of the current M-16 and M-16 derived weapons like deeply penetrating drill bits does not promise reliable stopping power so the question might not be whether the M-16 is a good rifle or not because it is or can be every good. The issue really is how many American soldiers are going to have to die trying to stop a determined enemy before the U.S. procurement bureaucrats finally decide to adopt a bullet that promises to be effective against the enemies we are likely to face. Certainly we can do as well or better than the Russians.

# The AK-47–world's most popular assault rifle

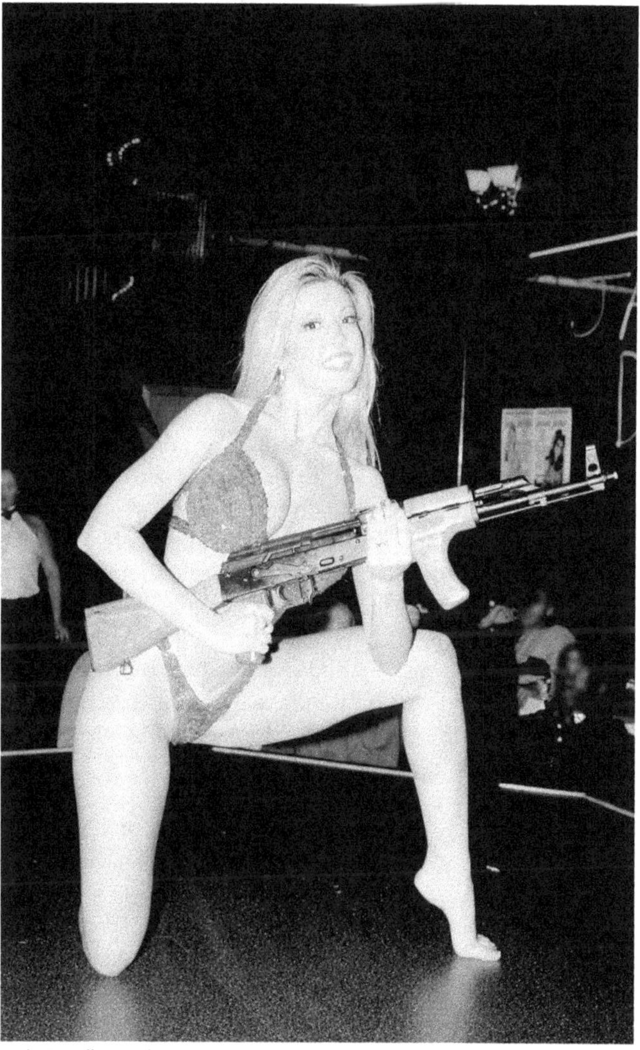

Jada Deville on the stage at Big Louie's at Fort Leonard Wood, Missouri with Vic Meyer's AK-47 in hand. Although Jada was one of the author's favorite feature entertainers, the author was very nervous during this photo shoot, and it's likely Jada was as well.

In some ways feature entertainer Jada Deville and the AK 47 assault rifle go well together. As a feature entertainer, Jada Deville is nearly as well known in the adult entertainment industry as the AK-47 is among gun aficionados. But after that the similarities end. Whereas Jada is utterly gorgeous, the AK-47 is downright ugly. Nevertheless, the AK-47 has equipped more than fifty armies during the later half of the twentieth century making it the most prolific rifle in modern History, a weapon that is commonly identified with the countries of the former Soviet bloc, the revolutionary left wing, and whether deserved or not, the drug dealer. How did this evolutionary weapon evolve and just how good is it?

The concept of the assault rifle started during World War II while the German armies were being bludgeoned to death by the Russians. With the exception of MG-42 equipped machine gun crewmen by 1944 the typical German infantryman was armed with either the Mauser 98 K bolt action rifle or a 9-mm submachine gun. Outstanding as far as bolt actions go, the 98 K was outclassed by our own M-1 which could deliver eight accurate shots out to very long range as fast as a man could pull the trigger. Good at ranges up to 100 yards, the 9-mm round used in German submachine guns simply didn't have the range required to successfully engage advancing Russian troops far enough out to inflict telling damage. It also lacked stopping power and couldn't be depended upon to put an enemy down with just one round. By the last year of the war, German engineers had developed a hybrid weapon that incorporated the best features of both the long range infantryman's rifle and the fast firing submachine gun. The weapon was the MP-44 which soon was nicknamed the assault rifle. Whereas both the American M-1 and the German 98 K Mauser fired full power rounds in the 2800 feet per second neighborhood, and the 9-mm submachine gun ran at around 1400 fps, the 7.92 mm Kurtz round for the MP-44 left the muzzle around 2200 fps, basically splitting the difference.

German studies of infantry tactics during both the First and Second World Wars showed that armed combatants rarely tried to engage their enemy beyond 300 yards. Since accurate fire beyond such distances was not considered necessary for most soldiers, full power ammunition requiring excessively large bullet and case dimensions soon became viewed as a liability instead of as an asset. At this late juncture of the war, the German soldier usually found himself heavily outnumbered by an enemy that was fanatically determined and supported by huge numbers of tanks. It became essential to throw as much lead out there in the shortest period of time starting at ranges greatly exceeding a hundred yards. This meant using weapons that could be fired on full auto (submachine guns typically fire on full auto) as well as semi. Full power ammunition simply could not be controlled on full auto because of excessive muzzle rise that left the shooter firing into the clouds after the first several rounds. Moreover, by adopting a weapon of intermediate range and power the German Army would be able to equip each soldier with far more rounds since each round would be much smaller and weigh less. Decisive stopping power and range out to three hundred yards, rapidity of fire, and ammo that was light enough that a man could carry several hundred rounds would be the ticket to stopping the Russian onslaught.

Like other brilliantly engineered German engineered weapons such as the Messerschmitt 262 jet fighter and the snorkel equipped submarine it was too little too late. The Germans were already beaten although the bloodletting would continue for many more months. By this time Mikhail Kalashnikov, an innovative and patriotic Russian arms designer, was already perfecting his own concept of the assault rifle, a short and stubby rifle with a selector switch for both fully automatic and semi auto fire that was ideally suited for paratroops, tanks corpsmen, and infantry riding in motorized vehicles.

It is unclear how much influence the MG-44 had if any upon Kalashnikov's work for accusing Kalashnikov of borrowing heavily from the German design, insults the genius of the Russian inventor. In 1949 the Soviet Union adopted Kalashnikov's AK-47 as its standard infantryman's rifle. By the early 1960's nearly every Communist nation was using the AK-47. By the 1970's the Soviet Union started replacing its 30 caliber AK-47's with more modern variants utilizing a high-powered 22 cartridge patterned after the American .223 round used in the M-16 rifle that had its baptism to combat during the Vietnam War.

Meanwhile American military doctrine followed the pattern successfully established by the full power semi automatic M-1 rifle during World War II. By 1960 a modernized M-1 in the form of the M-14 became the standard American infantryman's rifle. It would soon be replaced by the M-16 which fired a light weight 22 caliber bullet at over 3,000 fps. The event signaling the end of the M-14's brief reign as the primal U.S. combat rifle was the Vietnam War.

Although very reliable, and utilizing a larger 20 round box magazine holding shorter .308 or 7.62 mm rounds than the eight round clips feeding the longer 30-06 ammunition used by the M-1, the M-14's eight pound weight was not enough to keep its muzzle down on full auto. Officers commanding U.S. servicemen in Vietnam at first warned them to position their selective fire switches on semi auto and later M-14's were retrofitted so that they could only be fired on semi auto. Moreover, soldiers typically carried only a hundred rounds of the full power .308 ammo. The M-16, a new lightweight weapon manufactured from space age materials, gradually started to replace the M-14 in the killing fields of Vietnam. A rifleman could now carry his M-16 and several hundred rounds of the lightweight .223 shells and be able to fire the light recoiling weapon on full auto with great accuracy.

Our enemy, the NVA (North Vietnamese Army) and the Vietcong (Communist guerrillas) typically carried the AK-47 during the Vietnam conflict. Although the M-16 had greater range and accuracy than the AK-47, by this time serious problems arose with the M-16. By 1965 the weapon proved to be unreliable resulting in God knows how many American servicemen being found dead with jammed M-16's next to their bodies. Eventually most of the problems were corrected and the M-16 is still our predominant infantryman's weapon.

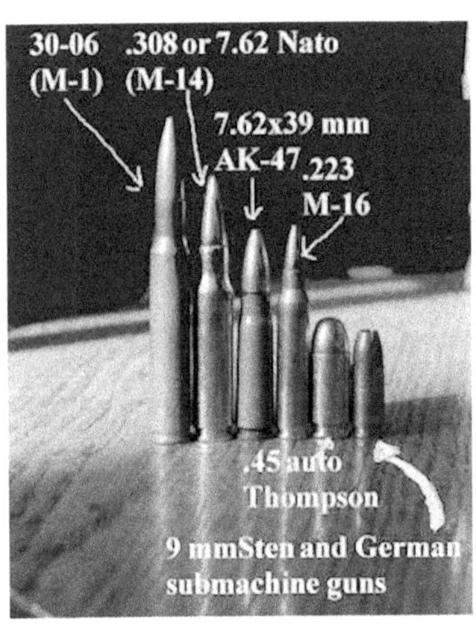


Compared to an M-1 rifle, the Thompson submachine gun, an M-14 or even the M-16 the AK-47 is downright crude in appearance. Wood stocks are cheaply turned out. The AK-47's sights are primitive compared to an M-16's. Major parts of an AK 47 are constructed from stamped steel and sheet metal. It's roughly finished and many AK-47's are painted to keep from rusting. But it's on the inside that counts. The AK-47's bore is chrome plated to avoid rust that promotes jamming and unacceptable accuracy. The gas mechanism that feeds and ejects live and spent ammo is very strong which contributes to an AK-47's ability to fire and keep on firing in all kinds of conditions. It is cheap and easily produced; it hits hard; and its 30 caliber bullet penetrates brush and other obstacles far better than the American .223 round.

The AK-47 is an ugly duckling but the bottom line is the gun is accurate enough to get the job done and you can do just about anything to it and it will keep firing. Its true beauty is experienced while firing it. Thanks to Vic Meyer, my nephew and I had at our disposal a Thompson submachine gun, a World War II fully automatic Riesling gun, a World War II British Sten submachine gun, and an AK-47. The Riesling was a horrible jammer, but the Thompson was a well-crafted instrument that was a blast to fire on full auto. The crudely made Sten with its relatively puny 9-mm ammo was a bit of a bore to shoot compared to the Thompson. The AK-47 was–on the other hand, THE WEAPON.

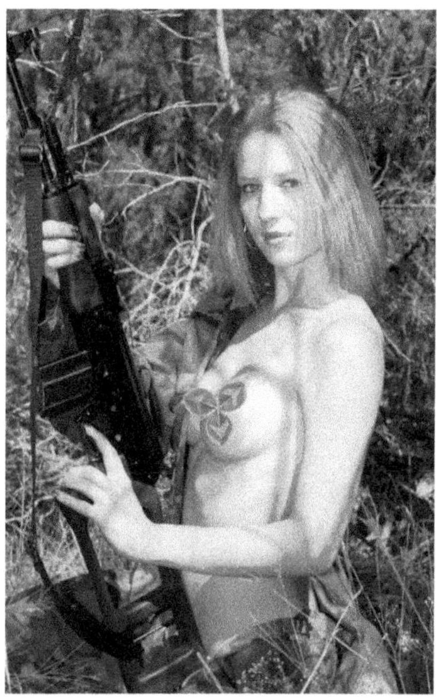

Mirage had been the author's favorite waitress when he was hired to shoot Club Maximus's M.S. Texas 2002, sitting next to him as he kept going up to the stage to shoot the latest contestant then returning to the table to put the digital images onto his laptop. A few months later, after an incredible performance the 20 year old waitress beat out nine seasoned feature entertainers to win the Texas Miss West pageant at the Maximus Abilene Club. Somewhere in Texas a few miles out of Wichita Falls the author took this picture of Mirage modeling his own AK-47. Mirage's pictures would be on the 2004 Xtreme Weapons calendar, but it would be Jada's that would appear in the actual gun article. In spite of her terrific talent Mirage never became a feature entertainer.

Although at close range, the .45 caliber bullets from the Thompson had earned a reputation as a terrific man stopper, firing it doesn't begin to prepare oneself for what is about to be experienced with the AK-47. One has to remember that the Thompson is limited to 100 yard affairs whereas the AK-47 will reach out and touch somebody out to several hundred yards. Its recoil is greater than the Thompson's. But its relatively low cyclic rate of fire on full auto makes it easy to limit one's bursts to three rounds or so. Learning to shoot low when you begin to squeeze the trigger comes naturally. The muzzle starts to rise as you listen to the loud report of its 7.62 millimeter ammo exploding in the gun's chamber. The first slug hits low. It's the second, third, or fourth round that hits the target every time. Shooting at a block of wood in the bushes, we watch shrubbery getting cut down by bullets and the block of wood being struck as we listen to the loud clunk as the bullet destroys it.

I love it. Now that's power. Sweet loving power in motion destroying everything in its path. And it's so easy to hit with. The Thompson might have been great in World War II and I love my M-1 with its even greater power than the AK-47, its great accuracy, and its ability to fire eight shots as fast as I can pull the trigger. But if you ask me which one I'd take into combat, I'm going to take the weapon that's going to give me the greatest chance of survival in the largest number of varying circumstances I'd find myself in. The winner is the AK-47. It might be ugly on the outside but it's utterly beautiful when you fire it. But I haven't shot the M-16 yet on full auto. But that's going to be next month.

> The author never did get around to firing the M-16 on full auto. He bought an AR-15 but it was semi auto only. Although he felt it was a terrific weapon, like most of his weapons, he sold it prior to moving to Thailand. The worse thing about moving to Thailand, was not being allowed to keep firearms there so he wound up selling most of the38 firearms he had acquired in the U.S.

# FAL----Right Arm of the Free World

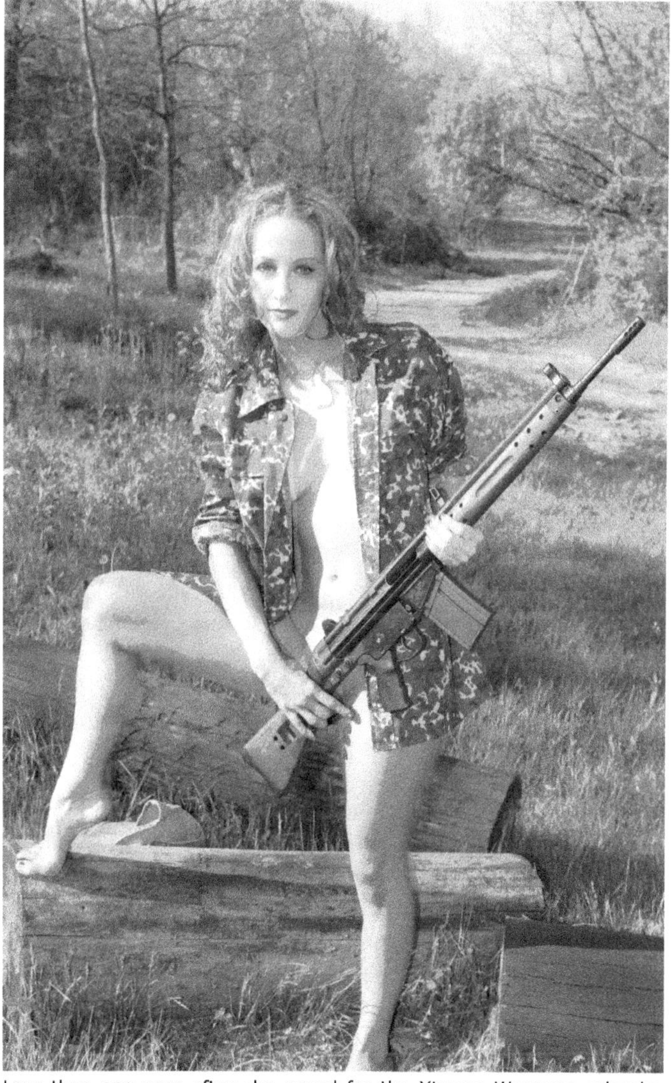

Less than one year after she posed for the Xtreme Weapons calendar Serenna Star will become 2005's Miss Nude World

In the early 1960's through the 1980's prior to the dismantling of the Soviet Union, first the .308 powered M-14, then the .223 caliber M-16 went to war with the American infantryman while his Communist adversaries relied on the robust Russian designed AK-47, a weapon that would ultimately arm over sixty nations worldwide. But what gun armed all those other countries of the so-called free world? For the most part, the weapon of choice was the FAL, produced by Fabrique National in Belgium, which ultimately armed over seventy nations. If this isn't enough to place the FAL on Jack Corbett's significant weapons list, consider that the U.S. came so close to adopting the FAL over the M-14 in the Mid 1950's that in January, 1955 training manuals were prepared at Fort Benning in the use and maintenance of the FAL. And even today many gun afficionados rate the FAL as a superior weapon to the M-14. Here's where these guys are wrong.

Although the M-1 Garand was indisputably the finest all around small arm of the conflict, during the waning months of WWII, the appearance of large numbers of German assault rifles demonstrated the need for new weapons capable of an even larger volume of firepower with realistic battlefield accuracy out to several hundred yards. The answer for the Russians was the AK-47 while the Americans and British underwent a twelve year search for a new battle rifle.

When the Nazis overran Belgium Fabrique National's leading arms designer fled to Great Britain where he started the FAL battle rifle project. The Brits wanted an intermediate powered cartridge that could easily be controlled on full auto, introducing a .280 caliber cartridge, which they tried to convince their American allies to adopt. But the powers that be of American weapons development were still stuck on the more powerful 30-06 round of the M-1 Garand. And these powers that be specified that a new round be should be introduced that was essentially a shortened 30-06 cartridge offering virtually all the power of its parent. They then rammed this .308 or 7.62 mm round down the throat of their British allies.

The FAL was redesigned for the .308 cartridge. Meanwhile American gun designers had been busy trying to convert the M-1 Garand into a slightly lighter rifle capable of firing from bottom feeding 20 round clips in both full auto and semi auto modes.

On both sides of the Atlantic neither the .308 caliber FAL or the modified M-1's proved capable of decent accuracy on full auto since the cartridge generated far too much recoil for the weight of the rifles. There were those evaluating the tests on both weapons' systems who felt the rifles should be produced without full automatic capability since they wasted ammunition while firing on full auto and should be redesigned at a significant weight savings through omitting the full auto option.

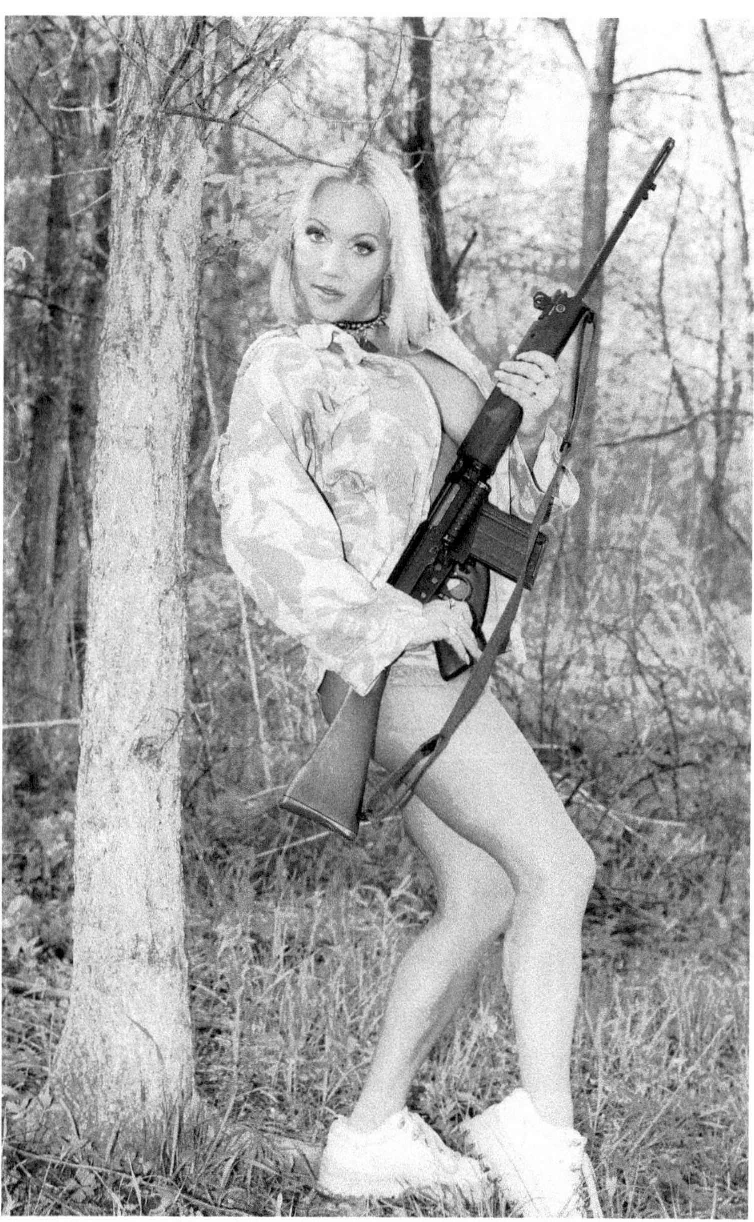

Carrie Bare with the FAL. Earlier she appeared with the M-16

However, had the smaller .280 cartridge been adopted both the U.S. and Great Britain might still be using the FAL today.

It has been argued that the U.S. chose the M-14, which is nothing more than an upgraded M-1 Garand over the FAL because 1. It is American made and 2. Springfield Armory (our leading producer of the M-1) had led our arms procurement decision makers into believing great cost savings would result from the M-14's using existing M-1 tooling, which proved later to be untrue. Although such considerations undoubtably influenced the U.S. military to adopt the M-14, the better weapon won out, a fact that all of you FAL lovers out there have failed to realize.

At the onset of our adopting the FAL over what would become the M-14, a batch of FALs and a batch of M-14 test rifles were shipped to the Arctic for final testing. In fact, the M-14 had already lost the competition and was only to be used as a bench mark for the FAL's final testing. But under frigid Arctic conditions, the FAL repeatedly experienced parts failures. Both Springfield and Fabrique National were sent back to the drawing boards for a grande finale of tests to see who would get the U.S. contract. Meanwhile Canada and other nations had already adopted the FAL for their standard battle rifles.

During this final knock down drag out fight for the U.S. contract the FAL was nearly three quarters of a pound heavier than the U.S. entrant. Its accuracy score was 141 points to the M-14's 166. The FAL's tested experienced an average of 6 to the M-14's 2 damaged or broken parts per 5000 rounds fired. Lastly, the FALS experienced 17 malfunctions to the M-14's 3 per 10,000 rounds fired. [2]

No doubt the FAL experienced continued improvement over the years of its service life. Neither weapon is as proficient for all around use on the modern battlefield as M-16's and AK-47's because of their lesser powered cartridges'

controllability on full auto as well as the fact that more than twice as many cartridges can be carried than the much heavier full powered .308 ammo chambered for the FAL or M-14. But fire an M-14 or an FAL, and you will be left with no doubts about the .308's immense capabilities. There is no question that it can level about anything in its path, that it retains its power way out there, and that it has immense penetrating power. So if I could take my pick from these two and the more modern types of assault rifles

---

[2] "U.S. Army M14 from John Garand to the M21", by R. Blake Stevens, Collector Grade Publications, p. 175

firing lesser powered ammo even at full auto, I'd choose the .308 chambered guns since firing 20 rounds of full powered ammo as fast as I can pull the trigger can do just about any job or handle any self defense scenario I can imagine short of being in an actual war zone. And out of the two .308's I've already chosen the M-14, since I already have one. It has a better trigger pull, better sights, and a better reputation for fine accuracy.

So why do so many gun connoisseurs prefer the Fal to the M-14? I suppose because it looks more like an assault rifle and because they figure it has withstood the test of time much better since the M-14 was phased out of combat in Vietnam hardly no sooner than it was introduced. But we were engaged in a major war(Vietnam) and already had an alternative weapon system available in the M-16. The harsh demands of unrelenting combat necessitated the best weapon for the task at hand. Those seventy or more nations that continued to use the FAL were not as severely tested.

www.ingramcontent.com/pod-product-compliance
Lightning Source LLC
LaVergne TN
LVHW010913110826
845149LV00013B/2341
*9780984893454*